Uplifting the People

religion and american culture

Series Editors   David Edwin Harrell Jr.

Wayne Flynt

Edith L. Blumhofer

Uplifting the People

Three Centuries of Black Baptists in Alabama

Wilson Fallin Jr.

The University of Alabama Press ■ Tuscaloosa

Copyright © 2007
The University of Alabama Press
Tuscaloosa, Alabama 35487-0380
All rights reserved
Manufactured in the United States of America

Typeface: Minion

∞

The paper on which this book is printed meets the minimum requirements of
American National Standard for Information Sciences-Permanence of Paper for
Printed Library Materials, ANSI Z39.48-1984.

Library of Congress Cataloging-in-Publication Data

Fallin, Wilson, 1942–
    Uplifting the people : three centuries of Black Baptists in Alabama / Wilson
Fallin, Jr.
        p.   cm. — (Religion and American culture)
    Includes bibliographical references (p.   ) and index.
    ISBN-13: 978-0-8173-1569-6 (cloth : alk. paper)
    ISBN-10: 0-8173-1569-1
    1. African American Baptists—Alabama—History. 2. Alabama State Missionary
Baptist Convention—History. I. Title.
    BX6444.A6F35 2007
    286′.176108996073—dc22

                                                                    2006038420

Contents

Illustrations

Preface

Historians and other scholars of the African American experience agree that the church has played a vital role in African American life in the United States. Primarily a religious institution, it became much more because of restrictions imposed on African Americans. The African American church served many purposes: refuge in a hostile world; promoter of business; sponsor of education; and dispenser of benevolence. The church was also the major preserver of African American culture. In the 1950s and 1960s the African American church and its pastors led the civil rights movement that overturned legal segregation in the United States.

The African American church experience has been documented in various forms. Several general studies provide an overall view of the black religious experience. Monographs on particular areas of black church life such as music, slavery, and culture have enriched our knowledge as well. Biographical studies on important figures such as Henry McNeal Turner, James W. C. Pennington, and Martin Luther King Jr. supplement other works. In recent times, historians have completed studies on the black church in local communities. In 1997 Garland Press published my book *A Shelter in the Storm: The African American Church in Birmingham, Alabama,* which documented the story of the African American Church in Birmingham from 1815 to 1963.

One of the most prominent and frequent ways that black churchmen have sought to document their history has been through denominational studies. This is not surprising since denominations have been a vital part of black religious life since blacks separated from white churches following the Civil War. Immediately, they formed conferences, conventions, and associations, which continue to the present day. Although at certain times, denominations prohibited blacks from speaking with one voice when they needed to do so, denominational histories are probably the richest source for understanding religion in the black community. Blacks were members of denominations and identified with their goals and aspirations. Black religious leaders gained support by affiliating with a particular denomination and were often denominational leaders. Several histories have been written about the National Baptist Convention, USA, and almost every Baptist state convention has published its own history.

Alabama has been a leader in the publication of black Baptist history. In 1895 Charles Octavius Boothe published his history of Alabama black Baptists titled *The Cyclopedia of the Colored Baptists of Alabama: Their Leaders and Their Work*. His book, which includes the history and origins of black Baptists in the state, as well as biographies of the early leaders, is an indispensable source for anyone researching the early history of black Baptists in Alabama. Without Boothe's pioneering study this book would have been much more difficult, if not impossible. In 1949 Stevenson Nathaniel Reid published a second history of black Baptists in the state, *History of Colored Baptists in Alabama*. His book duplicated Boothe's work to 1895, but he took up where Boothe left off and provided biographies of Baptist pastors and leaders to 1949. Both books, despite making a contribution, were narrow in their perspective and dealt almost exclusively with events and personalities within the denomination, a characteristic of all state black denominational histories.

This book goes beyond the usual black denominational history. It is a denominational history in that it tells the story of black Alabama Baptists, their origins, churches, associations, conventions, and leaders, but it reaches beyond the traditional studies. It attempts to show how black Baptists in Alabama responded to the wider world in which they found themselves. It discusses the response of black Baptists to slavery, disfranchisement, legal segregation, lynching, lack of state-sponsored education, and many other issues. In addition, it discusses the contribution of black Baptists and how they influenced and empowered black life. Particular emphasis is placed on the contributions of Alabama black Baptists in the areas of culture, education, politics, protest, and civil rights. This book is divided into the traditional periods of Alabama history: slavery and Reconstruction; post-Reconstruction; the Progressive Era; the World Wars; and the civil rights movement and beyond.

There is a personal note to this book as well. I grew up in a black Baptist parsonage in Alabama and the black Baptist church substantially influenced my values and perspectives. In addition, I have spent most of my adult life serving as president of the two black Baptist colleges in the state. I obviously have an appreciation for the denomination. Being an "insider" has given me information and insights not available to "outsiders." However, I have striven to be objective and, at points, critical of a denomination that I am a part of and deeply cherish.

One note of explanation is needed. In the history of Alabama black Baptists there have been four conventions. By far, the largest and most influential has been the Alabama Missionary Baptist State Convention, known until 1974 as the Alabama Colored Baptist State Convention. This convention, comprising more than a hundred associations and nearly fifteen hundred churches, provided the church's key leaders and educational institutions. The other conventions supported educational and other activities, but their numbers in no way compared to the Alabama Missionary Baptist State Convention. When I refer to the convention work of the state, I am referring to this organization unless otherwise stated.

Several themes are dominant throughout this study. Black Baptists developed a distinctive Afro-Baptist faith that sustained them in a state that was racist and hostile to their dreams and ambitions. Coming to Alabama during the period of slavery, African slaves combined their African religious emphasis of spirit possession, soul-travels, and rebirth with the evangelical faith of Baptists. As a result, an Afro-Baptist faith emerged. It emphasized most of all an ego-shattering conversion experience that brought salvation, spiritual freedom, love, joy, and patience. Worship was highly emotional, with much shouting, dancing, singing, and chanted preaching. The Afro-Baptist faith also stressed liberation from slavery and highlighted the exodus experience. Moses and Jesus were viewed as liberators who came to bring spiritual and physical freedom. As God delivered the Israelites, so he would deliver them. This faith formed the center of the religious life of slaves who called themselves Baptist. It gave them hope and meaning. Although black Baptists would add other theological emphases such as Landmarkism and Ethiopianism during the nineteenth century, the Afro-Baptist liberation theology developed during slavery remained dominant. This theology also sustained blacks during the periods of disfranchisement and segregation, and gave them hope during the Great Depression. Throughout the 1950s and 1960s, Afro-Baptist liberation theology remained at the center of the religious culture that sustained the civil rights movement.

The black Baptist church, along with other churches, served as the central self-help institution within the black community. Soon after the Civil War, blacks left white churches and formed their own congregations. Most of these were Baptist churches. Separate churches gave blacks an organization on which to build a stronger community. The church served not only as a place for worship but also as a location for social clubs, benevolent organizations, and political meetings. Church buildings doubled as schools. Churches helped blacks in Alabama develop a sense of unity and provided a way in which they could help themselves. The end of Reconstruction and the development of rigid segregation relegated blacks to a separate and unequal status and denied them access to political and other secular institutions. Through the church, blacks built institutions such as schools, banks, insurance companies, and welfare organizations. Eschewing communism and other radical organizations, black leaders sought to work within the system rather than to destroy it. They also chose to build their community by working with whites whenever possible. In this sense, they tended to be cooperationist rather than separatist.

After the Civil War, Baptists were by far the largest black religious group in Alabama. Reasons were numerous: the large number of black Baptist ministers; the liberation theology within their Afro-Baptist faith; freedom to form churches; and celebration worship. Indigenous leadership also emerged as a major factor. Other denominations, including Methodists, were led by bishops and ministers from other states. But within the Baptist denomination, local ministers organized churches and in 1868 formed a state convention with minimal outside assistance. Baptist pastors came from the bosom of the people, and this gave them an advantage over ministers from other denominations. They had a natural constituency through their church membership, were close to the people, and had an economic independence that most African Americans did not have. Throughout the church's history, Baptist pastors served in leadership positions. They served in the state legislature during Reconstruction, protested segregation and disfranchisement, built academies and colleges, and led the civil rights movement in the 1950s and 1960s. Often this leadership was symbiotic: Baptist leaders frequently took their cues from the congregations they represented.

The priority of education is also clearly evident. During Reconstruction black Baptists made the momentous decision to found a school, Selma University. When Reconstruction ended, limiting black political power, black Baptists turned increasingly to education. When the state legislature passed laws that severely decreased funding for black education, black Baptists formed more than thirty academies statewide. In Birmingham, black Baptists formed a college to educate Baptists in that area. The founders saw education as the key to uplifting the race. Furthermore, for them an educated ministry provided the religious order and correct doctrine that the denomination desperately needed for its survival and progress. Although the Alabama Colored Baptist State Convention gave contributions to Birmingham Baptist College and other academies from time to time, its major institution and primary focus remained Selma University. From 1873, when the motion was made to form a school, to the present day, support for Selma University has been the major aim of the convention.

This book addresses the significant role of women. Women constituted the majority of the black Baptist church membership. In addition, they served as the chief fund-raisers, youth workers, and missionary leaders. In 1886 E. M. Brawley, president of Selma University, founded the Alabama Baptist Women's Convention to provide support for the university. Through the years, the women's convention has made regular contributions, provided instructors, and funded buildings for the Selma campus. Although women leaders in the state have demanded a voice in decisions concerning the school and convention, they have not been revolutionary in their approach. The women's organization has remained an auxiliary of the convention and therefore subject to its direction. During the civil rights movement, women from black Baptist churches played an indispensable role as fund-raisers and demonstrators. One thing is clear: without women there would have been no effective black Baptist churches or organizations in the state.

The book also includes a comparison of white and black Baptists in Alabama. Although of the same faith and order, white and black Baptists developed differently. Both were theologically conservative, but black Baptists developed a broader social ethic grounded in their gospel of liberation. Whites developed a limited social ethic and came to different conclusions. As a result, whites and blacks grew apart with little cooperation throughout most of Alabama's history. Whites supported slavery and legal segregation, while blacks opposed such practices. Black Baptist pastors led the civil rights movement; white pastors remained neutral or voiced opposition. Only in recent times have the two groups attempted to reconcile, but continued differences on social, economic, and political issues have hindered the process.

This examination of black Baptists in Alabama highlights the largest and most influential denomination among people of color. The church was at the heart of the community that blacks developed in slavery and in a segregated, racist society. Black Baptist churches provided many needs. Most of all, black Baptists saw themselves as uplifting people of color. The term appears frequently in sermons and addresses of pastors during the period of legal segregation when blacks were building their own communities. "Uplift" connotes attempts by black churches to enhance the quality of life for black people in their communities.

This book would not have been possible without the assistance and support of many people. I am particularly indebted to Wayne Flynt for reading the manuscript and making many helpful suggestions. His constant encouragement proved invaluable. James Day, historian at the University of Montevallo, also carefully read the document and his observations were beneficial. Elizabeth Wells and Becky Strickland, librarians in the Special Collections Department of the Samford University library, were especially helpful. They repeatedly directed me to relevant sources in their collections. I am also indebted to Susan Vaughn, chair of the Department of Behavioral and Social Sciences at the University of Montevallo, for providing me with a flexible teaching schedule that allowed adequate time for research and writing. My other colleagues in the history department were most encouraging.

The love and support of my family made this project possible and bearable. Special thanks to my wife, Barbara, children, and parents for their support and encouragement. The memory of my father, Wilson Fallin Sr., drove me to complete this long project. He was a great lover of black Baptist history, and before he died a few years ago was my chief source for personal insight into many of the major figures discussed in this book. His was a life of service and dedication as father, preacher, pastor, history teacher, and humanitarian. He is gone but not forgotten. This book is dedicated to his memory.

There are others who are not named here, but none are forgotten. Thank you all.

Uplifting the People

1
Slavery and Reconstruction, 1701–1874

1
Slaves, Afro-Baptist Faith, and Black Preachers

In 1701 Jean Baptiste Bienville, lieutenant governor of the French Louisiana Colony, which included Mobile, wrote his government urging that African slaves be sent to help till the soil. In the 1720s African slaves begin to arrive in significant numbers. In March 1721 the *Africane,* a French ship of war, arrived at Mobile with 120 slaves from West Africa. It was followed in the same year by the *Marie* with 338 slaves. Later came the *Neride* with 238 slaves. The coming of African slaves to Alabama was closely tied to the history and development of slavery in the Americas. During the early decades of the sixteenth century, Europeans began to import Africans into the new world of the Americas to serve as cheap labor for their agricultural economies. About 10 million slaves were taken from Africa and sold in the Western Hemisphere. Of that number, about 500,000 were brought to the present-day United States.

Although African slaves came from a continent where they had developed their own religion, many of them accepted Christianity as it was introduced to them by their masters and by Baptist missionaries and pastors. Some who came to Alabama from upper south states such as Virginia, Tennessee, and South Carolina had already become Baptists. The acceptance and adherence to the Baptist faith by slaves who came to Alabama represents the origin of black Baptists in the state.

Slaves in Alabama and generally in the South worshiped and exercised their Christianity in two different settings. Slaves worshiped by themselves, in the "invisible church" as some scholars have described it, usually in the quarters where they lived or in secret meetings at designated areas. Away from the watchful eye of the slave master, blacks could more easily engage in their own distinctive style of worship and African heritage. In the "visible church" whites observed blacks in worship, often worshipped with them, and sought to control the slaves' religion. Blacks worshiped in a variety of ways in the visible church.

Baptist slave masters took their slaves to their churches where they became members. Most slaves worshipped in these biracial settings, a story that has just recently begun to be fully told. As the Baptist mission to slaves increased in Alabama and more slaves became members of white churches, white and black Baptists formed a number of "branch" churches or subcongregations where blacks worshipped by themselves but under the supervision of white Baptist churches. Whites also allowed blacks to form a few semi-independent churches in the state. These churches had a certain degree of autonomy but from time to time were limited by whites.

Whether worshipping in biracial churches or in separate settings, slaves developed a distinctive form of Christianity that combined African and evangelical features, especially those expounded and practiced by Baptist evangelicals. As a result, an Afro-Baptist faith emerged. Because of several factors, including the common ground slaves found between African beliefs and the faith of evangelical Baptists, most slaves gravitated to the Baptist church. In addition to slave preachers who led worship in the slave quarters and other unauthorized meetings, white Baptists licensed and ordained a few black ministers who possessed superior moral and spiritual qualifications, and who preached to both blacks and whites. Many of these ministers would become leaders in the African American community after emancipation.

Slavery and West African Religion

Slavery played an important part in the history of Alabama before 1865. Slaves first came to Alabama during the colonial period. But not until after the War of 1812—when the Indians had been defeated, several million acres of land became available to white settlers, and Alabama had joined the union (in 1819)—did slaves increase in significant numbers. Most came with farmers from the older southern states of Virginia, South Carolina, Georgia, and Tennessee, seeking quick profits from cotton production. These white settlers considered slavery absolutely essential for their agricultural success. During this period the slave population grew faster than the white population. The slave population grew from 42,024 in 1820 to 342,884 by 1850. In 1860 there were 437,770 slaves and 526,271 whites. More than 75 percent of Alabama's slaves lived in the Black Belt counties. The Black Belt comprised the twelve-county area in the southern part of the state extending from Barbour County to the Mississippi border. This area derived its name from the productive black soil in the area. It was ideal for cotton production.

Slavery in Alabama followed the pattern of other southern states. Work was the most important feature of a slave's life. Settlers brought slaves into the state to furnish cheap labor to tame the frontier conditions that existed. Defined as property, they were expected to work as one scholar has said from "sundown to sunup." The vast majority of slaves were field hands whose primary task centered around the production of cotton. This demanded planting, chopping, picking, ginning, and baling. These field hands usually worked by the gang system under the supervision of a driver who made sure that the work was done. When not producing cotton, field slaves mended fences, cut wood, and made shoes, candles, soap, and whatever else was needed on the plantation. Those slaves who were not field hands served as cooks, nurses, butlers, and carriage drivers. Slaves with skills were blacksmiths, carpenters, or brick masons.

Force and discipline were an integral part of the slave system, although there was often paternalism and goodwill between slaves and masters, especially on small farms, as evidenced by letters and other correspondence from slave owners. Slaves who refused to work, worked too slowly, were insolent or disobedient, or were caught stealing were beaten and subjected to various forms of punishment. On large plantations overseers usually rode horses and carried whips with them into the fields. Some wore pistols to discourage insubordination. Occasionally, masters called on the local patrols to whip slaves who ran away or were caught fighting. All adult white males in a community were required to serve on the patrol, a form of militia that theoretically rode the countryside to make sure no slaves were off the plantation without passes and no slave insurrections occurred. A few plantations had small jails for disobedient or runaway slaves, but planters discovered that jail was not a good solution for disciplining slaves and looked for other ways to discipline them. A slave who proved incorrigible was usually sold quickly before influencing other slaves on the plantation.

Contrary to popular perception, most slave owners were not large plantation owners. By 1860 large plantation owners held only 30 percent of Alabama's slaves. The majority of Alabama slaves were owned by yeomen farmers who had fewer than five, a figure in line with the rest of the South and with the 1860 census revealing that most slave owners in the United States had fewer than five. These farmers worked side by side with their slaves, and there were only occasional instances of brutal treatment, though slaves were denied basic freedom. Brutal treatment of slaves usually occurred on large plantations where there were overseers.

Slaves who came to the United States, including Alabama, came from the west coast of Africa or were descendants of those who came from that section of the continent. Although some West African kingdoms traded with the Muslims of North Africa, the economic life was essentially agricultural in a tropical climate. West Africans grew millet, wheat, rice, cassava, cotton, fruits, and vegetables. The family, clan, and tribe were the basis of social organization and ancestors were revered.

West African life and culture cannot be understood apart from religion. Some people practiced Islam, which developed in the cities of West African kingdoms. Most continued to practice the traditional religions. Unlike people in Alabama, most West Africans understood all life in religious terms, with no separation of the secular and sacred. Being in a tropical climate, which was often hostile and depended on agriculture, Africans saw themselves at the mercy of demonic forces that ravaged their crops. These evil forces produced drought, insects, and countless misfortunes. Magic, sorcery, religious ceremony, and ritual were considered essential for productive agriculture and life.

Several scholars of the West African religious experience have given a general picture of the religion that Africans developed over many centuries. Although these scholars have emphasized the diversity in religious practices, they have also shown that there were common features. In his pioneer study of more than three hundred West African tribes, Joseph Mbiti found that all had a notion of a God and Supreme Being. This God, however, remained aloof and uninvolved in the affairs of men. He was involved in the world through lesser gods that he created and that were sometimes seen as mediators between God and man. Most African communities therefore had a plethora of gods who represented the creator God and could be petitioned. They governed the forces of the world and affected the affairs of men for good or evil. At the shrines and cults of the gods there were usually priests whose job it was to offer worship, conduct proper ritual sacrifice to the various gods, and preside over periodic festivals. In addition to the gods, the sacred cosmos of West Africa included a powerful class of spirits who were associated with all living things but especially the ancestors. As the custodians of custom and law, the ancestors had the power to grant fertility and continued to be actively involved in the lives of human beings. The purpose of religion was to appease the gods, live in harmony with the spirits, and be possessed by the ultimate spirit. To be possessed by the spirit not only shielded a person from evil forces but also brought growth and fulfillment. If you were living in West Africa, as historian Mechal Sobel has forcefully pointed out, "you wanted to invite the force of the spirit to be with you."[1] A cosmos made up of spirits, gods, and ancestors was important to the African slaves that were brought to Alabama.

The Slave Community and the Invisible Church

Despite slavery being an institution of force and control, white masters allowed slaves to form their own communities. In these, slaves maintained many features of their African heritage, a thesis that the historical scholarship of John Blassingame, Albert Raboteau, George Rawick, Lawrence Levine, John Boles, and others has validated. Using slave narratives and other documents, they have shown that slaves preserved such African features as folktales, music, dancing, language, and funeral rites. Herbert Gutman showed that slaves also retained their important emphasis on the family, especially in its extended form. Although Alabama references are rather meager, the evidence in slave narratives, travelers' journals, and accounts by slave masters points overwhelmingly to the notion of African survivals in the slave community. Among the things most often mentioned were herbal medicines, funeral rites, and call and response styles in music.

As in Africa, religion was important in the slave community. It took several forms, not all of them Christian. Charles Joyner, in his study of a slave plantation in South Carolina, found that illegal or underground forms of worship, such as voodoo, witchcraft, and conjuring, existed side by side with Christianity. Alabama slave narratives testified to the same phenomenon. A former slave named Aunt Clussey testified that many people believed in conjuring. She recalled that one slave got sick and was conjured. The result was that "ants came out of her skin." Another Alabama slave, Henry Barnes of Mobile County, testified that there were "voodoo workers who could put spells on a person."[2] Conjurers and voodoo workers were respected because they had the power to heal and to tell fortunes. Their powers appeared to work. Slaves who went to church on Sunday often visited the conjurers on Monday. They wanted both spiritual powers at work for them.

Most slaves who were religious accepted some form of Christianity. It was in the slave community that the invisible church emerged with slaves worshipping by themselves, in the slave quarters or at certain designated areas. Sometimes, and especially when their masters were irreligious, slaves had to slip away to hidden "brush arbors" deep in the woods to preach, shout, sing, and worship. A former Alabama slave, Adeline Hodge, reported that because their master would not allow them to go to church, slaves met in the woods for prayer. In other slave narratives, former Alabama slaves asserted that there were long prayer meetings in the quarters at night. Two observers of slavery in Alabama witnessed slaves assembling at trees for worship. Trees were important places for slaves because, according to traditional African religion, the spirits of deceased relatives resided in them. In some cases camp meetings and protracted revivals provided occasions when blacks could worship by themselves. Some masters provided meeting places where blacks held their own worship services. For example, Alabama slave Anthony Abercrombie recalled that his master allowed slaves to build a brush arbor on the plantation for worship. Lee Cato, another Alabama slave, stated that his owner allowed slaves to build a church that "had a flo' and some seats" under a "roof of pine straw" and permitted them to worship there.[3] Many slaves preferred to worship by themselves because they resented being forced to go to white churches where they were admonished to obey their masters.

The Christianity practiced by slaves in their community was a synthesis of evangelical Protestant Christianity and African traditional religion. From evangelical Christianity, the slaves accepted the God of the Bible, Jesus as savior and liberator, and the emotional worship experience that was an integral part of camp meetings and protracted revivals. From their African past, they retained spirit possession, the ring dance and shout, and ritual sacrifice. Combining both elements, the slave's religion was different, a fact testified to by southern plantation owners and northern blacks.

Former Alabama slaves testified of their joy in these secret meetings, especially the singing. Oliver Bell said that although blacks on his plantation attended the white church, they preferred the services held in the quarters where slaves would sing and pray all night. To muffle their voices, they would turn the wash pots so that the sound would stay in the building.[4] In these meetings slaves sang songs they heard in the white churches but sang them differently. Among the favorite songs were the spirituals. Making no distinction between the sacred and the secular, the African American spirituals also expressed a desire for freedom and assurances that God would deliver the people. There was the constant identity with the children of Israel and their deliverance. "My Lord Delivered Daniel," "Go Down Moses into Egypt Land, Tell Old Pharaoh to let my People Go," and "Steal Away" were but a few spirituals that expressed the themes of deliverance and liberation. In addition, the spirituals showed the impact of traditional African survivals. Slaves often sang the spirituals in a call and response manner; some shouted them, and still others danced them. All of these reflected modes found in traditional African religions.

Important to the Christianity that emerged in the slave community was the slave preacher. An enigmatic figure who has been described in various ways, from a controller of blacks for the slave master to a flaming revolutionary, he was generally highly respected among slaves, who recognized the limitations under which he operated. Though a slave preacher might be acknowledged as such by whites, he had to get permission from slaves to preach to them. Pioneer Alabama slave preacher W. E. Northcross stated in his brief autobiography that after he was called to preach he asked the slaves in his area to allow him to preach to them. Generally illiterate, the slave preacher nonetheless knew the Bible and was able to communicate well to the slaves, who preferred him to the white preacher. Through him the slave heard the gospel that did much to sustain him, and like so much in the slave community, the practices of the slave preacher reflected both African and American religious tradition. He preached in a rhythmical style reminiscent of Africa and in an African American dialect, with gestures that evoked the powerful emotional and physical responses characteristic of slaves' worship. He also preached with vivid imagery that elicited a dynamic pattern of call and response from the preacher and worshippers. Like their African counterparts, slave preachers mediated between the natural and the supernatural forces that controlled their lives and those of the slaves they preached to.[5]

Although no full account of a secret service has been preserved in Alabama, slave narratives from Alabama and other southern states allow us to piece together how a secret service in a slave cabin or brush arbor must have proceeded. Typically, brush arbor meetings began when slaves created among themselves an understanding of the time and place for the meeting. They usually began with singing, both spirituals and lined hymns that they had learned in the camp meetings. Next came lengthy and emotional prayers. David McRae observed that "their prayers were full of fire, and often exceedingly vivid and impressive."[6] He also noted that women were as free to participate as men. The prayers often had overtones of liberation. Former slave Julia Malone saw women "stick their heads in the washpot and talk out loud." Her foster mother told her they were "prayin' for de Lawd to take dem out from bondage."[7] In some services testimonies from the group came after the prayers. Slaves testified concerning God's goodness and how he had kept them. Next came the sermon that began with normal prose and built to a rhythmic cadence, marked by exhortations and exclamations from the congregation. After the sermon came the shout. The shout incorporated the rhythm and dance, which moved worshippers into trance possession and communion with the spiritual world. The shout and trance were almost identical to the ring shout that slaves had practiced in their rituals in Africa. Some slaves maintained that the shout could go on for hours with some worshippers not ceasing until the "break of day." These services showed how slaves could take white ritual and create unique services with elements from the African and slave experience. Most who attended experienced spiritual liberation in these services that helped them endure the trials of their lives.

Alabama Baptists, Slavery, and Biracial Churches

The earliest white Baptists championed religious freedom but did not feel obliged to take a stand against slavery. During the period of the Great Awakening and the American Revolution, Baptists began to seriously question the validity of slavery as practiced among Christians. Many Baptists expressed strong opposition. For them the institution of slavery was opposed to nature and the gospel. Others opposed slavery but urged caution, not wanting to create tension or opposition from fellow Baptists. Still others expressed ambivalence toward the institution.

Among those expressing either ambivalence or opposition toward slave ownership were several early Alabama Baptists. One of these was Baptist pioneer Hosea Holcombe. He gave servants inherited from his mother's estate to his half brother because he did not feel he should own slaves. Lee Compere, a former missionary to Jamaica and president of the Alabama Baptist Convention in 1829, strongly opposed slavery. As late as 1840, Alabama Baptist leader E. B. Teague expressed doubts about whether the curse pronounced on Canaan was a legitimate justification for perpetual slavery.

Such concerns about slavery soon passed, primarily because of cotton's increasing importance and the accompanying conviction that profitable cotton production depended on slave labor. As Alabama Baptists became prosperous cotton farmers and increased their slaves, they began to defend slavery and project it as a positive good. Alabama Baptists turned to Scripture as their major proof for the support of slavery. They stressed Paul's admonition for slaves to accept their lot in life and the curse on Canaan found in the ninth chapter of Genesis.

One of the strongest and most effective apologists for slavery was Alabama

Baptist leader Basil Manly, who served as president of the University of Alabama and pastor of the First Baptist Church of Tuscaloosa. Although sympathetic to the spiritual needs of slaves, Manly developed an elaborate argument that summarized the main defense for Baptists not only in Alabama but throughout the South. For Manly, the entire Bible supported slavery. In the Old Testament he pointed to Abraham, the patriarchs, and the Mosaic law. In the New Testament he showed how Jesus, Paul, and the apostles supported the institution. Manly's defense extended beyond Scripture. He also defended slavery by using philosophy, history, political science, contemporary society, and the assumed inferiority of the slaves. Southern society, he contended, was superior and more just than other societies in the world. In this regard, he pointed out how much better off slaves were compared to the workers of Europe "where there were more strong bodies than there was food to fill them." Slavery was a positive good because blacks had been brought to the light of the gospel, Manly insisted. They were also being trained in how to develop Christian families. All attempts to free slaves, such as the Colonization Society's project in Liberia, had resulted in failure because slaves were simply an inferior people who needed the leadership of masters. It was a positive good that God had decreed, and the orderly functioning of southern society had proved to be superior to other societies. Manly declared that the institution was most beneficial to all concerned, both whites and blacks.

Alabama Baptists' defense of slavery grew stronger and more intense with the emergence of abolitionism. Through their state convention and through associations, they forcefully condemned abolitionists. In 1835 the Alabama Baptist State Convention issued a strong indictment, describing abolitionists as fanatics whose belief was contrary to the gospel of Christ and "calculated to oppress the slaves, to arm the assassins, to shed the blood of the good people of our state, and to alienate the people of one state from those of another." District associations such as the Alabama, Cahawba, and Mulberry issued similar attacks. In 1840 the Mulberry Baptist Association carried the following resolution: "Whereas the Anti-Slavery Convention at the North has had the unchristian impudence to publish and send to the Baptist of the South an address which we are disposed to treat with the utmost contempt and indignation, and do not at all thank them for their kindness, Therefore, Resolved that we commend our churches to commit to the flames all such instruments as may be received by any one of them, and hope as these fanatics regard our Christian feelings, they will withhold all such instruments in the future."[8]

Though Alabama's white Baptists vigorously defended slavery, planters provided opportunities for their slaves to worship. Slave testimonies have recorded that some owners built chapels and brush arbors on the plantation. Some wives of masters conducted Sunday school for slave children. Masters also took their slaves to camp meetings and protracted revivals, where usually both white and black ministers preached to them. The majority of Christian slave masters took their slaves to their churches, where many became members. It was in these biracial churches where most slaves worshipped during the antebellum period in Alabama. Recently, scholars of the antebellum South have more closely investigated these churches and the relationship that existed in them between slaves and whites. These churches showed great variety in terms of how much freedom was given to black members. Differences were also noted in such activities as voting, office-holding, and the right to preach.

Although there was diversity, some common patterns did exist. There was clear and definite inequality. Blacks usually sat in balconies or separate sections in the rear of most churches. Typically they could not vote and were not allowed to express themselves in their distinctive and emotional worship style. Often blacks were listed separately on membership lists; most included only the first name of blacks and the full name of their slave owners; some omitted the names of slaves altogether. Many white slave owners saw these churches as a means of control, with pastors reminding slaves to obey and be loyal to their masters. Sarah Fitzpatrick, a ninety-year-old former slave interviewed in 1938, who worshipped in a biracial Baptist Church in Tuskegee, recalled that, at the end of the sermon, the white preacher would look up into the balcony and remind blacks to obey their masters so that they could go to heaven when they died.

On the other hand, there were many positive features to relationships in the biracial churches. These churches allowed blacks a measure of equality that could not be found anywhere else in southern society. Blacks and whites primarily joined in the same way, through letters or testimonies of conversion. They were both dismissed by letter. They were often baptized in the same services, fellowshipped into churches in the same way as whites, and disciplined in the same way. In rare instances, blacks testified in cases of discipline concerning whites, something never allowed in the secular courts in the South. Although under Alabama law after 1832, slaves could not be taught to read and write, white ministers often taught them to read the Scripture and recognized the sanctity of their marriages. Many whites were sincere in their efforts to achieve spiritual uplift of slaves in the biracial churches. This concern and warm feeling was reflected at the time of death, when whites and blacks showed sympathy to each other's family. In many biracial churches whites and blacks were buried in the same cemeteries.

Numerous church histories of pioneer Alabama churches have left bits and pieces of information showing blacks as members, in some cases charter members, and making up a significant portion of the membership. An African American slave named Dinah was a founding member of the Ruhama Baptist Church located in what is today the city of Birmingham. By 1868 there were 37 African American members of the church. The Canaan Baptist Church, located in what is now Bessemer, had 37 slave members in 1837, with slaves worshipping in the balcony. The first slaves became members of the Salem Baptist Church located in Jefferson County in 1843. Whites worshipped in the front and slaves in the back, separated by a rail.

Some churches have provided more details of blacks in their churches. The Cubahatchee Baptist Church of Christ located in Macon County had, in 1856, 108 black members and 147 white members. Blacks were accepted into the church by letter, profession of faith, and on the recommendation of the slave master. Blacks were baptized in the same services as whites and then both groups were fellowshipped into the church. On the membership role, blacks were listed by their first names and as "servants of." Blacks were disciplined and excluded on some occasions, as were whites, for stealing, lying, poor church attendance, drinking, dancing, and adultery. It appears that on certain occasions black ministers were allowed to preach to the congregation. In 1842 a slave minister listed in the church records as "Caesar," obviously referring to Caesar Blackwell, preached to the congregation.

One of the most extensive records of relations between blacks and whites in biracial churches in Alabama is found in the church minutes of the Mt. Hebron Baptist Church, Leeds, Alabama. The Alabama historian Wayne Flynt has produced a rather detailed history of blacks in this church during the period of slavery and the limitations placed on them. Hosea Holcombe, pioneer Baptist leader, founded the Mt. Hebron Church in 1819 with 12 members. In October 1825 Peter, a slave, joined the church, the first slave to become a member. Of the 376 members between 1819 and 1865, 51 were slaves and 2 were free blacks. Most slaves became members by profession of faith, though some came by letter of transfer. Normally they were dismissed and given a letter when they desired to transfer to other churches, most likely when sold to other plantations. When a slave is mentioned in church records, the prefix "black brother" or "black sister" is usually appended; no slave was given a last name. With free blacks of color, the full name was recorded on the church rolls.

In some cases slaves became members even when their masters were not. Others joined at the same time as their masters. Still others became members before their masters, which hints at the notion that they may have influenced their masters and mistresses. For example, John, a servant of Isaac Cameron, entered Mt. Hebron as member number 72; his mistress, Sara Cameron, became member number 100. In some cases the master became a church member long after a slave. Rose, a slave of William Watson, joined the church as member number 78 long before her master who was listed as member number 266.

Mt. Hebron records show that whites were concerned for the spiritual welfare of the slave. In 1828 whites voted to build an annex for blacks. This demonstrated a desire to minister to the need of the black members, even if it meant using the financial resources of its members, and permitted the separation of the races that whites deemed necessary. Four years later, Anthony, a slave of Willis H. Jones, was given permission to preach. One may assume that his major task was to preach to the slaves of Mt. Hebron church and the surrounding area.

Like whites, blacks were subject to strict discipline. Blacks were disciplined for lying, irregular church attendance, stealing, drunkenness, and fighting. In 1833 Potter, a free black, was excluded for drunkenness and swearing. In January 1836 members excluded Bob and Abram for quarreling on the Sabbath. In August 1852 Elijah was excluded for lying. Records also reveal that slaves were disciplined for running away. Discipline of blacks was a part of the church's effort to maintain the moral life but was also a form of control.

Despite the rather liberal stance (for those times) on race relations, two disciplinary cases clearly demonstrate that church members were expected to observe strict limits in secular society. In 1855 three white males were excluded from Mt. Hebron for attending a Negro dance. Four months later, Mt. Hebron disciplined Aujdea Harris, a white female, for visiting the black quarters by herself. Her actions, which raised questions about sexual behavior, were deemed inappropriate. While a kind of quasi-spiritual equality could exist within the church fellowship, no such appearance of equality could be expressed in social life. Slaves were slaves, and whites were to keep their distance in secular society.

Increased Separation and Branch Churches

Beginning in the 1840s a noticeable spatial separation developed between whites and blacks in biracial worship. This took the form of separate services for blacks and sometimes separate buildings for black worship. The two primary reasons for this spatial separation were the increased number of blacks in biracial churches and the growing desire of blacks to worship in their own way and have a greater voice in their spiritual lives.

The increase in the number of blacks in biracial churches was due to the increased evangelization of slaves by white Baptists. Beginning in the 1840s Baptists in Alabama, like those in other southern states, began organized efforts for the conversion of their slaves. One of the primary reasons was a heightened interest in religion following the splits in the Methodist, Presbyterian, and Baptist churches over the issue of slavery. With the formation of the Southern Baptist Convention in 1845, Baptists in the South believed that God was getting ready to do something special through them. A part of this new expectation and heightened interest in religion was the growing belief of many Alabama Baptists that God had placed slaves in their midst so that they could be converted from heathenism to Christianity. The Salem Baptist Association expressed this view in an 1852 resolution, stating that God had brought blacks from Africa so they could be taught the Bible. In the light of God's action they urged all southerners to "rejoice that God had thought them worthy to teach Christianity to the Negroes."[9] A second reason was apologetic. The organized religious instruction of slaves served to contradict the abolitionist charge of the neglect of slaves. Abolitionist groups in the North denounced southerners for their neglect of the spiritual condition of slaves. By increasing their evangelization of slaves, white Baptists sought to show how false these charges were. The *South-Western Baptist* in 1854 said that if the proper interest could be awakened in the religious teaching of slaves, "the mouths of the abolitionists would be hushed."[10] A third reason was increased financial resources. With the emergence of the Southern Baptist Convention and general prosperity in the South, whites had more money to give. In 1853 Alabama led all southern states in giving to the Domestic Mission Board of the Southern Baptist Convention.

The Alabama Baptist State Convention joined other southern states in organized efforts to Christianize black slaves. The 1844 convention passed a resolution urging earnest efforts to evangelize slaves. Pastors were prompted to preach to them or provide some form of religious instruction. The next year the convention authorized the preparation of a simple booklet to be used to instruct slaves in the Bible and Christianity. In 1846 such a booklet, *The Catechetical Instructor,* prepared by A. W. Chambliss, was approved and printed.

Baptist associations in the 1840s also began to organize evangelizing slaves. For example, about the year 1846 the three Baptist associations serving Bibb County—Cahawba, Mulberry, and Tuscaloosa—voted to begin organized efforts to convert blacks. In each association, missionaries were appointed to preach to slaves. The Tuscaloosa Association appointed two part-time missionaries at an annual salary of four hundred dollars each. Other associations in Alabama followed a similar pattern. The Shelby County Association in 1852 appropriated funds for a part-time missionary. In 1848 the Yalabusha Association secured a minister to hold services for slaves at various plantations. In 1852 the Liberty Association near Montgomery assigned a minister to preach to slaves for three months. He reported that he had preached only twenty-one times because in many places there were no accommodations. Other missionaries reported similar difficulties, including slave masters who were content to have slaves worship in their churches and the fear by some masters that missionaries might espouse antislavery sentiments. Despite these difficulties, thousands of slaves accepted the Christian religion.

The impact of this vast increase of black converts affected the biracial churches. In some of these churches blacks outnumbered whites more than 10 to 1. The Elim Baptist Church of Tuskegee had 22 white members and 390 black members. In the Elam Baptist Church of Montgomery, blacks outnumbered white members 290 to 22. Others had a simple majority of black members. The expansion of black church membership vexed many white churchmen. Although blacks were segregated, some intermingling was unavoidable. White members were often jostled by crowds of blacks who blocked church entrances, and sedate services were often interrupted by emotional outbursts from the slave sections and galleries. Some churches in Alabama show whites making attempts to control blacks during worship. The Mulberry Baptist Church appointed a committee in 1855 to control what members considered the unchristian behavior of its black members during worship. The complications that accompanied the growth of black church attendance made many whites increasingly willing to consider removing blacks from their worship services.

Whites debated the best way to deal with the situation. Many pastors were motivated by a paternal concern for the soul of the slaves, a belief that religion would make it easier to control them, and a clear knowledge that their white parishioners had no desire to add to the already swollen black membership in their churches. One solution was to have separate services for blacks or separate facilities while insisting that slaves remain members of these churches, subject to the same discipline as before, and under the control of white members of the church. The First Baptist Church of Talladega followed this pattern. In 1850 the church began debating what best to do for its increasing black membership. In a conference held that year it was suggested that separate afternoon services be held for blacks. The main reason given was that blacks could understand the gospel when it was directly addressed to them. A committee of seven whites was appointed to attend the black services.

Blacks also wanted separate services. They wanted to worship in their own way, hold office, and have a greater control over their religious lives. Histories and minutes of biracial churches show blacks requesting to become deacons and preachers in larger numbers after 1840. In 1845 several slave members of the First Baptist Church of Tuscaloosa believed they had been called to preach and requested permission to do so. The white members first decided to postpone the matter indefinitely but later appointed six men to preach. When the issue arose over the legality of having services led by blacks, a white superintendent was appointed to be present at all such meetings. In 1846 the Wetumpka Baptist Church selected six black deacons and licensed two black preachers.

The spatial separation in the churches helped create a number of leaders for the black community, many who would play important roles in independent black churches after the Civil War. White Baptists recognized that they needed black leaders to maintain religious opportunities for their black members. Typically, black watchmen and deacons conducted special services for black members of Baptist churches on Sunday afternoons, held prayer meetings during the week, and presided at discipline meetings where blacks often voted to admit new members or release those having to move and discussed each other's behavior. Former Alabama slave Anna Scott remembered that the black deacon at her church would listen to professions of religion after the services until late into the night. He would then report the converts to the white preacher, who would question them further.

In addition to leadership, subcongregations created in blacks a growing sense of assertiveness and independence. This was reflected in disagreement over discipline. For example, at a church conference at Montgomery's First Baptist Church attended by both blacks and whites, the white moderator proposed the excommunication of Stephney, a slave charged with lying, keeping a house of ill repute, and working on the Sabbath. Whites agreed to excommunicate Stephney by a vote of seven to five, but black members voted to acquit him, nine to one. Because whites had the ultimate voice, Stephney was excommunicated. However, blacks' willingness to disagree shows how participation by blacks in these churches served as a liberating force.

Semi-Independent Black Baptist Churches

Although most slaves worshipped in the same church as their masters or in branch churches that whites supervised, a few churches had a kind of semi-independent status. Blacks took the initiative in forming these churches. Not having associations of their own, some of them received membership in white associations. Up to 1831, when Nat Turner led a revolt in Virginia, blacks served these churches as pastors and were allowed to preach freely to both slaves and free blacks. After 1831 they came under greater scrutiny from whites, who forced them to accept white pastors. Mechel Sobel lists 225 black Baptist churches that existed in the United States. There were at least 5 such churches in Alabama.

Hosea Holcombe, in his pioneer history of Alabama Baptists, lists two semi-independent black churches that existed in North Alabama during slavery. Both were members of the Flint River Association: the African Huntsville Baptist Church and the African Cottonfort Baptist Church of Lancaster. The African Baptist Church of Huntsville was founded around 1820 and entered the Flint River Association with 76 members. Reverend William Harris, a free black, was the first pastor. Later, he became a primitive Baptist and the church followed him. The date for the formation of the African Cottonfort Baptist Church is not known. It became a member of the Flint River Association in 1830 with 130 members. A slave named Lewis Jamison was its first pastor. In 1840 it boasted a membership of 190 people. Unlike the African Huntsville Baptist Church, it remained a missionary Baptist Church. No additional records of this church are extant, nor does it exist today.

Three black Baptist churches founded during the slave era have maintained their existence to the present. Two of these churches were established in Mobile: the Stone Street Baptist Church and the St. Louis Street Baptist Church. The third is the St. Phillips Street Baptist Church, now the First Baptist Church of Selma.

The Stone Street Baptist Church is generally considered the oldest black Baptist church in Alabama. A recent history of the church compiled by its members traces its origin to 1806. On this date an African church was founded in Mobile with "Uncle Jack," an African, as pastor, the history maintains. The uncertainty of records leaves this date clouded, as well as the true nature of this church. Was it a Baptist church? The best evidence seems to support the notion that a black Baptist Church existed in Mobile before 1841. Sources agree that, after the Nat Turner revolt, whites saw free blacks as a menace and sought to curtail all black assemblies. In 1841 the St. Anthony Street Baptist Church formed an African branch and urged blacks to join. The older Stone Street Church, needing a white sponsor, apparently merged with St. Anthony's colored branch. In 1845 another white Baptist church became sponsor of the black congregation: the St. Francis Baptist Church, now Mobile's First Baptist Church. The Cahawba Association accepted the African branch of First Baptist Church in 1847, which at that time had become constituted as a separate branch. It appears that the Stone Street Church exercised the same kind of autonomy that was present with the African Huntsville and African Cottonfort churches in north Alabama. Stone Street, however, had a white pastor until 1864, when Benjamin Burke, a black from Richmond, became the pastor.

The St. Louis Street Baptist Church of Mobile was founded in 1853. It was the result of a split in the Stone Street Baptist Church over a disciplinary case. An underlying cause was resentment over its white pastor, Kedar Hawthorne. The free blacks of Stone Street had never liked Hawthorne, possibly because of his autocratic methods in restricting their style of worship. At the time of the split, the members owed Hawthorne back salary. In 1859 St. Louis Street became a member of the Cahawba Baptist association, with Hawthorne serving as its pastor. Its pastors were white until emancipation. After emancipation, blacks became the pastors. Among these early pastors were Charles Leavens, I. Grant, A. Butler, and C. C. Richardson.

The St. Phillips Street Baptist Church was organized in 1845. It was composed of a separate white and black membership. These two congregations agreed to build together with the understanding that the white congregation would occupy the upper level and the blacks, the basement. This agreement was kept until sometime after the Civil War. The pastor of the black congregation was Samuel Phillips, a free black, who obtained his freedom as a reward for his services in the Mexican War. After the Civil War, whites paid blacks two thousand dollars for the basement.

Afro-Baptist Faith

Most black Christians during and immediately after slavery were Baptists. Estimates of the number of black Baptists in 1860 range from 150,000 to 400,000. Wayne Flynt estimates that when the Civil War ended in 1865, nearly half of all Alabama Baptists were African American. There were various reasons for the number of black Baptists. By the beginning of the Civil War there were more Baptists in the South than any other denomination, and therefore probably more Baptist slave masters. Slaves commonly joined the churches of their masters or ones that were accessible to them on their plantations. There were also a substantial number of black Baptist semi-independent churches in the South, many with large memberships. And democratic inclusiveness attracted blacks to the Baptist church. Especially in the late 1700s and the early years of Baptist expansion in the United States, there were few barriers to blacks becoming members of Baptist churches, being licensed to preach, serving as deacons, and generally using their talents. The only condition was that they fulfill the same high standard of moral uprightness that were expected of white members.

Another important reason for the growth of black Baptists was that the theology of Baptist evangelicals blended better than any other denomination with the sacred cosmos of the West African religion slaves brought with them. Although Methodists, Presbyterians, and Congregationalists were also evangelical, their faith and practice limited them in ways that Baptists were not. For example, many Methodist evangelicals protested against the holy dance, while most Baptist evangelicals allowed it to continue, and slaves viewed it as an integral part of their receiving the Holy Spirit. Slaves often found greater freedom in Baptist meetings. Baptist concepts of individual responsibility to God that required direct action by the individual through conversion and the belief in the dignity and worth of each person gave blacks greater opportunity for participation and religious experience than in any other denomination.

Some slave masters allowed their slaves to attend the church of their choice as long as they received a pass and returned at the designated time, as Alabama slave Sarah Fitzpatrick testified. The historian Eugene Genovese has pointed out that when given a choice, many slaves "overwhelmingly preferred the Baptists and secondarily the Methodist." After emancipation many former slaves became members of Baptist churches. Alabama slave Ellen King testified that during slavery she was a Methodist, but when she moved to Mauvilla after emancipation, she joined a Baptist church because there was no Methodist church in her community and she appreciated the freedom of the Baptists.

Mechal Sobel has shown the process by which slaves arrived at their faith and the importance of Baptist evangelicals in formulating it. Early slaves from Africa arrived with a sacred cosmos that emphasized the importance of ancestors, spirits, and man's journey to be one with the spirit, an event that brought fulfillment and growth. The earliest slaves were exposed to the liturgical Anglican religion, which conflicted with this worldview and diminished the sacred cosmos and the slaves' understanding of the holy. Beginning with the First Great Awakening, slaves found a religion similar to their own that emphasized emotion, spirit, and rebirth. Slaves found in Baptist preaching and polity a common ground upon which a coherent faith could be built that preserved and revitalized crucial African usages with the Christian understandings of salvation. This synthesis of African and evangelical elements created an Afro-Baptist faith.

For black Baptists three theological tenets were most important for their Afro-Baptist faith: conversion, the Holy Spirit, and baptism. The idea that a conversion experience was necessary to gain entrance into heaven was the central concept in Afro-Baptist Christianity. Former Alabama slaves who were Baptists remembered how they prayed and sought the Lord before conversion. Charlie Aarons insisted that he became converted only after "he sought the Lord both day and night."[11] Pioneer slave preacher W. E. Northcross recalled that he became converted and accepted the call to preach only after "a long session of fasting and praying."[12] The conversion experiences of Alabama slaves were similar to those from other states that Clifton Johnson recorded in the book *God Struck Me Dead*. In each case the person had an experience with God in which he was taken to the brink of hell and reborn through the mercy of Jesus. For Baptist evangelicals the process began with an awareness of utter worthlessness and led to a spiritual rebirth as the redeemed people of God. A person could not do it by himself; only through God's love, offered by way of Christ's sacrifice on the cross, could the sinner escape the torment of hell and find redemption. He would then enter the Christian brotherhood, a true community that set him apart and protected him from the wickedness of the world. This experience was similar to rituals in Africa in which initiates went through a process of purification before achieving rebirth.

Despite similarities with the conversion experiences of white Baptists, there were differences. Alabama Baptist pioneer and Baptist historian Hosea Hawthorne noted that blacks who joined his churches expressed themselves in a more visionary way than whites. White observers suspected African influence behind black visions and trances. Another major difference was the notion of a "little (white) man" who in these visions, or "trabels," led the sinner on his journey from hell to heaven. The notion of the "little man" or "man within man" was peculiar to the African experience. As time moved on, this little man became identified with Jesus. Jesus became the rock and the salvation for blacks. They could call on Him and find a friend who would cry and shout with them and also bring salvation, joy, and peace.

The Holy Spirit was also important. It filled the converted sinner with happiness and power that drove him to shout, sing, and sometimes dance. This pattern of motor behavior was in keeping with their African past. African American slaves tended to form rings when they would shout and dance. The ring symbolized the eternal cycle of birth, death, and reincarnation that were a part of traditional African ceremonies. In their religious services, slaves synthesized the African custom of spirit possession with the Christian doctrine of the Holy Spirit. Not surprisingly, Alabama slave narratives abound with testimonies from slaves of their Christianity bringing so much joy that they were led to shout when possessed by the spirit.

Baptism was the central symbol of spiritual death, rebirth, and initiation. Accompanied by song, shouting, and ecstatic behavior, baptism was the most joyous occasion, especially for Baptists. Alabama slaves remembered with enthusiasm being baptized in creeks or some similar body of water. Dressed in a white robe and attended by brothers and sisters, the candidate proceeded amid praises to the local pool or creek, symbol of the river Jordan, where he was "ducked" by the preacher. Many came up shouting for joy at being new in the Lord. One Alabama slave testified that when she was baptized you could hear shouting for ten miles. For some Baptists, this experience may have reminded them of the water cults in Nigeria and Dahomey. Methodists tended to sprinkle rather than immerse. Some black Methodists, however, asked to be immersed.

The African religion merged with the faith of evangelical Baptists to create the Afro-Baptist faith. The African creator God and the Christian God became one—a God close to man, who sent messengers to lead his black people home. Spirit force or power was still recognized, but it was exerted by God, Christ, and the Holy Spirit, as well as by holy men. The African idea of separable souls, of the "little me," found a proper place in the Afro-Christian cosmos, and the African goal of resolution and growth could be reached through a Christian life.

With the shout and the vision, the black slave knew his future, and he appropriated an African past. His African soul, with its essential self, found the means to travel to the Christian heaven while time past became the future.

Two other elements of the Afro-Baptist faith remained important. First, through their Afro-Baptist faith, slaves developed a sense of community, and their conversion brought them into a new community of faith. They were expected to live lives worthy of their redemption and salvation. They were to be separate from the evils of the world. This included monogamous marriage relationships. As black branch churches and semi-independent churches developed, black deacons took over the function of disciplining members who broke rules of morality, a task carried out with diligence. Many semi-independent black Baptist churches had covenants that prescribed rules of order and moral conduct. A part of Afro-Baptist life also included social activities such as picnics and dinners on the grounds. Slaves found support for each other and gained strength to endure slavery and the difficulties of life.

The notion of the Christian gospel as liberation was also a theme in the Afro-Baptist faith. This liberation was expressed in spiritual terms. They had been taken to the brink of hell and reborn through the blood of Jesus. This certainty gave black slaves a hope and freedom that could not be bought or taken away from them. This newfound spiritual freedom also gave slaves a yearning for physical freedom. They were convinced that God would free them from slavery in his own time. Black sermons focused on the deliverance of the Israelites, Moses, and Joshua. Jesus was seen as the great liberator. Just as God delivered Israel, he would deliver them. Baptists continued to sing Negro spirituals, which showed their longing for and the ultimate assurance of freedom.

A good example of the Afro-Baptist faith fostering spiritual and physical liberation is seen in the actions of Alabama slave Alexander Goldsby, one of Selma's notable black church leaders. Goldsby, a blacksmith by trade, became a deacon in the First Baptist Church because of his "good sense and genuine piety." In the 1840s and 1850s when black religious independence was being curbed, the white and black members of the First Baptist Church worked out a unique arrangement to govern their congregations separately yet remain within the same church. In 1845 Goldsby and other deacons installed a black preacher, the Reverend Samuel Phillips, who had received his freedom in the Mexican War. In 1850 black and white Baptists delineated separate spaces within the same building; they built a new church together with a lower level for black services and meetings and an upper level for whites. Each level had its separate entrance. As a deacon, Goldsby participated in the planning and maintenance of the physical as well as the spiritual church, so he might have had some responsibility for this unusual arrangement.

For Alexander Goldsby, religion was liberation as well as an opportunity for association and governance. Goldsby and a group of other blacks in Selma organized a small band to pray regularly for freedom. Each Friday night they met outside of town under a large oak tree. Goldsby later recalled that in order to determine whether a friend was approaching the tree, they had a password. Each uttered the password softly as he came under the bough of the tree, and was answered by any other who had come ahead. Then they seated themselves in the bushes to await the hour for prayer. This prayer ritual became legendary in Selma's black community. When the war ended, Goldsby and other church leaders fulfilled their wish for independence. After a dispute with whites over the ownership of the church's building, the black Baptists sold their interest in the church and built a new one. This building became the site of the original Selma University, which provided higher education for teachers and ministers among the freedmen.

Their newfound faith gave slaves the means by which they could understand their own experience as slaves. Although antebellum journals and writings in Alabama pictured slavery in paternalistic terms, it was a cataclysmic experience for slaves. Kidnapped from their homeland, brought to an alien environment, and forced into servitude, slaves survived through the comfort of their faith. Primarily through their worship, which included the singing of spirituals and other songs and the preaching of their ministers, slaves construed their servile state as merely a temporary phase that they would pass through to receive greater reward. If they remained faithful, like Daniel whom God delivered from the lion's den, God would vindicate them and give them greater blessings than their slave masters. God was no respecter of persons but was just and merciful. In addition to liberation, such themes as patience, equality, worth, and ultimate victory were prevalent themes in the Afro-Baptist faith.

Black Slave Preachers

The main disseminators of the Afro-Baptist faith among slaves were the preachers. Two types of slave preachers emerged in Alabama and the South: those who preached at the secret meetings and those sanctioned by white churches. Ministers who had no church or association credentials received no official white endorsement. Though recognized by slaves and sometimes even slave masters, they had no legitimate authority. Other black ministers were approved and recognized by white churches and associations. Some were lay preachers, usually deacons in black Baptist branch churches. These ministers worked chiefly among blacks but a few preached to whites as well.

Baptist revivalism created a kind of quasi egalitarianism across race lines. Although there were limitations on these relationships, white Baptists recognized blacks who were gifted in expounding the gospel and lived moral lives. Sobel pointed out that it was important that these preachers shared the sacred cosmos of their black congregations but were also able to speak to whites from the white Baptist worldview. Some of these black ministers were seen as reformers among blacks, moving them from superstitions that remained in their faith. White churches and associations licensed what they perceived to be worthy black ministers and were somewhat liberal in this regard up to the 1830s. For example, in 1822 the Liberty Association licensed two slaves to preach: Samuel Wheate and Job Davis. In 1825 a slave named Lewis requested and received ordination by the Round Island Church. Doc Phillips of Tuskegee was licensed to preach and often spoke to whites, especially at association meetings.

One of the most well known and best respected black Baptist preachers was Caesar Blackwell. He was ordained in 1828. So remarkable was his preaching ability that Reverend James McLemore, a leading pastor in the Alabama Association, took Caesar with him on preaching tours, where he preached to both whites and blacks. As a result, his reputation grew among whites. In 1828 Caesar's master died and a report was made to the Alabama Association that Caesar would be sold and removed from the association. The association acted promptly and raised $625 to purchase his freedom on December 15, 1828.

One of the reasons for Blackwell's popularity with whites was his excellent theology and his attempt to elevate black Christianity by purging it of what whites saw as African superstition. He studied Calvinist theology and loved to debate its major doctrines. If a listener began to shout while Caesar was preaching, he would pause and gently chide him. Blackwell insisted that believers give accurate testimony of their conversion and not merely rely on dreams, visions, and voices. Among his many converts were Nathan Ashby and Jacob Belser, who would be leaders and organizers of the black Baptist convention, which was formed during Reconstruction in Alabama.

Another slave preacher of renown in Alabama during this early period, one who preached to both whites and blacks, was Job. Job was brought from Africa to Charleston, South Carolina, in 1806 and sold to Edward Davis. While in South Carolina, Job learned to read and write, became a Christian, and in 1818 received his license to preach. Moving to Jones Valley in Alabama with his slave owner in 1822, he became a member of the Bethel Baptist Church, located ten miles from Canaan Baptist Church in Jonesboro. He left this church with twenty other members and became one of the founding members of the Roupe's Valley Baptist Church in Tuscaloosa County. Later Job's master moved to Pickens County, in the western part of the state. There Job became a member of the Pilgrim Rest Baptist Church. He died on November 17, 1835.

Job is most remembered as a partner with the white Baptist pioneer Hosea Holcombe. Job and Holcombe traveled as a team and preached together at revivals and camp meetings. Both whites and blacks respected Job and considered him to be a preacher with great power. Holcombe, in commenting upon the life and work of Job, said: "Few better preachers were to be found in Alabama in those days than Job. He lived the Christian and died the saint. He was generally loved and respected by all who knew him." One of the leading Methodists in the county, Bayliss E. Grace, recalled that Job was pious, devout, eloquent, and "those who came to scoff, remained to pray."[13]

The liberal attitude of whites toward black preachers changed with the Nat Turner slave revolt in 1831 and the abolitionist controversy. Nat Turner, a self-styled black Baptist minister, led a revolt in South Hampton, Virginia, in which several whites were killed. This revolt sent shockwaves throughout the South and led whites to look with suspicion on black preachers. As a result of Nat Turner's actions, most slave states, including Alabama, passed laws that prohibited blacks from preaching freely and controlled the manner in which they were licensed. For example, in Georgia, a black who wanted to preach had to obtain a license from a local court and be certified by three ordained white clergymen. An 1832 Alabama law required that "five respectable slaveholders" attend any service where blacks preached. In addition, the law stated that no free black could preach to slaves in Alabama without a license. All southern states passed laws against slaves learning to read. Even the highly respect Caesar Blackwell was asked by the Alabama Association to abstain from preaching for a couple of months because of reaction to the Nat Turner revolt. Similarly, a well-known black preacher named Chessley was ordered by his master not to preach and the order was sustained by a church committee, even though the committee confessed that the order was unjust. Chessley was only allowed to preach if three whites were present. "Doc" Phillips, another well-known slave preacher, refused an offer of freedom because as a free man of color in Alabama, he would have had a more difficult time preaching to slaves in Macon County, Alabama. Several churches that had been pastored by blacks up to the 1830s in Alabama were forced to have white pastors.

William Jenkins began preaching in 1852. He recalled that he was allowed to preach in the city of Montgomery and on plantations but was not allowed to read the Bible or a newspaper. Isham Robinson, who accepted the call to the ministry in 1850, said he was only allowed to preach in the presence of two slaveholders. Mansfield Tyler of Lowndes County began preaching in 1855. He testified that the work "was exceedingly difficult, as he was not allowed to know books and might receive only oral instruction on religious subjects."[14] Prince Murrell, who preached to blacks in the First Baptist Church of Tuscaloosa and the general area, received his call to the ministry in 1844. Murrell testified that he met many discouragements in his attempt to preach to and teach blacks. "Whites were often hostile and blacks apathetic," he maintained.[15]

The hardships encountered by many of these black ministers helped prepare them for leadership among black Baptists after emancipation. Exhorters such as Prince Murrell and Mansfield Tyler became pioneers in establishing churches and associations in their areas. After slavery, Tyler organized several Baptist churches in Lowndes County and was founder and first moderator of the Alabama District Association. Prince Murrell opened the first Sunday School for blacks in Tuscaloosa in 1866 and in that same year organized the First African Baptist Church.

William Ware of Jefferson County was another slave preacher who honed his organizational skills after emancipation. He was born into slavery on the Ware plantation in East Lake, seven miles east of downtown Birmingham, on October 5, 1837, and he was baptized into the Union Baptist Church in 1856. Although Ware had a limited education, he made strenuous efforts to learn to read the Bible. Like other slave preachers throughout the South, Ware was a folksy preacher who delivered his sermons with imagination and power. He also lived a strong Christian and moral life, which endeared him to white leaders like the Reverend A. J. Waldrop. The white pastor of the Ruhama Baptist Church said of Ware, "We never had in Jefferson County a man of more stainless character."[16] Because of his strong character and native ability, Ware was allowed to preach to both whites and blacks. After emancipation, two white ministers ordained Ware. Being the only ordained black Baptist minister in Jefferson County, Ware organized several churches in the area. In 1873 he helped found the Mt. Pilgrim Association for black churches in Birmingham and Jefferson County and became its first moderator.

The Afro-Baptist faith was a major focus in the lives of Alabama slaves. Merging African and evangelical religious elements, black Baptists created a religion that emphasized conversion and rebirth and that gave them spiritual certainty and a hope for physical freedom. It was also a way of viewing and understanding their slave experience. Long desiring religious freedom and repelled by discrimination in white churches, emancipated blacks began to renounce their old religious connections and form their own churches. These churches chose their own black pastors. Often led by former slave preachers, black Baptists in Alabama would also form other religious institutions to advance their freedom and uplift themselves and others.

2
God´s Gift of Freedom

On April 9, 1865, hemmed in by federal troops, short of rations, and with fewer than thirty thousand men left, Robert E. Lee surrendered at Appomattox Court House. General Ulysses S. Grant treated his rival with respect and paroled the defeated troops. Within weeks Jefferson Davis was captured, and the remaining Confederate forces laid down their arms and surrendered. After four years and more than 1 million casualties, the Civil War was over at last. Since the war had been fought primarily on southern soil, the area had suffered great physical destruction. Southerners lost their slaves, and former Confederate states would experience extreme economic, political, and social privation for many years.

Alabama was hit particularly hard by the war. Thousands of Alabama soldiers had been killed. Agriculture was left in shambles. Union soldiers had destroyed railroad tracks as well as sixteen of the seventeen blast furnaces in the state. Federal troops occupied cities and many small towns, and their presence often led to deep resentment. After the war, Alabama entered the Reconstruction period and the ordeal of gaining readmission to the Union. One key issue involved deciding the fate of approximately four hundred thousand blacks who received their freedom as a result of the war. For most whites, the postwar years were a distressing, even tragic, time.

For blacks, Reconstruction represented a period of deep concern about their future, but it also brought jubilation and release. Many blacks, including Baptists, were convinced that God had answered their prayers for deliverance. For them, Reconstruction was both an opportunity and a challenge. They could now build their own community. Blacks manifested their new freedom by forming their own independent religious organizations. Black Baptists in Alabama and other southern states broke from white churches and formed their own congregations with blacks as pastors. Because of lack of funds, black Baptists often worshipped in primitive conditions. Despite inadequate facilities, these churches became the central institutions within the black community. Pastors emerged not only as religious leaders but also as social and civic leaders. Many of these Baptist pastors came together in 1868 to form a state convention. In turn, the convention founders established associations in their local communities.

Reconstruction was also a time of black political activity. For the first time, blacks throughout the South were allowed to vote and to elect their own political leaders. Because of their liberation theology and holistic view of the church's role in the community, it is not surprising that Baptist ministers were among the political leaders and officeholders. In some cases their churches provided a base for their political activities. Baptist laymen and pastors became Alabama state legislators; others held local office. Baptists impacted the political process and emerged as the fastest-growing black denomination in the state. During Reconstruction black and white Baptists, while having some things in common, basically went their separate ways—and they developed different interpretations of the Civil War and Reconstruction.

Black Baptist Churches

By 1860, one year before the Civil War, blacks comprised one-half of the membership of the Baptist churches in Alabama. Following the war, the Alabama Baptist State Convention and associations urged blacks to remain in their churches. Reasons included a fear that blacks would be unduly influenced by northerners, a paternalistic feeling of responsibility for blacks, and the belief that blacks, as an inferior race, could not successfully go their own way. In 1865 the state convention issued a resolution stating that whereas the convention recognized the right of former slaves to leave if they desired to do so, their changed political status in no way "necessitated a change in their relation to our churches." The convention further stated that "their highest good will be served by maintaining their present relations to those who know them, who love them, and who will labor for the promotion of their welfare."[1] Baptist leaders also ordered renewed evangelical work among blacks by means of lectures, private instruction, and Sunday schools. In 1865 the Alabama Association, located in the Montgomery area, appointed a committee to deal with the question of blacks in white churches. The committee urged churches to retain blacks in their membership. The committee reported that "blacks had no money to build churches." It agreed with the Alabama convention that "the change in the civil relationship did not necessitate a change in the spiritual relationship."[2]

Even though the Baptist convention and some associations urged blacks to remain, some whites feared that blacks would try to take over, especially in those congregations where they were in the majority. Therefore, several Baptist groups placed conditions on blacks' remaining in their churches and made it clear they expected antebellum relations to continue. Blacks could remain members, but whites would make the ultimate decisions and fill all positions of leadership. The Central Baptist Association suggested to its churches that "in view of the recent political changes, all the privileges of church membership, except that of controlling us by numbers be extended to our black members. If they cannot conform to our selection of officers, they should be accorded the privilege of forming separate organizations."[3] In 1864 a Talladega church asked the Coosa River Baptist Association what it should do about its black members. The association responded that "if the black membership was small, they should be encouraged to remain. On the other hand, if numbers were large and blacks wanted to separate, the church should not hinder them."[4]

After emancipation many blacks began to leave white churches and form their own congregations, despite the pleas of some white groups that they remain. By 1874, the year in which Reconstruction ended in Alabama, the process of separation was complete. A desire for independence and self-determination as well as the opportunity to worship as they desired motivated blacks to establish their own churches. Having developed their own worship style, blacks wanted a setting in which they could listen to and react to their own preachers, singing, dancing, and shouting. In their own churches, they could do so without being circumscribed or looked down on by whites. Their churches also promoted equality. In the biracial churches, whites had relegated them to balconies or other separate seating areas and prohibited blacks from voting on church matters. By organizing their own churches, freedmen gained some measure of freedom over their lives and the opportunity to develop pride and self-respect. In addition, with the dissolution of old communal bonds, these churches provided former slaves with a caring community.

The process of separation was more complex than has been suggested by some historians. In some cases the break occurred almost immediately after the Civil War, with blacks taking the initiative. Excited about their new freedom and confident of the future, these blacks did not hesitate to strike out on their own and to start churches without the assistance of whites. For example, during slavery blacks worshipped in the balcony of Marion's Siloam Baptist Church. After emancipation a group left the Siloam Church and began to worship under a brush arbor. In 1871 these worshippers joined another group of blacks from Siloam; together they purchased land and constructed a building, naming their church the First Colored Baptist Church of Marion. The church exists today as the Berean Baptist Church. Similarly, the Morning Star Baptist Church of Monroeville began when newly freed blacks began to worship under a brush arbor until they could purchase land and construct a building.

In some instances, black churches that formed shortly after the Civil War emerged as extensions of plantation chapels. These buildings had been constructed by owners for slave worship. After emancipation, many former slaves continued to worship in these buildings. In a few instances, these congregations formally constituted churches. For example, blacks formerly owned by William Jenkins, a slave master from Talladega, continued to worship on the Jenkins plantation. Eventually, they founded the Africa Baptist Church, and Jenkins deeded the land to the congregation.

In other cases, immediate separation of churches occurred as the result of strong black leadership. In October 1865 black members of the First Baptist Church, Tuscaloosa, asked to form a separate church. Whites and blacks understood that Prince Murrell, a black preacher and leader among the black members of the church, would become the pastor. Born a slave in South Carolina, Murrell came to Tuscaloosa with his mother and six brothers and sisters. Later he bought his freedom, learned to read and write, and started to preach. Murrell's love for freedom and independence spread among the black church members. Whites refused the request to constitute a separate church and also declined to ordain Murrell so he could serve as pastor. Charges were brought against Murrell, and he was expelled from the First Baptist Church. Shortly after this incident, Murrell led a majority of the black members into organizing the First African Baptist Church. He became pastor and served in that capacity for thirteen years.

Other black churches were organized at the initiative of white pastors. In 1865 black members comprised a majority in the Mt. Pleasant Baptist Church of Lawrence County, as well as many of the biracial churches in the Tennessee Valley. White members at Mt. Pleasant and in other churches of the Muscle Shoals Association feared that blacks would try to use their numbers to gain control. Pastor Josephus Shackelford therefore suggested that the black members form their own congregation. Reverend Shackelford assisted blacks in organizing a separate congregation known as the Mt. Pleasant Colored Baptist Church. In similar fashion, the Reverend W. M. Grimes, pastor of the Canaan Baptist Church of Bessemer in 1865, agreed with both black and white members that blacks should seek another place of worship. He led the black members in constructing a frame building in the Old Jonesboro community. He preached to the group for several years until they obtained a black pastor.

Not all blacks separated immediately from white churches. In some cases, black members asked to remain in white churches. For example, black members of the Ruhama Baptist Church of present-day East Birmingham chose to remain with the white members, agreeing not to claim equal rights but to observe former relationships. Separation did not come until 1868 when the black members withdrew and formed the Mt. Zion Baptist Church. Obadiah Woods, formerly one of the largest slave owners in the area, gave land for the building. Similarly, in 1866 white members of the Mt. Zion Baptist Church, Alexandria, suggested to blacks that because of their new status they were free to leave. Nevertheless, blacks chose to remain, and separation was delayed until 1871.

In some biracial churches one group of blacks left, and others remained. For example, seventeen members of the Alpine Baptist Church of Talladega County requested letters of dismissal in order to form a separate church in 1867. Those letters were granted, but other blacks chose to remain as members of the Alpine church. In that same year a black minister, David Welch, received permission to preach to the blacks that remained members of the white church. Even so, black and white services remained separate, and Welch could not administer the ordinances until given permission. As late as 1868, blacks reported cases of discipline to the white church for their approval.

Overall, black separation from white churches took place in stages between 1865 and 1874. A pattern developed in which blacks pressured whites for concessions until they finally asked for separation. Although whites initiated the final separation in some instances, the process usually began with blacks asking permission to worship by themselves. Subsequent requests focused on black deacons and preachers or on separate buildings. Finally, black members issued a formal request for separation. In some cases, whites allowed blacks to worship in their buildings until separate facilities were completed. Frequently, whites assisted blacks in constructing a building or in locating a new structure.

Church histories and minutes reflect the gradual separation that occurred in many Alabama Baptist churches between 1865 and 1874. The First Baptist

Church of Jacksonville and First Baptist of Wetumpka were representative of many churches. In the First Baptist Church of Jacksonville, black and white members worshipped together during the antebellum period. Shortly after the war, the pastor held separate services for white and black members. In July 1866 the church agreed to name two blacks as deacons. In that same year, blacks asked that they have their own preacher and church. White members agreed and they assisted in the search for a pastor. Ned Wyly, a member of the black branch, was licensed to preach in January 1867 at the request of his fellow black members. White and black deacons met in June 1867 to schedule separate meetings for whites and blacks in the same building. Finally, in 1869 whites gave black members letters of dismissal. Both groups continued to worship in the same church building until 1870, when whites and blacks completed a new structure for the black congregation. However, some black members remained in the First Baptist Church until 1873.

After the Civil War blacks and whites continued to worship in separate services at the First Baptist Church of Wetumpka. In 1866 rumors circulated concerning the political nature of black Baptist meetings. Suspicious whites initiated a thorough investigation when blacks requested that whites give permission for two of their number to preach. Following a meeting of the elders with the black congregation, the investigating committee found no truth to allegations of political activities. In keeping with the committee findings, the committee recommended that Green Taylor and Mark Rose be allowed to preach among the blacks members of the church as well as in the immediate vicinity. Eventually blacks began to feel increasingly uncomfortable and restricted, and the black congregation ultimately formed its own church and erected its own building.

By 1870 the vast majority of churches had separated into white and black congregations, although some blacks remained members of white churches. Most whites realized that blacks were dissatisfied with the old arrangements, and blacks were finding their own way in political affairs as well. But many whites resented black pressure and felt a sense of betrayal. An 1869 report made to the Bigbee Association of Greene County concluded that "because of their ignorance and want of confidence in whites produced by evil men, we suggest separation."[5] Obviously this report reflected the political context of Radical Reconstruction: despite white advice, blacks were cooperating with Republican "carpetbaggers" and "scalawags."

Several reasons accounted for the gradual nature of black separation from white churches. The times were dangerous for blacks after the war and many former slaves encountered hostility in cities like Selma and Montgomery. Some returned to their former communities. In these communities and in a biracial church some blacks felt more comfortable. The warm feelings and good relations that existed during the antebellum period had not completely dissipated. Many whites showed continuing paternalism and goodwill toward blacks. In addition, blacks simply had no money to build new structures. They had helped build the biracial church buildings and obviously felt some degree of ownership. In at least two instances blacks attempted to occupy the existing building. In the Eufaula Baptist Church, blacks negotiated successfully and whites sold them the church building. Blacks were thwarted in their attempt to acquire Selma's St. Phillip Street Baptist Church when whites threatened violence.

The most important factor affecting black gradualism was that black Baptists in biracial churches needed time to understand the full meaning of their newfound freedom. Blacks in states such as Virginia and Tennessee, where federal troops had been present for some time, had the opportunity to experiment with various forms of freedom and semifreedom. Not until the spring of 1865 did Union troops arrive in the Black Belt where most Alabama slaves lived, informing them of their freedom. Freedom meant different things to different people. For some blacks it meant instant separation, while for others it meant gradual spatial separation. Though northerners may have influenced some former slaves's understanding of what freedom might entail, for most blacks the idea of complete separation developed only over time. While appreciating northern financial, educational, and organizational assistance, black Baptists did not allow northerners to control their religious lives. In fact, northerners believed that the religion of Alabama black Baptists needed considerable reforms, a view with which blacks disagreed. Baptists in black Alabama churches continued to worship in their own way despite criticism from northern missionaries and teachers. They determined for themselves that emancipation meant God's deliverance and an opportunity to express their own religious views and style of worship. None of this could be accomplished while they were under white control, and by 1874 practically all black Baptists had departed from biracial churches.

Although some white congregations gave buildings to blacks and in other instances assisted blacks in constructing churches, most black Baptist churches began in primitive settings. Many began in log cabins or under brush arbors, open-air churches that consisted of four posts with a covering of brushes and leaves. Over time these churches moved to more permanent structures. For example, the Morning Star Baptist Church of Monroeville began by worshiping in a brush arbor but later moved to a log house under a nearby grove of oaks. Because of the dirt floor and cracks in the logs, many worshippers left the church with tick bites. Hence, the church earned its nickname as "the tick church." Eventually, the Morning Star membership constructed a frame building and began worshipping there in 1887. Similarly, the first building of the Good Hope Baptist Church of Monroe County when it was organized in 1871 was a rough log house; it was replaced later by a hewed-log house and finally by a frame building. The Amity Baptist Church, also in Monroe County, started in a brush arbor located near the Amity community cemetery. The congregation purchased land from one of its members and constructed a frame building in 1877. Birmingham's Sixteenth Street Baptist Church began in a tinner's shop on the fringe of the downtown area.

Despite primitive conditions, churches became the center of life for the black community during Reconstruction. Churches became social hubs, educational centers, and meeting places for political gatherings. The church constituted the one institution that blacks controlled and where members expressed their hopes and goals through religious liturgy. Because of its unique role in the community, black pastors would exert considerable influence during Reconstruction.

Formation of State Convention

By December 1868 black Baptists had established approximately fifty churches in the state. Among these were the Stone Street and the St. Louis Street Baptist Churches in Mobile, the Columbus Street Baptist Church in Montgomery, the St. Phillips Street Baptist Church in Selma, the First African Baptist Church in Uniontown, the Salem Baptist Church in Greensboro, the First African Baptist Church in Eufaula, the Mt. Olive and the First Baptist Church of Lowndesboro in Lowndes County, the Mt. Olive Baptist Church in Tuskegee, the Africa Baptist Church in Talladega, and the Mt. Pleasant Baptist Church in Madison County. With the establishment of these and other black Baptist churches, the foundation was laid for a statewide organization.

On September 29, 1868, a notice appeared in the *Alabama State Journal* calling for a meeting to form a black Baptist convention. Fifteen people from the Montgomery area issued the call for the purpose of promoting missions and evangelism among freedmen. On December 17, 1868, sixty people met at Montgomery's Columbus Street Baptist Church to form the convention. Twenty-six people representing twenty-seven churches were qualified as delegates.

The Columbus Street Baptist Church, later known as the First Colored Baptist Church, exerted considerable influence at the initial meeting of the convention. All the initial officers were members of this church, and Columbus Street hosted the first three sessions. Located in the largest city on the edge of the Black Belt, this congregation was known for its large building, its membership that included some of the key political and business leaders of the black community, and the missionary vision attained from its strongest benefactor, I. T. Tichenor.

The relationship with Tichenor stemmed from the church's formation in the basement of the white First Baptist Church of Montgomery in 1866. Prior to this formation, blacks worshipped as a separate congregation in the basement where white and black ministers preached to them on Sunday afternoons. However, as a branch church its actions were subject to supervision by the white congregation. After the Civil War, blacks remained in the same relationship for one year, but they became uncomfortable with this arrangement and pressed for separation. Under Pastor Isaac Taylor Tichenor's leadership, white members purchased land for the black church. Tichenor made an extended trip through the North to raise funds for the new church. When that effort proved unsuccessful, he secured a loan locally, and on July 28, 1867, approximately six hundred members formed the Columbus Street Baptist Church. Within eighteen months the church had grown to nine hundred members.

The missionary spirit inspired by Tichenor apparently affected Nathan Ashby, the first president of the Alabama Convention. Ashby preached to slaves under the tutelage of Tichenor and emulated his missionary emphasis. Tichenor exercised considerable zeal during his two pastorates at First Baptist before the war. He served as a missionary to Indians, held protracted meetings for blacks, preached to slaves, and was an active member of both the Alabama Baptist State Convention and the Southern Baptist Convention. After the war, he urged white Baptists to work for the education and evangelization of the freedmen. Speaking to the white Alabama Association, he reminded them that "if Southern Baptists [do] not assist blacks the Yankees will."[6]

The all-black Consolidated American Baptist Missionary Convention also influenced the convention's formation. In particular, William Troy, first president and general agent for the convention, and Frank Quarles, who was a member of the executive committee, provided guidance. Troy preached the opening sermon and Quarles gave advice and counsel. Delegates expressed gratitude for Quarles's counsel by making him a life member at the second convention. Quarles served as pastor of the Friendship Baptist Church in Atlanta and became the first president of the Georgia convention upon its formation in 1871.

The Consolidated American Baptist Missionary Convention was the result of a merger in 1866 of the Northwestern and Southern Baptist Convention and the American Baptist Missionary Convention. Formed in New York City in 1840, the American Baptist Missionary Convention emerged when black Baptists in the Northeast felt that the white Baptist convention had not taken a strong stand against slavery and had neglected missions on the African continent. The primary motive for the formation of the Northwestern and Southern Convention in 1864 was to establish missions among the freedmen in the border and southern states. The merger of these two conventions constituted the first attempt to build a national convention among black Baptists in the United States. Convention leaders emphasized the need to send black missionaries into the southern states to form churches, associations, and conventions. National convention officers believed that southern blacks should provide their own leadership rather than relying on established white leadership. Other major concerns included the importance of ministerial education; the care of widows of deceased ministers; the cooperation with Bible, Sunday school and tract societies; and opposition to the use of intoxicating beverages. These became immediate concerns for the Colored Missionary Convention of Alabama.

Although two white northern groups, the American Baptist Publication Society and the American Baptist Home Missionary Society, missed the initial session of the Alabama convention, they provided support in the early years as the black Baptists struggled to establish their work. Most notable among groups exerting no influence and providing little support were the white Baptist churches of Alabama. Though they claimed various reasons for their inactivity, the real reason was almost certainly race relations. White Baptists in Alabama simply could not adjust to the new conditions that freedom brought. They were not prepared to treat blacks as equals, and they feared that continued association with black members would foster social equality. So whites defended their actions by citing a lack of funds, the reluctance of blacks to accept aid, and the influence of northern missionaries. By 1869 white Baptists in Alabama praised segregated churches as benevolent organizations, despite their lack of concern for freedmen. By 1870 working relationships between white and black Baptists were almost completely severed and would remain so for many years.

The formation of the Colored Baptist Missionary Convention was also the result of what some historians have called the "spirit of the times." The period immediately after emancipation was one of religious organization among blacks. Black Methodist groups formed conferences, and Baptists established conventions throughout the South. Kentucky led the way in 1865. North Carolina organized in 1866, followed by Virginia and Arkansas in 1867. Other states followed suit including Mississippi (1869), Georgia (1870), Tennessee and Louisiana (1872), Texas (1875), and South Carolina (1876). Not surprisingly this spirit carried over into Alabama.

Of the twenty-six delegates present at the initial 1868 convention, most came from the Black Belt. Six came from Montgomery; four from Tuskegee; and two each from Greenville, Uniontown, Auburn, and Lowndes County. There were no delegates from Mobile or North Alabama. Slow communications accounted for the lack of participation from those areas. However, the missionary Washington Stevens went to Mobile in 1869, and his visit contributed to the presence of Reverend B. Burke, pastor of the Stone Street Baptist Church, at the 1869 convention. North Alabama responded more slowly partly because of its physical isolation from the rest of the state. Moreover, residents of the northern part of the state often identified more with Tennessee than with Alabama.

The convention's most important positions consisted of president, corresponding secretary, recording secretary, and missionary. Every person initially elected to these positions was a member of the Columbus Street Baptist Church. All were former slaves who had advanced themselves despite the limitations of a white-dominated society. Each was literate and at least three officials owned considerable personal property. Their Christianity was permeated with a desire for doctrine, discipline, evangelism, and missions.

Convention delegates elected Nathan Ashby as president. Born in Fredericksburg, Virginia, August 5, 1810, Ashby was taken from his grandmother at age sixteen and sold with some horses to traders who brought him to Alabama. A carpenter by trade, he purchased his freedom at age thirty-two for nine hundred dollars. After moving to Montgomery and gaining his license to preach around 1845, he preached to black members of the First Baptist Church of Montgomery. Montgomery courthouse records dated 1865 reveal that Ashby was then fifty-five, married, and the father of two children. He was literate, a mulatto, and had property valued at two thousand dollars, which made him one of the most prosperous blacks in Montgomery. Ashby was ordained to the ministry in 1867 by the Reverend I. T. Tichenor, the pastor who had assisted him in preaching to the slaves at First Baptist Church. When the Columbus Street Baptist Church organized later that year, Ashby became pastor. He led the congregation for three years until he became ill and was unable to perform his pastoral duties.

Corresponding Secretary James A. Foster was born a slave in Kentucky. After emancipation, he came to Alabama and joined the Columbus Street Baptist Church; he was ordained to the ministry by Ashby and Tichenor. Foster pastored for a time in Mt. Meigs before succeeding Ashby as pastor of the Columbus Street Baptist Church. During those two pastorates, he baptized ten thousand people and preached four thousand sermons. In addition to his pastoral duties, he was a trustee of the state normal school (now Alabama State University), a trustee of Swayne Schools, and moderator of the Spring Hill Association. Charles O. Boothe, pioneer historian of black Baptists in Alabama, described him as "a man who was a liberal giver toward causes, a strong pastor, a dedicated family man, and a lover of missions and education."[7] Foster held many convention positions during the Reconstruction period, and he served as president from 1873 to 1875.

The recording secretary, Holland Thompson, was a deacon of the Columbus Street Baptist Church. Born a slave in Alabama, he worked as a waiter at the Madison House Hotel in Montgomery. Having learned to read and write while still a slave, Thompson had his marriage legalized by 1866 and opened a small grocery store. By 1870 he owned city real estate worth at least five hundred dollars and personal property valued at two hundred. Although a layman, Thompson exerted considerable influence during the early years of the convention. His position required a literate person at a time when few blacks could read and write. In addition, he issued circular letters for the convention, printed and distributed minutes to churches, and made a yearly report to the convention in the early years of Reconstruction.

Because of the importance of missions and evangelism to the convention, the missionary exerted influence second only to the president. The convention hired a missionary to carry out its evangelical initiative by forming new churches and strengthening those already in existence. Washington Stevens was elected missionary at the first convention. Other than his membership in the Columbus Street Baptist Church, little is known about his personal history.

However, in his first report to the convention in 1869, he stated that he had "traveled 2,422 miles, preached ninety sermons, baptized 60 candidates, ordained 21 deacons, and organized three churches." He also reported that he had traversed "the state from Mobile to northern Alabama."[8] In spite of his prolific efforts, Stevens was not reelected. Rather, Prince Murrell of Tuscaloosa became missionary for the convention.

Four documents adopted at the initial meeting spelled out the convention's purpose and structure. The constitution was the most important of these documents, and its second article clearly stated the convention's purpose: "It shall be the object of this Convention to propagate the Gospel of Christ, and to advance the interest of his kingdom, by supplying vacant churches as requested; by sending ministers into destitute regions within our reach; and by planting and building up churches wherever a favorable opportunity offers, and also to promote the educational interests of the destitute. This Convention shall in no case interfere with the internal regulations of churches or associations."[9] The convention's basic and overriding concern was to provide some form of order.

Coming out of slavery and moving away from white churches, blacks were prone to move toward all types of religious beliefs and practices. Spiritualism, voodoo, fortune telling, palm reading, and other African survivals presented a threat to their Christianity. An 1868 report of the white Alabama Baptist State Convention's Committee on the Religious Instruction of the Colored People maintained that the religious condition of the freedmen was deteriorating rapidly. "Naturally superstitious and credulous," the report stated, "no delusions are too absurd to find entrance into their minds."[10] Although this report may have reflected some bias because whites resented the fact that blacks had chosen to go their own way, it does possess some truth. Black Baptist growth and development exhibited little order or structure, and convention minutes from the Reconstruction conventions indicate that founders sought orderly development above all else.

To promote order, the convention leaders stressed the need for doctrine and education. In 1870 the convention issued a circular letter to its churches maintaining that the Scripture provided the only basis for doctrine and discipline. Minutes of the 1872 convention minutes include a document titled "Articles of Faith and Practice," issued by James Foster, pastor of Columbus Street Baptist Church and a convention officer. Foster's document stressed such evangelical themes as authority of the Scripture, salvation by faith, the atonement of Jesus Christ, divine election, and the resurrection of the body. In addition, a sermon preached by Mansfield Tyler and carried in the 1874 convention minutes stated unequivocally that immersion was the only true form of baptism.

Education was of special importance to the convention founders as well. In its initial session of the 1868 convention, members established a committee on education, and the following year a resolution passed encouraging delegates to do all in their power to establish Sabbath schools. In 1870 the convention advised its churches "to build schoolhouses and churches in their own means, declining all union proffered by others, unless absolutely necessary."[11] In 1872 a proposal called for a Sunday school convention to establish a more uniform system for Sunday schools in the churches. The Sunday School Congress took form slowly, but Sunday schools did begin to enroll in the convention. The educational concern of the convention peaked in 1873 when William McAlpine made a motion that the convention establish a theological school to train ministers, and five men, including McAlpine, were appointed to serve as managers for starting the school. According to convention historian C. O. Boothe, "this threw new life into the convention and signs of activity immediately appeared."[12]

Morality ranked as another major concern of convention founders. Marriage was the primary moral issue that concerned black Baptist leaders during Reconstruction. Prior to emancipation black marriages were not considered legal, and black families often were separated because of economic factors. After the Civil War, leaders of the convention spent much of their time performing marriage ceremonies. Boothe reported in 1895 that James Foster, pastor of Montgomery's First African Baptist Church and a leader among black Baptists, had performed more than six hundred marriages during his two pastorates.

Temperance constituted yet another important moral issue. Convention leaders were convinced that Alabama's black community could not elevate itself unless excessive alcohol consumption was curtailed. Consequently, the first session of the convention passed a resolution stating that "the use of intoxicating drink as a beverage was injurious and most destructive to morals and urged pastors to influence their members to abandon its use." Four years later, Prince Murrell introduced a similar resolution and encouraged ministers to discontinue the use of intoxicating drinks and make every effort to promote temperance. This resolution was strengthened the following year, and all pastors and Sunday school superintendents were asked to speak on temperance at least once per month.[13]

District Associations

Two African American associations predate the state convention—the Eufaula Association and the Bethlehem Association. The Eufaula Association formed in 1867, one year before the state convention, due primarily to efforts by Reverends William McCoo and Jerry Shorter, and deacons J. E. Timothy of Eufaula and Byrd Day of Glenville. The Bethlehem Association of Monroe County was founded in 1868, just a few months before the convention.

Other associations were formed between 1869 and 1870, and two of the principal founders had been delegates to the state convention. In 1869 Mansfield Tyler created the Alabama District Association, which comprised several churches in Lowndes County. The following year, William McAlpine organized the Rushing Springs Association composed primarily of churches in Talladega County. In addition, the Shelby County Association and the Muscle Shoals Association in North Alabama formed in 1869, and the Old Pine Grove Association was organized in Bullock County in 1870.

Between 1870 and 1874, a number of associations came into being. In 1871 black Baptists formed the Colored Bethlehem Association in southwest Alabama, the New Cahaba Association in Dallas County, and the Salem Association in southeast Alabama. The Dallas and Uniontown Associations began in 1872, and in 1873 the Wills Creek and Mud Creek Associations organized in Etowah and Jackson County, respectively. In 1874 black congregations formed the Lebanon Association in Pickens County, the Morning Star Association in Coosa and Elmore Counties, the Mt. Pilgrim Association in Jefferson County, the Spring Hill Association in Montgomery, and the Union Association in Greenville. By the end of Reconstruction at least nineteen associations had been formed in Alabama.

Although few association records exist from the Reconstruction period, these groups apparently followed the same pattern as and expressed similar concerns to the state convention. Formed by leaders of the state convention, associations focused on order, discipline, doctrine, education, and morality.

Black Baptists and Reconstruction Politics

Even though Alabama blacks experienced many changes after the Civil War, they were relatively slow in becoming active in politics. Whites denied the ballot to them until the Reconstruction Acts of 1867 enfranchised blacks and called for constitutional conventions in ten southern states. Before this time, blacks expressed themselves through rallies, barbecues, and political conventions. Even so, official statements remained moderate in tone. Blacks exercised caution so as not to give the impression of challenging their former masters directly. For example, at the first Colored Convention held in Mobile in November 1865, the participants adopted a resolution that called for peace, friendship, and goodwill toward all men. Convention delegates, most of whom were ministers, urged their fellow freedmen to work industriously, to educate their children, to live moral lives, and to avoid fighting among themselves.

As blacks became more politically active they comprised a majority in the Republican Party, and became more assertive, demanding greater economic and political rights. Meeting again in Mobile in May 1867, the second statewide Colored Convention revealed increasing growth in black expectations. After two days of debate and deliberation, delegates adopted a series of resolutions calling for a public school system, relief for the aged and homeless, and military assistance to counter election abuses. Blacks also proclaimed their right to sit on juries, ride on all public conveyances, and sit at public tables. Later, they issued a proclamation to the people of Alabama insisting that blacks should have the same rights as whites.

Encountering organized politics for the first time in the summer of 1867 during voter registration preceding the state's constitutional convention, many blacks registered to vote and overwhelmingly supported the call for a convention. Election results indicated that 71,730 blacks and 18,553 whites voted for the convention and that 5,583 whites were opposed. Seventeen of the delegates were black. In addition, fifty-seven blacks served as voting registrars, and this experience produced a group of future leaders for the state. Ten of the seventeen delegates continued to be active in politics, with most serving in the state legislature.

Black delegates to the constitutional convention showed no spirit of revenge toward whites. With few exceptions they showed little interest in restricting the rights of former Confederates. Rather, blacks focused on more pragmatic matters. They stressed issues such as voting, education, land acquisition, and other concerns important to uplifting the black race. Despite the desire for land among blacks, their representatives were unwilling to entertain programs that called for radical redistribution. Moreover, black votes indicated some ambivalence on the question of integration. Overall, blacks voted against segregated schools, hotels, and public transportation but they did not press the issue. Apparently, blacks did not want to unduly alienate a majority of whites.

With approval of the new Alabama constitution, blacks for the first time gained election to political office in the state. Although many served as officials in their local communities, they sought to make their greatest impact as state legislators. In the 1867 election, 27 blacks won seats as representatives and I was elected to the state Senate. Between 1877 and 1884, 105 blacks served in the state legislature. They continued the trend established by delegates to the constitutional convention by promoting an attitude of pragmatism and racial uplift.

Black churches were in the forefront in the advocacy and exercise of political rights during Reconstruction. They served as places for political rallies and Republican Party meetings. Local Union Leagues, Republican Party organizations pledged to the principles of equal rights, also often met in church buildings. Black ministers reflected the people's enthusiasm for politics and their hopes for full citizenship, and many of them felt the need to become political leaders. Black Baptists, armed with their Afro-Baptist faith that stressed liberation and a holistic ministry, would exert political influence. Five outstanding Baptist leaders were among those who served as black legislators: Holland Thompson, Alexander Curtis, Lloyd Leftwich, Mansfield Tyler, and John Dozier.

Holland Thompson, a layman from Montgomery, became the most prominent of the early political figures affiliated with the Alabama Colored Baptist State Convention. One of the people who formed the Colored Baptist State Convention in 1868, he was elected corresponding secretary, a position that made him a powerful figure in the early years of the convention. His work at Montgomery's First Colored Baptist Church also aided his political success. Thompson was one of three people who purchased the lots for the church, and he became the first president of the Sabbath school. Two years later, he became president of the 180-member missionary society attached to the school.

In addition to his religious involvement, Thompson's participation as leader of the Union League's Lincoln Council assisted his rise to prominence in state politics. In May 1867 he was elected as a delegate to the first Union Republican State Convention. In September of the same year, he won approval from the Montgomery County Convention to nominate five delegates—two white northerners, two white southerners, and one black to serve as delegates to the state constitutional convention. In addition, Thompson was one of the few black officials chosen to serve on the first state Republican Executive Committee.

Thompson's political rhetoric, like that of most early black political leaders, was conciliatory in his early years, but unlike many black leaders he placed the highest priority on making the new southern homestead law a more effective means of providing land for the freedmen. Even as he encouraged blacks to become more assertive in attaining land and challenged the policies of President Andrew Johnson, he consistently attempted to allay white fears. He spoke out against the confiscation of white-owned property, encouraged blacks to forsake hard feelings toward whites, and called only for civil and political rights, believing that social rights would come in due course.

Thompson's demands for equal rights for blacks would become stronger over time. In 1869 he was elected to the Montgomery City Council where he focused on improving living conditions for blacks. He took special interest in the condition of streets in the black community. Concerned for the poor, he advocated soup kitchens, aid for poor families, and increased wages for street workers, most of whom were black. During his years on the council, Thompson advocated the employment of black policemen, a cause in which he achieved notable success. Thompson also emphasized education, championing the council's allocation of funds for Montgomery's schools and serving as the only black member of the city's five-man school board.

Thompson's work in politics was most pronounced as a state legislator, having been elected to a two-year term in 1868 and again in 1870. During both terms he was one of three blacks in the five-man Montgomery delegation. Like most freshmen legislators, he moved cautiously through his first year in office. However, in the 1869–70 sessions, he became very active in debate and introduced several controversial bills. As he had done as a member of the city council, Thompson promoted legislation that would benefit blacks, either directly or indirectly, and became one of the most militant spokesmen for black rights. He sponsored a bill that established a savings association in Montgomery. He unsuccessfully sought to establish the office of Montgomery county advocate to defend people who were unable to hire lawyers. He was equally unsuccessful in trying to defeat legislation aimed at impeding the growth of black political power. As with other black legislators, Thompson sought an end to the exclusion of blacks from public facilities by advocating equal treatment without demanding integration. Education remained a prime concern, and he sponsored bills designed to provide educational opportunities for the freedmen of Alabama.

Thompson performed ably as a state legislator, but he failed to gain renomination in 1872, a turn of event that would lead to his demise as a political figure. Thompson's fall was the result of a number of factors: his aggressiveness at introducing bills to benefit blacks, which alienated many white Republicans; persistent factionalism in the Republican Party; conflicts within the First Colored Baptist Church; declining health; and personal family problems. He would hold no political office after 1875.

Another Baptist layman, Alexander H. Curtis, was one of the most effective Baptist legislators, especially in terms of longevity. Born a slave in Raleigh, North Carolina, in 1829, he came to Alabama with his master in 1839. He moved to Marion in 1848, became a barber, and was able to save enough money to purchase his freedom for two thousand dollars in 1859. Afterward, he went to New York, but returned to Marion after the Civil War where he reopened his barbering business and became a successful merchant and farmer.

In 1861 Curtis joined the Second Baptist Church in Marion and became a staunch member of that congregation. He was a delegate to the Alabama Colored Baptist Convention in 1873 and became an active member of the convention. Seven years later, convention delegates then meeting in Eufaula appointed Curtis to a committee charged with laying the groundwork for establishing a Baptist school. Although Curtis advocated Marion as the site for the institution, the committee and convention established the school at Selma. Curtis proved a valuable force in starting the institution known today as Selma University.

Curtis was also a major force in establishing another school. In 1867 he and six other people from Perry County incorporated Lincoln School in Marion. The following year the trustees transferred the school's property to the American Missionary Association. Lincoln School evolved into a state-supported normal school by 1874; later it was moved to Montgomery, where it became Alabama State University.

Curtis began his political career in 1870 when he was elected to the House of Representatives. Serving one term in the House, he became a state senator in 1872 and served three terms. In addition, he served as a delegate to the 1868 Constitutional Convention, which met in Montgomery to draft a new postwar constitution. In addition to his support of public and private education, Curtis also attempted to garner equal rights for Alabama blacks. He supported the amended Civil Rights Bill of 1873 that entitled all citizens to equal accommodations on common carriers. Although not an advocate of social equality, he felt strongly that blacks should enjoy the same privileges as whites in all public places and events. In 1874 he was a delegate to the Equal Rights Association that supported the Civil Rights Bill and urged blacks to remain in the Republican Party.

Lloyd Leftwich, a Baptist minister, served in the Alabama legislature as a member of the House of Representatives from 1872 to 1876. Born a slave in Virginia in 1832, Leftwich settled with his master in Forkland, Alabama, near the end of the Civil War. Somehow, either by hard work or a stroke of good fortune, he was able to purchase his master's plantation. As a legislator he supported public education and those causes that provided opportunities for blacks to own land. A devout Baptist, he donated land from his plantation for the construction of a community church and an elementary school for the black residents of Greene County. The Lloyd Chapel Baptist Church in Greene County still bears his name.

One of the most outstanding Baptist pastors and denominational leaders who served in the Alabama House of Representatives was Mansfield Tyler. Born a slave near Augusta, Georgia, Tyler joined the Springfield Baptist Church, a large black church that had more than a thousand members and whose pastors were blacks. When he was about eighteen, Tyler moved with his master to Alabama. At twenty he was converted and accepted his call to the ministry. He often commented on the difficulties experienced by slave preachers who were discouraged from holding any kind of meetings and had to preach to black congregations that met in secret to express their spiritual feelings. On some plantations, slaves could hold religious meetings provided a white person were present. These experiences, Tyler explained, helped prepare him for leadership.

After emancipation, Tyler moved to Lowndes County. He learned to read and organized a Baptist church in his community in 1867. The next year he was ordained. The following year, he organized other churches in Lowndes County. One of these was the First Baptist Church of Lowndesboro where he baptized a thousand people. A few years later he organized a Baptist church at Whitehall where he baptized five hundred people. Tyler was instrumental in establishing several other churches in Lowndes County. So influential was Tyler that some referred to him as the Baptist "pope" of Lowndes County.

Tyler also became a leader among black Alabama Baptists, helping to establish the Alabama Baptist State Convention in 1868. Later, when Selma University was founded, he became the first chair of the school's board of trustees; he served in that capacity for twenty-seven years. During his tenure as chair, the board established the Tyler Medal in his honor. It was given annually to the student with the best oratorical skills. From 1867 to 1886 Tyler served as president of the Alabama Colored Baptist State Convention. During the peak years of his career, few men held more influence over Alabama Baptists.

Tyler served in the Alabama legislature from 1870 to 1872. For Tyler, the key to the success of blacks rested in getting an education and acquiring property. His work in the legislature advocated programs that made it possible for blacks to achieve those goals. High among his concerns in the legislature was building a strong public education system.

John Dozier's role as pastor provided a base for his political activities. Born a slave in Virginia in 1800, Dozier learned to read and write. His owner, president of a college in Virginia, also taught him to read Greek before granting him his freedom. Unfortunately, Dozier's master had sold his wife and son to a plantation owner in Alabama. After Dozier obtained his freedom, he came to Alabama in search of his family, finally settling in Marion. After reuniting his family, he went to Uniontown, where he established the First Colored Baptist Church.

Dozier's political career began in 1867 when he served as a delegate to the second Freedmen's convention. This meeting professed its faith in the U.S. government and opposition to the treatment of blacks at the hands of white Alabamians. Delegates declared that "blacks should have the same rights, privileges, and immunities as enjoyed by white men."[14]

Dozier served two terms in the Alabama legislature from 1870 to 1874. Assuming office at age seventy, he was the oldest of the black legislators. Three major issues were central to Dozier's political and ministerial life: land ownership, education, and civil rights. He bought a 320-acre farm in Perry County that was valued at sixteen hundred dollars. While in the legislature he served as a trustee of Lincoln Normal School and voted for measures designed to improve the public schools. In addition, he favored the Civil Rights Bill of 1873 that legally prohibited discrimination on common carriers, in hotels, and in schools, and in places of amusement such as theaters. However, Dozier opposed integrated schools because he felt such an action would hurt the Republican Party.

Black Baptist leaders in the Alabama legislature performed well, especially when one considers the limitations and restrictions that were placed on them. From the outset of Reconstruction their interests were often at variance with those of white Republicans. Consequently, many white Republicans formed alliances with Democrats rather than advance legislation that benefited blacks. Internecine conflict between blacks and whites was common within the Alabama Republican Party. Although blacks made up the majority membership of the party, they did not share equally in the important offices. In addition, many blacks felt that both scalawags and carpetbaggers shared common prejudices against them and did not accept them as equals.

The work of all blacks, including Baptists, was also noteworthy because of the intimidation they faced. Terrorist groups often targeted black churches and ministers who were politically active. Black churches that opened their doors to the Union League and the Republican Party were subject to attacks. The Liberty Baptist Church of Sumterville was burned apparently in retaliation for having allowed Republicans to meet there. Richard Burke, a Baptist minister, teacher, and Union League organizer who served in the state House of Representatives from 1868 to 1870, was killed after rumors circulated that he advocated arming blacks. Jessie Duke, editor of the *Baptist Leader* and a political activist in the Republican Party, was forced to immigrate to Arkansas after publishing inflammatory editorials.

In spite of threats and intimidation these black Baptist legislators, like their counterparts in Georgia, South Carolina, and Louisiana, showed no bitterness toward white southerners. These Christian men held beliefs that taught them to be generous and forgiving, and to eschew vindictiveness. Even as they fought for programs to enhance blacks, they did not want to alienate or to punish whites. They made no attempt to pursue radical programs, to confiscate white-owned land, or to proscribe the liberties or rights of white citizens. They knew that whites still had the economic power, and they sought to win both their trust and support. Most of all, these black leaders promoted legislation that would benefit blacks throughout Alabama. Education, economic opportunity, acquisition of land, and basic civil rights in terms of equal access to public facilities remained their major goals.

The Nature of Black Baptist Religion

By the end of Reconstruction black Baptists had become one of the most effective and largest movements in the African American community of Alabama. One reason for this was their worship pattern. Taking the language, ritual, and biblical traditions from the sermons, hymns, and catechism lessons learned in slavery, black Baptists integrated and transformed them into their own religious services. Worship in black Baptist churches in Alabama during Reconstruction was highly emotional. Chanting, singing, preaching, and praying dominated the services. Sermons, delivered in a chanting pattern, were designed to uplift, liberate, and provide security in a hostile world. Pianos and organs were almost nonexistent. Singing was congregational. Negro spirituals and lined hymns were most common. Shouting was expected and encouraged. Utterances of strong emotions during services was a result of the unique worship developed by African Americans during slavery in which they combined African and evangelical Christian elements. Worship also represented a response to the harsh conditions under which blacks lived and worked. During Reconstruction most blacks were forced into a system of tenancy known as sharecropping. The sharecropper often ended the year in debt to the landlord, year after year. In their worship black Baptists heard sermons on Old Testament characters like Moses and Joshua, and on the return of Jesus Christ when there would be no more hunger and pain but beauty and sunshine. This caused them to erupt in joy and celebration.

Such emotional and joyful worship was one of the reasons that black Baptists expanded much faster than the Congregational, Presbyterian, and Episcopal churches. In practical terms, none of these churches could compete with Baptists. Their liturgical worship services failed to address the needs of an oppressed people who needed a more emotional experience. Blacks turned toward Baptist churches, which continued to combine African and evangelical elements and to provide an environment in which they could witness the heartfelt moving of God's spirit among his people. In addition, these other denominations did not attract blacks because of a dearth of African American pastors, due in part to educational requirements. Blacks preferred churches presided over by their own ministers, churches where they could express their own cultural and religious heritage.

The black Baptist movement was also the most indigenous of all the religious groups. Pastors from within the state provided key leadership. When the state Baptist convention was formed, a few men from the all-black American Baptist Missionary Convention provided some advice, but they gave no guidance or support after the initial meeting. In contrast, other religious groups in Alabama, including the black Methodists who constituted the second largest group, had leadership that came primarily from outside the state and the local community. Most Methodist bishops came from other states, and they depended on other state conferences to provide their pastors and leaders. For example, when the AME Alabama Conference formed in 1868, there were only seven local preachers. The bishop, five of the traveling elders, and ten of the deacons had transferred from established conferences in Georgia and Louisiana. Because northern religious groups like the Presbyterian and Congregational denominations had strict educational requirements, ministers who came to Alabama were primarily white. A limited number of educated northern blacks served in Alabama churches, but many of the early black Baptist leaders had been slave preachers. Others, like Prince Murrell and Nathan Ashby, had gained their personal freedom but continued to minister to slaves. Baptist ministers came from the bosom of the people and sought to minister to the needs of their congregations. This gave black Baptists a tremendous advantage over other religious groups.

Although black Baptists exhibited worship patterns, ecclesiology, and theological beliefs similar to those of white Baptists, they increasingly drew away from white congregations as the Reconstruction era came to a close, although some biracial activities continued. For example, H. E. Taliaferro, former editor of the denominational paper and a respected minister among Southern Baptists in Alabama, pastored a black church in Mt. Meigs and continued to pastor black churches until 1872. Other white ministers preached revivals for black churches throughout the state in the 1860s. However, such biracialism became the exception near the end of Reconstruction. By that time separation was well under way and the process brought with it recriminations, increasing racism, and segregation. As early as 1868 the Alabama Baptist Convention reported that race relations were deteriorating, basing its conclusions on black superstition and idolatry. An article published in the denominational newspaper in that same year argued that blacks were subhuman and should be crushed. By 1869 the white state convention no longer submitted reports on black evangelism, indicating that the majority of white Baptists had lost interest in the evangelism or education of blacks.

Differing interpretations of the ways in which God acted in history also contributed to the increasing separation between white and black Baptists. White Baptists emerged from the Civil War period with the view that God had chastised them and given them a special mission—to maintain orthodoxy, strict biblicism, personal piety, and traditional race relations. Slavery, they insisted, had not been sinful. Rather, emancipation was a historical tragedy and the end of Reconstruction was a clear sign of God's favor.

On the other hand, black Baptists viewed the Civil War, emancipation, and Reconstruction as God's gift of freedom. They appreciated opportunities to exercise their independence, to worship in their own way, to affirm their worth and dignity, and to proclaim the fatherhood of God and the brotherhood of man. Most of all, they could form their own churches, associations, and conventions. These institutions offered self-help and racial uplift, and provided places where the gospel of liberation could be proclaimed. As a result, black preachers continued to insist that God would protect and help them; God would be their rock in a stormy land.

Reconstruction ended in Alabama in 1874. As in other southern states, northern capitulation, violence from southern terrorist groups, and internecine conflict within the Republican Party contributed to the decline in federal authority. Consequently, black political power was greatly diluted. Still, black Baptists held onto their statewide organization, a theology that emphasized self-help and liberation, and a focus on education. By remaining true to their goals, black Alabama Baptists sought to extend their influence and uplift of blacks through churches and associations as well as through their convention in a state that would attempt to thwart the advancement of people of color after the end of Reconstruction.

2
Post-Reconstruction, 1874–1900

3
Church Life, Expansion, and Denominational Concerns

In October 1870 a group of armed whites broke up a Republican campaign rally at Eutaw, the county seat of Greene County, Alabama, killing four blacks and wounding fifty-four other people including whites. This incident, known as the "Eutaw riot," was designed to discourage Republicans, black and white, from voting. The Eutaw riot along with similar acts of violence would help end Radical Reconstruction in Alabama four years later.

Beginning in 1874 conservative Democrats reestablished political leadership in Alabama. Some called these men Redeemers because they presided over the defeat of the Republican Party and the restoration of white supremacy. Others referred to them as Bourbons, after the reinstated French monarchy. They promoted spending policies that severely reduced money for social services and education. Those policies would negatively impact Alabama into the twenty-first century. Among the post-Reconstruction leaders were advocates of the New South who insisted that industrialization and commerce were key to the South's revitalization. A number of newspaper editors took the lead in this effort; other advocates were prominent Alabama Baptists Isaac Tichenor and Benjamin Riley. Although neither man subscribed to the virulent racism of the times, both were strong advocates of southern orthodoxy and sectionalism.

The post-Reconstruction period was one of deteriorating race relations and a hardening of racial lines. Bourbon Democrats consistently used racial fear to maintain power. Historian Rayford W. Logan referred to this period as the nadir of race relations in the United States. Racial violence increased with the lynching of almost two hundred African Americans in Alabama between 1882 and 1902. Fewer blacks served in the state legislature than had during Reconstruction. And black subordination was a major plank in the southern Democratic platform during this era.

With such potential violence arrayed against them and the dilution of black political power, the church assumed an even greater role in the black community, particularly in Alabama's Black Belt. Ministers continued as important leaders, and churches increased along with the formation of new associations. The Colored Baptist Missionary Convention, formed in 1868, went through a period of rapid growth, organization, and expansion. In many ways, this constituted the formative period for black Baptists in Alabama. They established most of their educational and convention organizations during this time, and women formed a state convention as they assumed a greater role in Baptist life. As the number of churches, associations, and state conventions increased throughout the United States, church leaders envisioned a convention that would unite all black Baptists in one organization. Alabama Baptists exerted considerable influence in forming the Baptist Foreign Mission Convention, the forerunner of the National Baptist Convention, USA, Incorporated.

The Black Baptist Church in the Black Belt

After the end of Reconstruction most blacks continued to live in Alabama's Black Belt, a twelve-county rural area in the southern part of the state extending from Barbour County in the east to the Mississippi border in the west. Most blacks in this area were sharecroppers. In this tenancy system, which could be as exploitative as slavery, the plantation owner equipped the sharecropper with mules, seed, fertilizer, tools, land, food, and a house in exchange for the family's labor. Often the sharecropper did not earn a profit and remained in debt to the landlord year after year.

African American life was hard in all respects. Most blacks lived in one- or two-room cabins with leaky roofs, barely sustained by a monotonous diet that consisted primarily of salt pork, molasses, turnip greens, and coffee. Because of the poor diet and substandard living conditions, African Americans were most susceptible to diseases such as tuberculosis, pellagra, pneumonia, and diphtheria. Despite the presence of a few private schools and some feeble efforts to provide public schools, educational opportunities for African Americans remained abysmally poor. Whites had little regard for African American life, and blacks were easy targets for lynching, particularly during times of economic depression. In addition, life was often boring, especially for the young who yearned for more social activities.

The church provided the main source of comfort, support, and cooperation for African Americans in the Black Belt. Blacks turned to their local congregations to supply many needs. Since the overwhelming majority of blacks in the state lived in the rural Black Belt, these churches mirrored more than any others the typical church life that existed among blacks in Alabama. Some town and city churches existed, but they were in the minority. Their importance became more pronounced in the early years of the twentieth century.

Black Belt churches were overwhelmingly Baptist, and they dominated the religious life of the state. By 1890 there were 61,030 black Baptists in the Black Belt, by far the largest number of any denomination. This proliferation stemmed from the days of slavery when there were more Baptist slave masters than any other denomination. Slaves usually joined the churches of their masters, and many continued in those denominations after emancipation. African American Baptists emphasized freedom and spontaneity in worship, significant roles for laypersons, and congregational polity that allowed black Baptists to form churches and appoint ministers of their own choosing without formal educational requirements. All these factors, along with the freedmen's desire to maintain their cultural roots and freedom from white control, contributed to the proliferation of Afro-Baptists.

Baptist churches throughout the Black Belt followed an organizational pattern typical of churches in other rural areas of the state. For example, most congregations met only one Sunday per month. Their pastors were usually itinerant, bivocational, farmer-preachers who held business meetings on Saturday night and conducted worship services the next morning. Business meetings also provided a forum for church discipline, a practice that was taken seriously by black Baptist congregations.

Overall, Black Belt churches were first and foremost worship centers. Worship services consisted primarily of praying, singing, and preaching, with spirituals and meter hymns constituting the music. Eventually, churches began to have choirs, nonetheless music remained a churchwide activity. At services on an Alabama sharecropping plantation in 1894, Henry Morehouse, secretary of the American Baptist Home Mission Board, heard plantation songs, standard hymns, and gospel tunes, all of which were lined out. Sermons were designed to inform, as well as to move the worshipper through emotional appeals. The strong emotions expressed in worship resulted from unique worship patterns developed by African Americans during slavery and as a response to the harsh conditions under which most blacks lived and worked. African American ministers frequently preached on Old Testament characters like Moses and Joshua.

They also emphasized the return of Jesus "when there would no more cold, hunger, and pain, but plenty of food, beauty, and sunshine for all."[1] Observers of African American religion in the Black Belt noted a strong element of joy.

For black and white Baptists, conversion formed a central place in their life and worship. The purpose of worship was to glorify God and lead the unsaved into a conversion experience. Black converts from 1865 to 1920 have given vivid accounts of these experiences. These experiences normally occurred in the late teenage years or in early adulthood, thus indicating the role of conversion as a rite of passage in rural black communities. One convert who left a brief account of her conversion at the Antioch Baptist Church in Hale County in 1899 stated that after the revival service on Tuesday night she became more conscious of her sin than ever before. "Her feeling of dread for her sin caused her to become ill and restless." While sleeping on Thursday night she had a dream that "Christ came and touched her, saying that her sins had been forgiven and she was now a part of his family."[2] This person recounted the experience of her conversion to the revival meeting on Friday night and became a member of the church. Such experiences constituted the norm for membership in black Baptist churches.

These conversion testimonies continued well into the twentieth century and are an important part of the worship experience of black Baptist churches today, in rural and urban Alabama. One of the most moving conversion stories comes from Ned Cobb, a sharecropper in Alabama whose life story has been recorded in *All God's Dangers: The Life of Nate Shaw*. Converted in prison, Cobb recounts the spiritual experience that overpowered him. Imprisoned for defending his neighbor's property (who like himself had become a member of the Southern Tenant Farmer's Union, an organization that sought to challenge the rural southern social order), Cobb began to pray. After days of prayer in his cell, he found himself "leaping everywhere, in a trance," while the other prisoners looked on. "All of a sudden," he recalled, "God stepped in[to] my soul. Talk about hollerin' and rejoicing, I just caught fire Good God almighty, I just felt like I could have flown out the top of that jail."[3] This testimony, which he gave to a rural Alabama congregation, generated much emotion and excitement.

Special worship services included baptisms, foot washings, revivals, and funerals. Black Baptists looked forward to the baptismal service with great anticipation. For many this event represented the central event in their lives. Most baptisms were communal gatherings that carried with them great significance. Being lowered into the water symbolized the cleansing of sin. The emergence from the water represented one's birth into the Christian community. Most baptismal ceremonies followed a pattern. Typically, the pastor led the procession of church members followed by converts dressed in white robes. Singing fervently, worshippers moved to the riverbank. There, after prayer, more singing, and exhortations, the converts were baptized, and they usually came out of the water shouting "Glory to God." In the afternoon, the congregation returned to the church to hear more preaching and to join in congratulations and singing.

Although the baptism of Ned Cobb did not follow the typical communal service, his account nevertheless reveals several key features of the baptism service. Cobb recalled that on the day of his baptism he wore a blue robe over his best Sunday suit. Church deacons escorted him to a nearby creek where the pastor waited. After the immersion, Cobb celebrated in the traditional way by shouting and praising God. In his testimony he remembered that, although the weather was cold, he felt warm and happy. "I felt, when I hit the air—and it was early winter when I stepped up out of that water—I felt like somebody done poured a kettle of warm water over me. I weren't cold a bit. And I commenced [shaking] hands all around and laughing and going mad for joy."[4]

Many black Baptist missionary church leaders did not approve of foot washing as an ordinance; nevertheless, the practice continued among certain rural Alabama churches. Some missionary Baptist churches joined the Black Belt primitive Baptists in these services. Like the baptism ceremony, foot washing had a communal function. Sometimes it accompanied a regular service but most often it was a separate ceremony, often held on Christmas Eve. At one foot washing in the 1890s, the ceremony began with an evening supper. To begin the ritual, the pastor washed the right foot of the head deacon, and the deacon returned the favor. The minister then tied a towel around his waist, washed the foot of a man in the congregation, and handed over the towel, the process passing from one male worshipper to another. A similar ceremony took place among females. After the washing, worshippers moved church benches to make room for a ring shout led by a layman. During this part of the service "worshippers danced around a perfect circle with twitches and jerks of the body."[5]

Black Baptists regarded the revival as the "spiritual festival of the year." It doubled as a "homecoming day" for people of the community who had moved elsewhere and as a general holiday season for average working people. Everything came to a halt in the local community, and services were conducted two or three times a day. Services were filled with emotion, and preachers gifted with the ability to chant sermons, sing, and shout drew the largest crowds. Worshippers sang special revival songs rather than the more traditional hymns that were considered appropriate for Sunday schools and more formal religious services. Even at colleges where leading ministers were trained, administrators encouraged the periodic revival as an outlet for the pent-up emotions of students.

Funerals allowed communities to come together to mark the passage of souls. Friends and neighbors remained with the deceased during the three days between death and burial. Pallbearers bore the white-sheeted coffin to church and placed it in front of the pulpit, after which preaching began. Ritual wailing filled the air from the church to the grave. Funeral music like the popular hymn "Hark from the Tomb a Doleful Sound" illustrated the older style of slow, a cappella singing, with verse couplets read by the minister.[6] Overall, funerals served as times of celebration when the deceased went to a place of happiness and peace. Afterward merriment and joy prevailed as family members and friends enjoyed a meal together.

Besides their various worship functions, Baptist churches in the Black Belt served a social purpose. With families and neighbors scattered over a wide area, the church held subcommunities and families together. By singing together, eating together, praying together, and engaging in other forms of fellowship at their churches, black Baptists maintained a sense of community. As a social institution, the church offered relief from the physical stress of life through church suppers, picnics, and carnivals. Special church services such as weddings, funerals, revivals, and baptisms served as both social and religious functions. The Baptist association meeting also provided a time for socializing and happiness. It met once a year and was eagerly anticipated.

Some Baptist churches served as the educational centers for their communities. After the Civil War, churches supplemented the work of the Freedmen's Bureau and the northern benevolent societies like the American Missionary Association. Churches often housed the schools operated by these agencies. Sometimes pastors doubled as teachers, especially before the establishment of public schools for African Americans. Some African American churches established their own schools. In 1887 the Baptists of Alabama founded Selma University. In 1889 the African Methodist Episcopal Church of Alabama founded Daniel Payne College in Selma. In 1898 the African Methodist Episcopal Zion Church of Alabama started Lomax Hannon College in Greenville, Alabama. Baptist associations also operated many schools in Alabama.

Pastors filled the key role in the churches. Most were literate, but few had no formal education. African Americans in Baptist churches expected their pastors to know the Bible and to be able to arouse the congregation. The preachers often accomplished this with a chanting tone. The meaning of his words would be lost in the rhythm of the sounds he made in concert with the loud amens of the congregation. Sermons, particularly in the churches of the common people, contained vivid imagery and parables. They frequently included references to Moses, the liberator of the Israelites, and to God's reward for Abraham's unquestioning faith. The glories of heaven and the torments of hell were also common themes. Some popular sermons were often repeated during camp meetings and revivals. One of the most popular was "Dry Bones," based on Ezekiel's experience where the scattered bones of a human skull came together, symbolizing the rebirth of the sinner as a follower of God. Another widely popular sermon was "The Eagle Stirs Her Nest," referring to how mother eagles stir their young from the nest to teach them to fly, portraying God's concern and love for his people. "The Prodigal Son" was a sermon that gained widespread acclaim. Through the emotional power of worship, conveyed through the mesmerizing sermons of the preacher, African Americans received a sense of worth and the fortitude and faith to face a hostile world.

Church and Association Growth

During the last quarter of the nineteenth century, churches and associations grew at an unprecedented rate. The number of churches grew because of black migration into new communities and separation from other congregations. For example, blacks moved into Brighton, a small community in Jefferson County, to work at the Woodward Iron Company. By 1886 two furnaces were in operation and Woodward was a prosperous industrial community. Nearby, the town of Brighton sprang up along the streetcar line to the east of the Woodward furnace and served primarily as a residential community for people working at Woodward and at the coal mines at Mulga and Dolomite. As early as 1883 blacks living in Woodward formed the Shady Grove Baptist Church. After a few years, members moved the church across the highway to the larger Brighton community and renamed themselves the First Baptist Church of Brighton. As Brighton expanded, members left the First Baptist congregation to form churches that were closer to their homes. Residents formed the Oak Grove Baptist Church in 1908 and another group left First Baptist Church to form the Shiloh Baptist Church in 1911.

With the enormous growth of churches, new associations formed to meet the local needs of church members. The Alabama Association, consisting of churches in Montgomery, Lowndes, and surrounding counties, was the largest association in the state in 1874. At that time several churches in rural southwest Alabama broke away to form the Union Association. Similarly, in 1884 churches in the rural section of north Alabama broke from the Muscles Shoals Association to form the Flint River Association. The St. Mary Association came into existence in 1891 when churches in the Dothan area left for the East Alabama Association. In Jefferson County, several churches in Bessemer broke from the Mt. Pilgrim Association to form the Bessemer Association in 1895.

Between 1875 and 1900 at least thirty-seven associations came into being in Alabama, making this the most fertile period for the planting of such organizations. Among these were the Autauga Association (1882), the Bibb County Association (1885), the Mobile Sunlight Association (1885), the Alabama Middle Association (1887), and the East Dallas Association (1900).

Most associations in Alabama followed a similar pattern. Their annual sessions usually convened in September or October, with meetings beginning on Thursday night and culminating on Sunday evening with a giant preaching service. Delegates from the member churches brought annual dues plus letters indicating the numerical and financial status of their respective congregations. In addition to paying annual dues, churches were expected to give to schools, welfare projects, and other association causes. Every association had a constitution, a statement of faith, and rules of decorum. Sessions were filled with sermons, speeches, and reports from standing committees. Practically every association distributed minutes of its meetings to its membership churches, informing them of resolutions from standing committees on issues of doctrine and polity that churches were expected to heed.

The primary purpose of the associations was to promote missions and Christian education, and to maintain proper doctrine and discipline in the member churches. They supported missionaries who preached the gospel, organized new churches, founded and operated schools, and gave financial support to widows, orphans, and the needy. While most association constitutions stipulated that they could merely advise churches, they did possess some coercive power over the churches in their membership. They could expel churches and thereby deprive them of the fellowship of other churches, thus placing a stigma on the congregation. Practically every association maintained a grievance committee whose purpose it was to solve problems within local churches. Churches found guilty of teaching false doctrine or engaging in practices that deviated from standard Baptist practices could be reprimanded or ousted from the association. Ministers were subject to the same disciplinary actions. In 1886 the grievance committee of the Eufaula Association recommended that the Bethlehem Baptist Church be readmitted to the association. However, it warned the association that "if the former pastor were reinstated, the church would forfeit its membership."[7] The former pastor, Reverend John Messer, had been found guilty of teaching false doctrine.

Association meetings also provided a time of socializing. Delegates usually stayed in the homes of host church members. They were fed and entertained in a hospitable manner. Large crowds attended the general meetings; the singing was fervent; and ministers preached with gusto and power. Everything came to a stop in the community. Baptists looked forward to these occasions, especially to meeting friends they had not seen in many months. Hospitality committees in Alabama associations consistently praised the local church and community for their great hospitality.

State Convention Growth and Expansion

By the turn of the twentieth century, there were seventy-six associations affiliated with the Alabama Colored Baptist State Convention. These associations included 1,846 churches with an aggregate membership of 186,212. At the 1900 annual meeting, 200 churches registered and sent delegates, a significant increase over the 27 churches that had originally enrolled at the convention of 1868. The Alabama convention was one of the largest black Baptist conventions in the nation. Several auxiliaries, agencies, and journals were formed by the convention between 1875 and 1900 that leaders and delegates viewed as important in meeting the needs of its constituents and growing the convention. Among these were the *Baptist Leader,* the Mission Board, the Sunday School Congress, and the Baptist Young People's Union, later known as the Baptist Training Union (BTU).

Publishing a newspaper was one of the first projects undertaken by the state convention. Alabama Baptists joined other black southern conventions as they, too, began to publish papers. The name of the Alabama paper was the *Baptist Pioneer,* later changed to *Baptist Leader.* Its main purpose was to inform black Baptists about the work of the state convention, particularly its educational efforts. The official voice of black Baptists, it began operations in 1878. The *Baptist Leader* was the first denominational paper published by blacks in Alabama.

William McAlpine was the first editor, with C. O. Boothe and John Dozier serving as his assistants. McAlpine was succeeded by A. N. McEwen and then C. M. Wells. A. F. Owens served as editor in 1884–85. During the tenure of these men, the paper was printed in Selma. By 1895 J. H. Eason had become editor, publishing the paper from Anniston. Other people who served as editors during the paper's early period were Professor W. M. Austin, Mr. J. C. Duke, Reverend R. T. Pollard, Reverend A. J. Stokes, and Mr. J. C. Leftwich.

The paper struggled during its early years, primarily due to lack of funding. At its inception the paper was published by Selma University. Because of declining finances at the school, it was turned over to a stock company, but the arrangement proved unsatisfactory. Finally, the *Baptist Leader* was placed in the hands of the state convention. Publication was sporadic through 1900, but the paper remained an important part of the convention's goals and activities. Leaders were convinced it was necessary to inform Baptists in the state concerning their activities and goals, especially the status of Selma University.

In addition to publishing the newspaper, the convention formed the state mission board in 1881. Its stated purpose was "to spread the gospel by holding institutes, supplying churches upon request, and by planting and building up churches where they were needed."[8] To carry out its functions, the mission board hired a corresponding secretary and missionaries. The board also raised funds for its missionary endeavors and submitted an annual report of its activities and finances to the convention.

The major leaders of the convention comprised the officers of the board and served as its earliest missionaries. These leaders were convinced that a mission board was necessary to coordinate the mission emphasis of the group. The first officers were Mansfield Tyler, chairman; H. N. Boney, secretary; and Charles White, treasurer. Those serving as chairman of the board to 1900 included William R. Pettiford, A. N. McEwen, J. P. Barton, and William Madison. Some of the general missionaries during this period were C. O. Boothe, N. P. Boney, William H. McAlpine, C. L. Purce, and Robert T. Pollard.

From 1878 to 1900 the Alabama missionaries worked jointly with other mission boards. C. O. Boothe, the first general missionary, worked under joint appointment with the American Baptist Publication Society. In 1895 the state mission board entered into a cooperative arrangement with the American Baptist Home Mission Society, the Southern Baptist Convention, and the white Alabama Baptist State Convention, appointing Robert T. Pollard as general missionary, William H. McAlpine as state missionary, and C. O. Boothe as district missionary. This cooperative work came to an end in 1898, at which time the state convention divided its missionary work into five districts.

The idea for another statewide convention stemmed from excitement that grew over the erection of Susie Stone Hall, a women's dormitory and dining hall, on the campus of Selma University. In 1889 the state convention assembled in Selma to lay the cornerstone for the new building, and Silas Jones offered a resolution for the formation of a Sunday School Congress. Jones insisted that such a convention was needed to promote the growth of Sunday schools and to train lay leaders. Those opposed believed that a separate convention was unnecessary and would create undue division. His resolution, after much heated debate, was referred to the next session of the general convention. Sunday schools registered with the regular state convention that year.

The following year, the convention met at the Sixth Avenue Baptist Church in Birmingham. Reverend D.T. Gully offered a resolution to organize a Sunday school convention. At this time there were about one thousand Sunday schools in the state. The resolution passed, and a committee was appointed to organize the convention. Serving on this committee were Reverends J. P. Barton, L. F. Bryant, G. P. Johnson, and Professors R. B. Hudson and James S. Berry. In 1891, at a meeting called by the committee at the First Baptist Church, Union Springs, the Sunday School Congress was born. Its first officers were Reverend Silas Jones, president; Professor E. W. Knight, secretary; and Reverend D. T. Gully, corresponding secretary.

In spite of the founders' enthusiasm, the Sunday School Congress struggled during its early years. In the second annual session some delegates attempted to discontinue the organization and return authority to the regular state convention. Among these were many strong leaders in the convention, but pressure from Sunday schools in small towns kept it alive. In addition to grass-roots support, the convention also survived because of financial and operational support from the American Baptist Publication Society and the loyalty and tenacity of its first three presidents: Silas Jones, C. M. Wells, and J. C. Leftwich.

In the 1890s the Baptist Young People's Union (BYPU) began in U.S. Baptist churches. These groups, which met on Sunday afternoons, were designed to train young people in church work. In 1893 John C. Leftwich proposed a resolution to encourage churches to establish local BYPU programs in Alabama. The formation of the Alabama BYPU Congress resulted from the work of Professor T. H. Posey. After attending the BYPU Convention of America in 1898, Professor Posey made a glowing report to the Sunday School Congress. Delegates decided to organize an Alabama BYPU Congress at once. Posey was elected the first president, but the next meeting of the BYPU Congress elected Benjamin Barnes as president and S. B. Brownlee as secretary. At this time, only four unions existed in the state. The convention encouraged the growth of BYPU organizations in Alabama churches and served as a forum for training lay leaders.

Women's Movement in Alabama

From the beginning, black women played an indispensable role in the formation and maintenance of black Baptist churches in Alabama. In practically every congregation, they outnumbered men. Women directed fund-raising efforts especially for the construction of church buildings by holding bazaars, bake sales, dinners, and other events. In addition, they provided hospitality, often furnishing lodging and preparing meals for the pastor and visiting ministers. Women also played an important role in planning district associations and convention meetings, and arranging accommodations for the messengers of member churches.

Despite their numerical strength and active service, black Baptist women in the state experienced a hierarchical gender relationship, common to both white and black churches in the South. Almost universally, black Baptist leaders in Alabama agreed that women should not serve as ministers and deacons. Nor were women allowed to be delegates to state convention meetings. At the 1887 meeting of the Alabama Baptist Convention, Harrison Woodsmall, a white missionary for the northern-based American Baptist Home Mission Society and the first president of Selma University, suggested that women should be able to serve as convention delegates. William McAlpine, one of the black leaders of the convention, proposed a counterresolution denying women the right to serve as delegates. McAlpine's resolution, which was promptly passed, proposed that women could be honorary members but not official messengers. Even though black Baptists held great respect for Woodsmall and admired his work among them, they had no intention of changing their established views on gender.

The formation of the women's convention constituted a giant step forward in expanding the educational work and support of the Alabama State Convention. Edward M. Brawley, then president of Selma University, was the leading figure in the convention's formation. Influenced by William J. Simmons, who established a women's convention in Kentucky to support State University, Brawley sought to organize a similar convention to support his school.

After visiting the Kentucky Women's Convention, Brawley returned to Selma and called a meeting to organize the Women's Baptist State Convention of Alabama. Leaders assisting Brawley included William McAlpine, Robert T. Pollard, C. S. Dinkins, and C. L. Purce. The convention was formally established at Selma's Tabernacle Baptist Church on January 27, 1886. The purpose of the convention as stated in its original constitution was "to promote the cause of Christ by working to enhance Selma University and by engaging in as much mission work as possible." The meeting lasted three days and raised forty-one dollars, which was donated to Selma University.[9]

Officers elected at the first meeting were president, Frances Nickerson; vice president, Emma Ware; secretary, Florence Birney; and treasurer, Amanda Tyler. Others serving as president before 1900 were Anna Brooks, Amanda Tyler, and Eliza Washington Pollard. The secretary for much of this period was R. J. Fisher, wife of C. L. Fisher, pastor of the Sixteenth Street Baptist Church in Birmingham. Female leaders of the convention in Alabama, like other states, were teachers or wives of ministers or educators. Of the first four presidents elected to office in the Alabama Women's Convention, two were teachers and all were wives of outstanding ministers. Eliza Pollard, president from 1894 to 1904, was one of the first graduates of Selma University, a successful teacher, and wife of the Reverend Robert T. Pollard, a leader among Alabama Baptists and the fourth president of Selma University. Mrs. Charles Dinkins, Mrs. Edward Brawley, Mrs. Charles Purce, and Mrs. A. A. Bowie, members of the board of managers of the women's convention, were all married to ministers associated with both Selma University and the state convention. Mrs. Amanda Tyler, third president of the convention, was married to the Reverend Mansfield Tyler, chairman of the board of trustees of Selma University during its first twenty-seven years.

The organizational structure of the black women's state conventions followed that of the male-directed conventions. The Alabama convention, like its male counterpart, appointed a field missionary to canvass the state and to organize local societies. The convention sought to represent women in every black Baptist church in the state. The Alabama convention met annually, usually on the same date and in the same vicinity of the annual meeting of the male-based state convention. Locations varied within the state, and individual churches selected delegates, who paid their own transportation costs to and from the annual meetings. Unlike many other women's conventions, the Alabama convention did not prohibit men from delegate status. During the sixth annual session, which met in 1891 at Eufaula's Second Baptist Church, some of the prominent male leaders of Alabama, including William McAlpine and J. H. Eason, registered as delegates. Men commented on papers, prayed, preached, and submitted reports. However, the women made the major decisions. They elected their own officers and set policies and programs for the convention. Moreover, the Alabama convention executed its work through committees that dealt with education, finance, temperance, and new societies.

True to its original intention, the convention made education in general, and support for Selma University in particular, its primary objective. In 1889 the women noted the importance of "preparing skilled workers in our religious organizations" and maintained that education would solve the race problem in America. The committee on education recommended that the women's convention endeavor to expand student enrollment at Selma University and introduced a motion to earmark all future contributions for the construction of a girl's dormitory. In 1890 the Baptist Women's State Convention represented ten thousand women in sixty church societies. At the sixth annual meeting the following year, the Alabama women emphasized their role as fund-raisers and argued that the Christian church must assume the burden for education. More importantly, they asserted that support of Selma University remained the primary responsibility of black Baptists in the state. Three years later, the women's state convention described Selma University as the "child of Baptists of Alabama" and praised its work in educating leaders of churches and Sunday schools.

Throughout its early years the women's convention tried various means of raising money for Selma University. One of the most ambitious plans was "Sisters' Day," proposed in 1891. The daylong celebration would acquaint church members with convention activities and try to win their financial support. In his history of black Baptists in Alabama, Charles Boothe recalled several public exhortations by women who hoped to inspire congregations to follow their example of giving. The president of a women's mission band, he recalled, told him that each member of her congregation had taxed themselves a nickel per month. A poultry-raiser testified that she set aside one of her hens specifically for missionary work income, then donated to her society all the money received from the sale of that hen's eggs and chickens.

In addition to its support for education, which included raising funds for Susie Stone Hall on the Selma University campus, the convention promoted other endeavors. For example, in 1895 the convention began to publish guides for the missionary societies to be placed in every church in Alabama. These guides contained sample constitutions for missionary societies, district associations, and children's groups. Bible lessons were also included. By 1900 the *Baptist Women's Era*, a convention publication, was published "to convey the works and goals of the convention." Mrs. Eliza Pollard served as the first editor.[10]

Missions gained increasing importance for the women's convention. In an 1893 letter the warden and inmates of the state's prison school thanked the convention for its visit and concluded that women had the greatest positive influence on prisoners. During the 1900 convention, the women's missionary societies resolved to visit the prisons in their respective areas. Missionary groups were encouraged to take their work into the homes of the poor to hold Bible studies and prayer meetings. In the final two decades of the nineteenth century several societies engaged in house-to-house visitation, Sunday school, and temperance work.

The Women's Convention generated self-assertiveness, and in some instances, aggressive, behavior, including protests of the actions of male-led conventions. In Alabama, unlike Tennessee and other states, male leaders were generally supportive of the women's organization. But this did not stop some women from expressing a degree of autonomy in interesting ways. For example, in 1889 a female messenger presented a paper titled "Women's Part in the General Work of the State and Her Relation to the State Convention," in which she complained that the male convention did not feel the need to assist the women's convention, although it expected women's assistance. Nevertheless, the speaker urged other women to assume an unselfish position toward men. Although Alabama women passed a resolution in 1892 to exercise more care in the treatment of the brethren, minutes of the Alabama convention recorded that the men continued to complain that women did not allow them to talk enough during their meetings.[11]

The *Baptist Leader* served as the most important means through which black Baptist women asserted their views and disseminated news of their state conventions as well as information of general interest to women. In 1892 the Alabama women's convention appointed Mrs. Eliza Pollard to write a column on women in the *Baptist Leader*. Issued out of Selma at the time, the *Baptist Leader* served as an important instrument in promoting the work of the women's convention. Ms. Alice E. McEwen, a graduate of Spelman College and active member of the Alabama convention, became an associate editor when her father, the Reverend A. N. McEwen, was editor of the *Baptist Leader*. The black

Baptist women in Alabama used the paper to promote pride in Selma University and to advertise their fund-raising efforts. During the early 1890s the Alabama Baptist women's convention assisted in the weekly circulation and distribution of ten thousand issues of the paper.

The women's convention greatly accelerated the work of women in their local communities and at the state level. Men still made the more important decisions in local churches, but women's roles as missionaries and fund-raisers had been heightened. By 1900 more than sixty societies were represented at the state convention. In addition, many associations formed women's conventions; these were also reported to the state convention. In that same year, six district women's conventions registered, including groups from the Mt. Pilgrim, Shelby Springs, and Bibb County associations.

In 1889 the cornerstone was laid for Stone Hall. The women of Alabama had succeeded in their first educational project and would continue as a significant force among African American Baptists. In 1891 Selma University's trustees reported to the convention that other buildings were needed, especially a new chapel. Alabama women began to raise funds for that project. Perhaps the women's conventions' most important role was to heighten self-worth and a sense of usefulness among black Baptist women. In "How the Church Can Best Help the Condition of the Masses," Miss Hardie Martin of Montgomery assigned responsibility of leadership "to the clergy, to the black Baptist press, and to female missionaries who visited the homes of the common people."[12]

Denominational Concerns

Continual growth and expansion created a host of concerns and problems. One of the most pressing challenges for denominational leadership in Alabama was pastoral support. In general, Baptist ministers were poorly paid. Association records reveal the paltry pastoral support. For example, in 1881 the highest salary paid by a church in the Colored Bethel Association was $125 per year, and many pastors received less than $100. The Blandon Association, located in Clarke and Choctaw Counties, provided even less support. In 1885 the highest paid pastor received $75 per year, and the lowest received $21. In 1890, in the Brownville Association, which included Lee and Russell Counties, salaries ranged from $400 per year to $25. Pastors in urban areas received higher salaries, but payments were still inadequate. In the Mt. Pilgrim Association, located in urban Birmingham, pastors with churches of 100 or more members received between $1,200 and $500 per year in 1897. The highest paid pastor was Thomas W. Walker of Shiloh Baptist Church, the city's largest congregation with a membership of 782; he received $1,200 annually. The second highest was J. Q. A. Wilhite, pastor of the Sixth Avenue Baptist church with a salary of $840. Walker's salary was probably the highest in the state.

There were several reasons for the poor pay of pastors. First, blacks in Alabama were poor, often destitute. Also, the Baptist laity did not realize the value of a trained, full-time minister. Finally, some parishioners, influenced by hyper-Calvinism common to white churches during this period, believed that paying pastors was unscriptural. As a result, black Baptist churches made little effort to adequately compensate their pastors. Most black pastors were forced to make ends meet by farming, teaching, or working as common laborers. Many ministers pastored several churches, holding the monthly business conference on Saturday night and preaching at the worship service the following day.

To stimulate churches to provide better pastoral support, convention and association leaders made speeches and initiated various resolutions. The Colored Bethlehem Association passed a resolution in 1891 that stated that pastors could not give adequate attention to their church duties because they were forced to work with their hands. Each church, the resolution continued, had a responsibility to adequately support its pastor. In 1892 the East Perry Association passed a similar resolution maintaining that no pastor could be effective unless he had liberal support from his church thus enabling him to give time fully to the work of the word of God. Similar resolutions came from the Brownville and the Gilfield Associations. In the 1893 session of the Alabama Association, William Pettiford, financial agent for Selma University and pastor of Birmingham's Sixteenth Street Baptist Church, presented a lecture titled "Duties of Churches toward Pastors" in which he lamented the poor support that Baptists provided for their ministerial leaders. He insisted that the denomination could never progress until it gave financial freedom to its ministers.

To assist ministers in receiving better overall compensation, associations took a strong stand against ministers who advertised they would pastor churches for less money than that received by current pastors. These associations also resisted the practice of some churches calling other ministers as their pastors without having paid their former ministers. Resolutions condemning such actions came from several associations. In 1891, for example, the Bethlehem Association of Sumter County issued a resolution that "any minister who sought a pastorate by agreeing to preach for less money than the former pastor would not be received by the association."[13] In 1892 the Colored Baptist Union Association strongly urged ministers not to take a church until the former pastor was paid.

A second concern for black Baptists involved continuing relationships with white Alabama Baptists. During slavery, white Baptists had initiated and promoted special missions to evangelize blacks. Also, immediately after slavery, some white clergy and churches attempted to aid black churches directly. Numerous examples of interracial cooperation followed emancipation. Some white ministers even pastored black churches. However, Reconstruction politics and the willingness of black Baptists to listen to and receive support from white northern missionary agencies contributed to less cordial relations between white and black Baptists in the South. As historian Robert Praytor has suggested, by 1870 the attitude of white Baptists toward their black brethren went from "concern to neglect."[14] White Alabama Baptists and their leaders mirrored the growing racist sentiment of the time: they sanctified segregation, subscribed to the idea of black inferiority, and were, at best, ambivalent toward black education.

Nonetheless, black Baptist leaders sought to revive relations with their white Baptist brothers and to garner support for missionary and educational work. In 1873, when both conventions met in Tuscaloosa, black delegates asked representatives from the white convention to fellowship with them and to offer advice on the school project they were attempting to start. They also asked white Baptist pastors to provide lessons in theology to their ministers.

In 1876 the white Baptist convention responded by stating its desire to assist black Baptists, but delegates were divided on the issue. Some were opposed to any kind of assistance or relationship. Those supporting some form of continuing association with their black Baptist brothers had various views on the subject. Some believed that white influence would mitigate the superstition and bad theology prevalent among black preachers. Others thought their help would reduce the influence of northern Baptists. A third group maintained that since blacks had been faithful to whites during slavery and the Civil War, they deserved the help of their white Baptist brothers. Regardless of the different views held by individuals, white Baptists as a group did attempt various forms of cooperation.

In 1881 white Baptists entered into a cooperative program for the benefit of blacks. They agreed to provide support for black missionaries, whose work included holding ministers' institutes. The convention hired C. O. Boothe, who conducted twenty-three institutes. Unfortunately his work was short-lived. Receiving little financial or moral support from white Baptists, Boothe resigned on December 31, 1881, and was not replaced. In the 1890s the state mission board attempted to revive the cooperative work by employing W. H. McAlpine to hold institutes for blacks. Again, because of poor support, McAlpine made little progress, and the convention abandoned the work in 1897.

Eventually, Southern Baptists in Alabama terminated their cooperative work with black Baptists. Growing racial antipathy continued ties between black Baptists and the Northern American Baptist Home Mission Society; and conflict within the white convention between the Home Mission Board and the Committee on Evangelization of Colored People combined to destroy the endeavor. The historian Daniel Stowell provided meaningful insight into why cooperation between white and black Baptists was so difficult during this period. He suggested that an understanding of post-1865 southern religion must begin with an understanding of Southern Baptist attitudes and perspectives following the Civil War. White Christian leaders insisted that they had not lost the war because of evils inherent in slavery or secession. Rather, they had lost because they had not been pure enough in their religion. God, however, had not permanently forsaken them. To the contrary, the war was his chastisement for greater purposes, namely maintaining religious orthodoxy and white supremacy. According to southern Christians, northern religious groups were heretical in their faith and the idea of reunion with them was unthinkable. They organized churches and denominational structures to thwart the efforts of northern missionaries in the South. Also, underlying all southern Christian decisions was the consistent belief in the inferiority of the black race. Southern religion did all in its power to maintain white supremacy, which they viewed as a God-given mandate. With this kind of thinking on behalf of whites, and with the blacks' thirst for independence and their willingness to receive advice and support from northerners, any form of meaningful relationship was impossible. In the end, black Baptists resolved to operate their own programs, seeking greater support from northern Baptist societies. With few exceptions, no meaningful relations or communication existed between black and white Baptists in Alabama until the 1970s.

Ministerial conduct and morals constituted another critical concern for black Baptists. Because of their leadership positions and prestige, black ministers were subjected to numerous temptations, especially relations with women in their congregation. One of the most prevalent criticisms leveled against black

Baptist ministers involved their moral conduct. To counter this accusation and maintain the dignity of the ministry, Alabama associations and the state convention took strong stands against immoral behavior by their ministers. Countless examples in association and convention minutes reveal disciplinary actions against deviant ministers.

The degree of seriousness that black Baptist leaders in Alabama placed on disciplining those who were immoral is reflected in the actions taken against leading people in the convention. For example, in the 1895 convention, A. N. McEwen was the focus of a lawsuit by an unmarried woman in his church. McEwen refused to submit his case to a council of pastors in the Sun Light District Association of Mobile where his church was a member. A resolution from the state convention informed the association of its duty to drop his name from the roll and notify the Franklin Street Church of its decision. Fortunately, McEwen changed his mind, went before the association council and was cleared. At that time McEwen was one of the best-trained men in the state convention, editor of the *Baptist Leader,* and a vice president of the National Baptist Convention. Consequently, his fellow preachers expected him to live above moral reproach, as the convention actions indicated. After being cleared of charges, McEwen continued to be a leader in both the state and National Baptist Convention. At the same convention a resolution told pastors not to encourage or recognize the work of evangelist J. W. Douglass because there were suspicions of bad character.

Alabama Baptists and the Formation of the National Baptist Convention

In 1894 there were 1,584,210 black Baptists in the United States. Baptist organizations consisted of 437 district associations, 18 state conventions, and 13 women's state conventions. Yet no formal national organization had been formed to bring all black Baptists together. Ministers who had received formal education, many in the schools supported by the Baptist Home Mission Board, were instrumental in creating such an organization. The path to the formation of the national convention included three previous attempts to form a national body. In 1880 black Baptists from various states met in Montgomery, Alabama, and formed the National Baptist Foreign Missions Convention, whose major purpose was missionary work in Africa. In 1886 black Baptist leaders from across the nation but mostly from the South met in St. Louis, Missouri, and formed the

American National Baptist Convention. Under the presidency of the Reverend William J. Simmons, the convention stated its purpose in ambitious terms:

1. To promote piety, sociability, and a better knowledge of each other.
2. To be able to have an understanding as to the great end to be reached by the denomination.
3. To encourage our literary men and women and promote the interest of Baptist literature.
4. To discuss questions pertaining especially to the religious, educational, industrial, and social interests of our people.
5. To give an opportunity for our best thinkers and writers to be heard.[15]

In 1892 the National Baptist Educational Convention was launched in Savannah, Georgia, as a concerted effort to facilitate the growth of black educational institutions, to encourage dialogue among black educators, to furnish scholarships for students, and to promote the employment of black graduates. The Reverend W. Bishop Johnson, pastor of the Second Baptist Church, Washington, D.C., was the leading figure in forming this organization. Johnson had organized the Sunday School Lyceum movement, and with the formation of the educational convention, he attempted to federate all schools owned, controlled, and managed by black Baptists.

In the early 1890s attempts to combine these three bodies and others into one convention failed. However, the spirit of the Tripartite Union lived on in the minds and hearts of several prominent black Baptist pastors. The Reverends S. E. Griggs, L. M. Luke, and A. W. Pegues led a movement at the 1894 meeting of the Tripartite Union in Montgomery, Alabama, to unite black Baptists all over the country. They developed the form, structure, and machinery of an organization to serve that objective. A committee was appointed and the three bodies adjourned with plans to meet in Atlanta.

On September 24, 1895, at Atlanta's Friendship Baptist Church the Committee on Plans and Constitution made its report to the Tripartite Union. The report was adopted. In the same year the Foreign Mission Convention, the National Baptist Educational Convention, and the American National Baptist Convention consolidated to form a new national convention with the Reverend E. C. Morris of Helena, Arkansas, as president.

Baptist leaders from Alabama participated in all three conventions. Mrs.

A. A. Bowie was elected educational secretary for the American National Baptist Convention. However, Alabama leaders played their largest role in the foreign mission convention. The inspiration behind this organization came from William W. Cooley. While serving in Africa for the Southern Baptist Convention, he was convinced of the need for American blacks to serve on the mission field in Africa. Returning to America after four years in Africa, he began to travel around the country, espousing his views of foreign missions and encouraging others to send missionaries to Africa.

On November 24, 1880, at the First Baptist Church, Montgomery, about 150 black Baptists from eleven states—delegates from churches and associations—met to discuss the issue and form an organization. At this meeting they decided to call themselves the Foreign Mission Convention of the United States of America. The purpose was to support, with money and personnel, the mission work in Africa.

In addition to hosting and housing the meeting, several Alabamians played a leading role in the formation of the convention. William McAlpine was elected the first president, serving from 1880 to 1882. The second and third presidents were also from Alabama: J. Q. A. Wilhite and James A. Foster. Robert T. Pollard of Selma served as a vice president, and William R. Pettiford became secretary in 1882. When the three conventions were combined in 1915, the National Baptist Convention adopted the 1880 founding date of the foreign mission convention as its beginning to establish the chronology for its annual meetings.

The demise of Reconstruction did not defeat the spirit of black Baptists in Alabama. On the contrary, the church became the major institution in the Black Belt where most blacks lived, filling many of its constituents' needs. Among these were worship, education, and social life. A women's convention was formed and would play an important role in black Baptist life. With its expansion, several problems and denominational concerns emerged. Its outstanding leaders would be significant in establishing a national organization for black Baptists. Other important events took place during this formative period for black Baptists in Alabama. Chief among these was an emphasis on education, along with concerns for a broad range of social, racial, and theological issues.

4
Education, Black Nationalism, and Sociopolitical Concerns

The late nineteenth century was not only a time of church, association, and convention growth and consolidation, it was also a period in which education became a critical concern for black Baptists. With the end of Reconstruction, the dilution of black political power, and increased violence against blacks, black Baptists turned increasingly to education as the key to uplifting the race. The state convention founded Selma University, and associations throughout the state formed academies and schools. In addition, black nationalism emerged among black Baptists with its call for independence from white interference and control. Alabama Baptists would experience a split in the convention as a result of separatist thinking and the popularity of black nationalism among a minority of pastors. As churches and pastors continued to exercise a leadership role in the black community, associations issued resolutions on a host of social and political issues. In some instances, the Colored Baptist State Convention sent delegations to the governor and the legislature to press for increased justice toward blacks in the state.

Educational Goals

No issue concerned black Baptists more than education. Coming out of slavery, blacks craved formal education. They flocked to schools sponsored by the Freedmen's Bureau and the American Missionary Association. In slavery, blacks had seen that educated whites held power; they now wanted such power for themselves. During Reconstruction black Baptist churches formed Sunday schools and allowed their buildings to be used for Freedmen's Bureau schools, and some ministers served as both pastors and teachers.

After the end of Reconstruction in 1874, education became the number one goal and aspiration of black Baptists. Although blacks in Alabama continued to vote and participate in the political process as best they could, they increasingly promoted education as the principal method of achieving black uplift. Education received considerable emphasis among associations, and many viewed it as the primary means of black survival, liberation, and equality with whites.

A sampling of association resolutions indicates the serious approach by black Baptists concerning the need for education. In 1889 the East Dallas Association maintained that education was necessary to improve people. It broadened their minds and taught them how to act. That same year, the Early Rose Association stated that young blacks were perishing for lack of education. It was absolutely essential for racial uplift. In 1890 the Mt. Pleasant Association insisted that if blacks were to stand on an equal footing with other races they must educate their children. The Cahaba Association of Perry County in their annual session the same year maintained that education was necessary to build pride and respect. The Colored Bethel Union Association summarized the importance of education when it urged its members in 1891 to let education be the watchword of everything they did. The Canaan-Pickensville Association in 1900 insisted that "no people could succeed in ignorance. Education of the race," the resolution stated, "was absolutely essential. It was educate or perish."[1]

Ministerial training ranked as an equal concern with secular education. Associations and the state convention issued annual resolutions calling for ministerial preparation. Most of these resolutions encouraged ministers to attend Selma University or the local association school. Several associations mandated that no minister could be ordained who could not at least read and write.

Associations gave several reasons for training ministers. In 1890 the Snow Creek Association of Etowah County maintained that "ministerial education was absolutely necessary in advancing the kingdom of God. An ignorant minister made for an ineffective preacher, therefore ministers should be prepared to teach. Unless they were trained, they could not uplift the people. If doctors and lawyers needed preparation, then ministers had the same need," the resolution concluded.[2] The Spring Hill Association of Montgomery County in the same year also stressed that education was necessary for leadership. They contended that a minister who did not subscribe to schools and letters fell behind and ceased to be a leader. Most associations used the Bible to support their desire for educated ministers. These association leaders often pointed to Paul's letter to Timothy in which he urged Timothy to study so he might be approved unto God. Other associations pointed to the example of Jesus who trained his disciples before sending them out. The Colored Baptist State Convention meeting in 1878 resolved that "without an educated clergy, Baptists would fall behind other denominations in the state."[3]

Association Schools

To provide general and ministerial education, associations established schools. One of the major reasons was the feeling that the public schools were inadequate. High schools for blacks were nonexistent in the state, and conservative Democrats, who regained power from the Republicans in 1874, limited public funding for education. Black schools received a disproportionately small share of the inadequate amount of money devoted to education. The state constitution of 1901 legalized this policy of discrimination.

Poor public education for blacks prompted leaders of the Baptist associations to call on black Baptists to sacrifice on behalf of their children. An 1892 resolution from the Colored Bethlehem Baptist Association maintained that education in the county schools was making slow progress. As a result, the association voted to begin a school in 1893. A resolution from the Early Rose Association called upon its members "to sacrifice what they spent on vices like drinking and give it to the support of its high school."[4] The Flint Hill Association maintained that the public schools were impure and voted to start its own school in 1894.

Existing records indicate that at least thirty association schools existed in the state from 1875 to 1915. These schools were called by different names—colleges, institutes, high schools, and academies—and were formed for different purposes. For example, the Autauga Academy was founded in 1888 primarily to provide ministerial training. The Mt. Pleasant Association started a female institute in 1890 to train local girls. Several associations organized high schools, since few existed in the state for blacks. Among these were Canaan-Pickensville (1883), Gilfield Association (1887), Auburn Association (1890), and Geneva Association (1902). Most educational institutions started by Baptist associations were elementary schools, and the majority included industrial arts departments in which sewing and agriculture were taught.

Several association schools were highly successful. Among these were the Eufaula Baptist Academy, the Thomasville Academy, the Bethlehem Baptist Academy, the Courtland Academy, the Marion Baptist Academy, the Anniston Normal and Industrial College, and the Union Springs Normal School. Marion Baptist Academy was founded in 1880 when several Baptist families, convinced that education was essential for the advancement of their children, came together to seek ways to provide better academic and religious training in their community. Among the founding families were the Hogues, Greens, Billups, Billingsleys, Jenes, Petersons, Scotts, Davises, Fosters, Underwoods, and McGhees. The Hopewell Baptist Association raised money to purchase eight acres of land. A few years later, two other Perry County associations, the New Cahaba and East Perry, added their support. Together, these associations built a two-story building to house the institution.

The school, which began as Marion Baptist College, was renamed Marion Baptist Academy. William H. McAlpine, pastor of the Berean Baptist Church, served as the first principal. He was succeeded by C. S. Dinkins, Samuel Bacote, and R. T. Pollard. Dinkins and Bacote pastored the Berean Baptist Church while serving as school principal. Three of the four eventually served as president of Selma University. For much of its history, the institution provided elementary training through the ninth grade.

In 1893 the Snow Creek Baptist Association started the Anniston Normal and Industrial College. As with Marion Baptist Academy, it began as an elementary school going to the ninth grade and also taught industrial arts. By 1915 its enrollment included 85 pupils and four teachers. Its physical plant, covering eight city blocks, consisted of three frame buildings, two of which served as dormitories. In that year, the school's income totaled fifteen hundred dollars, of which four hundred came from the Snow Creek Association, and the remainder from tuition and contributions.

The Union Springs Normal School, founded in 1900 by the Baptist associations of Butler County, was effective in educating blacks as well. Three associations joined forces so that the black children in the area would receive a formal education. In 1913 the school counted 365 elementary and 35 secondary students. The physical plant consisted of a one-story building and one block of land. There were five teachers (one male and four female). The annual income reached approximately sixteen hundred dollars, three-fourths of which came from the Baptist associations in the area.

The state convention gave little financial support because funds were limited and some Baptist ministers viewed other academies as a hindrance to the development of Selma University. However, the state convention generally endorsed academies because there were tremendous local educational needs and they recognized that everyone could not attend its main college, Selma University. Many convention leaders served as principals and deans of the academies. For example, James H. Eason served as editor of the *Baptist Leader* and as dean of theology at Anniston Normal and Theological School. C. M. Wells became president of the Sunday School Congress of Alabama and served concurrently as principal of Opelika High School, an institution operated by the Auburn District Association. During the 1880s and 1890s the Eufaula Academy, Anniston Normal and Theological School, and Courtland Academy received endorsements from the convention. Efforts were made by leaders to coordinate the work of these academies so they did not hinder the work at Selma. In the 1890s the convention called for the academy leaders to meet with President C. S. Dinkins of Selma University in an effort to coordinate and not duplicate education in the state. Leaders of the convention wanted to ensure that association schools remained feeder institutions for Selma University.

Selma University

The formation of Selma University constituted the most ambitious project of black Baptists in Alabama and was the primary focus of the Alabama Colored Baptist State Convention. Black Alabama Baptists, like blacks elsewhere, were concerned about the poor public education for blacks in the South. In order to produce well-educated ministers and teachers, state conventions established black colleges. Selma University was one of the few black Baptist colleges founded in the last decades of the nineteenth century initiated almost solely by blacks. Similar institutions included State University in Kentucky (1873), Arkansas Baptist College (1887), and Virginia College and Seminary (1887). Other black Baptist schools were formed after emancipation but they were initiated by whites or the American Baptist Mission Society. Among these institutions were Shaw University (1865), and Bishop (1881), Spelman (1881), Morehouse (1867), and Natchez (1885) Colleges.

The process of founding Selma University began in 1873 when William McAlpine made a motion at the annual convention meeting in Tuscaloosa that the convention "plant in the State of Alabama a theological school to educate our young men." C. O. Boothe, a convention member, reported in his book *Cyclopedia of the Colored Baptists in Alabama* that this motion injected new life into the convention. With white Baptists meeting in the same city, the convention formed a delegation to solicit their advice concerning the school. The white convention insisted that the effort was impractical and suggested that blacks attend the school that the American Baptist Home Mission Board was starting in Atlanta. Despite this admonition, the black Baptists of Alabama, at McAlpine's urging, began the process of establishing their own school.[5]

State conventions from 1874 to 1876 laid the groundwork for the institution. The 1874 session appointed a committee to manage the school project. Among those chosen were William McAlpine, Charles O. Boothe, Alex Butler, H. J. Europe, and Holland Thompson. Delegates authorized McAlpine to serve for six months as missionary and agent of the convention. The following year, McAlpine and Boothe were selected to search for a suitable site. In 1876 McAlpine turned over one thousand dollars he had raised for the proposed school.

The convention of 1877 was one of the most memorable in relation to the founding of Selma University. After much discussion and debate, the convention chose Selma over either Marion or Montgomery as the school's location. The trustees recommended Harrison Woodsmall to be president, and the convention promptly accepted him to lead the school. On January 1, 1878, five years after McAlpine presented his initial resolution, the school opened as the Alabama Baptist Normal and Theological School in the St. Phillips Street Baptist Church. Four students were enrolled. Harrison Woodsmall was assisted by the Reverend William R. Pettiford. In the same year, the trustees completed negotiations to purchase the "Old Fair Grounds" in Selma at a cost of three thousand dollars. The physical plant consisted of thirty-six acres of land, a large amphitheater, and several other buildings. The structures were repaired at a cost of seven hundred dollars and then used for classrooms and dormitories.

During its early years, the school changed names several times. On March 1, 1881, it was incorporated as the Alabama Normal and Theological School. In 1885 the name was changed to Selma University. In 1895 it became Alabama Baptist Colored University. Finally, in 1905, the name was changed again to Selma University, the name it has retained.

Financial support was a critical factor in the early years. Funds came primarily from blacks, who were often both poor and illiterate. But the American Baptist Home Missionary Society adopted the school in 1880 and began to give support. The society gave $2,000 that year, an additional $3,500 in 1892, and in 1890, $6,000. The latter gift included $2,600 for the building of Susie Stone Hall, a new four-story building that cost about $7,000. Among other things, the building provided a much-needed dormitory for female students. Regular funds given by the society were used to pay the president and many of the teachers. The 1878 convention minutes indicate that the American Baptist Home Missionary Society and other northern agencies were supporting three white teachers at that time.

Funds donated to Selma University were small compared to gifts given to other schools by the American Baptist Home Mission Society. For example, in 1895 Selma University received only $1,500 from the society, whereas Spelman Seminary (now Spelman College) in Atlanta received $17,204. Schools like Selma University, which were controlled by black trustee boards, received considerably less than schools like Shaw University, Virginia Union University, and Bishop College that remained under the society's control. One of the reasons was white paternalism and racism, which affected the North as well as the South. Although the American Baptist Home Mission Society promoted humanitarian projects, its leaders and constituency believed that blacks were not as competent as whites to operate institutions of learning. This kind of thinking, exhibited by many northern mission societies, helped foster black nationalist views among black religious leaders. In many states, they demanded control of their own institutions, even if it meant refusing funds from the Home Mission Society. Nevertheless, contributions from the society were essential to the operation of Selma University. In 1895 funds raised by Selma University totaled $4,083.50 with more than one-third ($1,500.00) contributed by the Home Mission Society.

Before 1900 Selma University had five presidents: Harrison Woodsmall, William H. McAlpine, E. M. Brawley, Charles L. Purce, and Charles S. Dinkens. All were dedicated men who made significant contributions to the institution. Their personal sacrifices and financial contributions often kept the school afloat during uncertain times.

Harrison Woodsmall, a white minister and missionary, served as the first president. Woodsmall came to Alabama as a missionary of the Indiana Baptist State Convention in 1876 to conduct ministerial institutes among black Baptists. Because of his relationship with the Indiana Convention and other northern Baptist missionary agencies, his effective teaching among black pastors, and his superior theological education, black Baptists viewed him as the best person to lead the school. He was elected president in 1877.

Woodsmall was born on June 9, 1841, in Indiana. His parents, Jefferson H. Woodsmall and Malvina Wilhite, were farmers who migrated from Virginia. After attending county schools, Woodsmall entered the State University of Indiana at sixteen; he remained there until the Civil War began. In June 1861 he enlisted in the 14th Indiana Regiment, serving primarily in Virginia, and was wounded at the battle of Antietam. He rose to the rank of major in the 115th Indiana Regiment.

After the war, Woodsmall entered law school at Ann Arbor, Michigan, and then practiced law in Indiana for about six years. During that period, he took an active part in Sunday school, temperance work, and politics. He gave up the practice of law and entered the ministry. After working briefly among the blacks of Indiana, he entered Southern Baptist Theological Seminary. After graduation, he worked under the auspices of the American Baptist Publication Society, the American Baptist Home Mission Society, and the Indiana Baptist State Convention, holding ministerial institutes for black ministers in Georgia, Alabama, Tennessee, and Kentucky.

Woodsmall's contributions to Selma University's early years were numerous. Under his direction, buildings were repaired and transformed into men's dormitories and classrooms. In 1879 he erected a frame chapel and additional schoolrooms. He also secured both money and teachers for the institution. His wife soon joined him as an instructor, and she, along with her husband, attracted white teachers from the North, including Dr. M. Stone of Ohio and several female instructors from white Baptist missionary boards. In 1880, largely due to Woodsmall's influence, the American Baptist Home Mission Society began to give two thousand dollars annually for teachers' salaries.

By 1881, the last year of Woodsmall's presidency, the school had educated more than one hundred ministerial students and an equal number of teachers. Approximately eighty Selma University alumni were teachers in Alabama public schools that year. Alumni also taught in other states. The enrollment had reached nearly three hundred.

In an address to the 1882 Colored Baptist State Convention titled "The Theological and Bible Teaching Work of the Alabama Baptist Normal and Theological School," Woodsmall discussed the school's mission, especially as it related to its ministerial program. He asserted that the mission was to train pastors for the state's six hundred black Baptist churches and to furnish teachers for Alabama's fifteen hundred public schools.

For Woodsmall, ministerial training was the more important because of its crucial role in elevating black Baptists in particular and the black race in general. The most critical need was finding qualified pastors. Since ministers provided necessary leadership for the churches, a lack of qualified pastors meant congregations could not fulfill their mission. Woodsmall also believed that ministers influenced their people in this world, as well as preparing them for eternity. The pastor's job, therefore, was more important than anyone else's, even earthly rulers. Because of the significant role of ministers and the paucity of qualified men, Woodsmall believed the school's mission to educate and train ministers was crucial.

In his address, Woodsmall outlined five ways in which the institution trained its ministers. First, it provided the rudimentary skills of reading, writing, spelling, and speaking. While not undervaluing Greek and Hebrew, Woodsmall suggested that the basic skills were more important since few ministers could read the word of God correctly. Second, the school inculcated a thorough knowledge of the Bible, as well as techniques for how to study it and teach it. Preaching constituted a third function of the ministerial program. Woodsmall insisted on extemporaneous preaching. He believed that black men were natural orators who were handicapped by manuscripts. A fourth tenet of the ministerial program was building a concern for missions and evangelism. To this end, the school advanced the importance of building Sunday schools, missionary societies, and temperance unions. Finally and of key importance for Woodsmall, was producing men of character. Woodsmall argued that "morality and spiritual character was essential if ministers were to be fit leaders of the colored race of the South. Ministers needed not only to be trained but also to be examples for the people."[6]

In 1881, at Woodsmall's urging, William McAlpine became president of the school, while Woodsmall continued to direct instruction. McAlpine, a former slave, had done more than any other black Baptist to get the school started. He made the original motion to found the institution and became the chief financial agent in raising funds. McAlpine's tenure only lasted for two years (1881–83), but he guided the school through a critical period of transition. He resigned in 1883 in favor of E. M. Brawley of South Carolina who, according to McAlpine, was more capable because of his superior formal education.

E. M. Brawley, the third president of the school, was one of the best-educated black clergymen of his day. Born a free black in South Carolina in 1851, he became the first member of his race to attend Bucknell University in Lewisburg, Pennsylvania, after having attended several African American institutions, including Howard University.

He graduated from Bucknell in 1875 and was immediately ordained to the ministry. Brawley became a missionary to South Carolina for the American Baptist Publication Society. After assisting in the formation of Sunday schools, churches, and associations, he helped establish the South Carolina State Convention. He served as corresponding secretary and financial agent of that body until he accepted the presidency of the Alabama Baptist Normal and Theological School.

Brawley's major contributions to the school were twofold. He established the Women's State Convention of Alabama as a means of providing financial support to the institution. He also reconstructed the academic program, beginning the college department and changing the name of the institution to Selma University. His dedication to preserving the institution was evident when he mortgaged his personal library to keep the school afloat as bills mounted. Brawley resigned in 1885 because of his wife's poor health and moved back to South Carolina.

Brawley was succeeded by C. L. Purce, one of Brawley's protégées. Born a slave in South Carolina in 1856, his master moved him and other slaves to Georgia to prevent their being confiscated by Union soldiers during the Civil War. Purce was converted in 1875 and became a devoted member of the Morris Street Baptist Church of Charleston, South Carolina. During this time Purce became acquainted with Brawley, who encouraged him to obtain a strong education. Purce graduated form Benedict Institute (now Benedict College) in South Carolina and from Richmond Institute (now Virginia Union University). After graduating from Richmond Institute he returned to South Carolina and spent the summer as Brawley's private secretary. In 1884 he joined Brawley at Selma University where he became an instructor of Greek and Latin. Purce became president in 1886.

Purce was one of the most popular men to hold the office. He was a strong preacher and teacher, as well as an outstanding administrator. At the time he assumed office, the school's debt totaled seven thousand dollars. Much of the debt was liquidated during his tenure. To reduce the debt, the school sold six acres of land; the Baptist Home Mission Society gave a one-time gift of six thousand dollars; and in 1890 there was a successful financial drive under the leadership of Purce and his financial agent, J. Q. A. Wilhite. William Pettiford, president of the convention during that year, also provided leadership and support.

Purce resigned in 1891, and Charles S. Dinkins succeeded him as president. Born a slave in Canton, Mississippi, in 1856, Dinkins showed a remarkable propensity for learning. He graduated as valedictorian from Roger Williams University in 1877. Five years later, he completed his work at Newton Theological Seminary, one of the first blacks to graduate from that institution. Before becoming president of Selma University, Dinkins held several important positions: faculty member at State University of Kentucky; pastor of York Street Baptist Church, Louisville, Kentucky; teacher of languages at Selma University; pastor of Second Baptist Church, Marion, Alabama; and principal of Marion Baptist Academy.

Assuming the presidency in 1893, Dinkins helped steer the school during a period of considerable debt. He succeeded in bringing the debt under control and promoted several building programs. The south wing of Susie Stone Girls Dormitory was completed during his tenure, and Dinkins also laid plans for the construction of a building that would bear his name—Dinkins Memorial Chapel. During his tenure the name of the school was changed to Alabama Baptist Colored University. Dinkins died suddenly in 1901 while still president of the institution. Charles O. Boothe completed his unexpired term.

At the turn of the twentieth century, Selma University emphasized the training of teachers and ministers. Its normal school constituted its strongest program and the one with the largest attendance. Of the 382 students enrolled in the institution in 1900, 124 were enrolled in that department. After completing this program, graduates could become teachers in state and county schools. The second largest program, with 57 pupils, trained students for the ministry. Most of these students were pursuing the two-year Bible training course. The school offered a three-year classical course in Bible, but few students pursued this route. These two programs included courses in Bible and theology, as well as some high school courses such as English and history. There were six college students in 1900; they were required to take languages such as Latin, Hebrew, and Greek.

In addition to the normal, ministerial, and college programs, Selma University had several other curricula. The school's preparatory department, offering an academic program below high school, enrolled 112 students. In addition, 135 students were listed in the model school that was designed to teach farming and trades. However, this program received only a small space in the 1901 catalog, and the names of students were not listed with the academic programs.

From 1878 to 1900 Selma University graduated 142 students from its normal school and 15 from its college program. Since most of its graduates were teachers and preachers, clearly the college was making a valuable contribution to the two most vital institutions in the black community in Alabama—the church and the schoolhouse.

Black Nationalism

In the 1880s and 1890s black nationalism emerged as a potent force in the African American community. It fostered racial consciousness and group solidarity within the black community and led to African American demands for economic and political control of their own institutions and lives. For many the concept also promoted an awareness of their African roots and a desire to reunite in some way with their African brothers. For others it spawned an appreciation of African American culture and history.

No person was more influential in promoting black nationalism in the South than Bishop Henry McNeal Turner of the AME Church. The first black U.S. Army chaplain, Turner served in the Civil War. He was active in Georgia politics after the war and was elected to the state legislature. In 1880 he became a bishop of the AME Church. The Republican Party's acquiescence on political rights for blacks, increased violence, and emerging Jim Crow laws led to Turner's disillusionment with U.S. policies. Turner's nationalist position included promoting immigration to Africa, respect for black history and culture, and black control of black institutions. Turner had a strong impact on black Baptist religious leaders such as Charles S. Morris, financial secretary of the National Baptist Convention. Exercising a leadership role, he achieved his greatest impact in religious circles with his call for black religious organizations to control their own institutions. At the organizational meeting of the National Baptist Convention in 1895, Turner told the delegates "to spurn all white men, and to worship a black God."[7]

In effect, the black church had adopted a type of nationalism since its initial separation from white churches after the Civil War. In the 1880s and 1890s this separatist philosophy intensified, mainly because of what blacks saw as the betrayal of the Republican Party, a rising tide of racism and violence, and paternalism and condescension by northern mission board and agencies. Debate emerged in black denominations as to how much assistance should be received from white groups and what part they should play in black denominational life. Two groups emerged: separatists and cooperationists. Separatists called for total separation from all forms of white control. Cooperationists believed that blacks were not yet able to support their own schools and publishing houses and therefore called for a continuing relationship with northern mission boards.

Debate between separatists and cooperationists resulted in numerous schisms. Among black Baptists, three issues were paramount: the promotion of African missions, the rise of black denominational publishing houses, and the control of educational institutions. In the area of African missions, the two groups battled over the degree of cooperation that should exist between the Foreign Mission Convention and whites in establishing missions in Africa. When the Foreign Mission Board moved its headquarters from Richmond to Louisville, cooperationists established the Lott Carey Foreign Mission Society in 1897 and continued to work closely with whites.

Schism over publishing centered on the American Baptist Publication Society. For years black Baptists had depended on the American Baptist Publication Society for its literature. Even though black churches provided a major market for the literature, the society did not publish articles *by* blacks. This led to separatists organizing the National Baptist Publishing Board. Frequent debates occurred within state conventions as to which publishing house should be supported.

The most vociferous debate focused on the control and operation of educational institutions. This debate was especially bitter in three states—Georgia, Texas, and Virginia. In each state, separatists formed schools controlled by black trustees and sought to remain free from control by the American Baptist Home Mission Society, the organization that operated Baptist schools in those states.

Alabama Baptists were influenced by the growing black nationalism. In an article in the *Colored American Magazine,* President R. T. Pollard expressed his pride in Selma University's being operated and controlled by black Baptists in Alabama. Charles O. Boothe, in his history of black Baptists in the state, extolled the progress that Baptists had made since slavery. In several urban associations, Alabama leaders called on blacks to patronize black professionals and businesses. T. W. Walker, moderator of the Mt. Pilgrim Association of Birmingham, gave an address in 1897 on why black businesses should be supported. His position was verbally sanctioned by William Pettiford and Charles O. Boothe who were present at the meeting. Resolutions were issued by several associations, including the Alabama Association of Montgomery County in 1900, urging the support of black businesses.

Ostensibly, Alabama black Baptist leaders supported the cooperationist view, while appreciating, building, and supporting black institutions and enterprises. They continued to work with and to receive support from northern Baptists and other whites. In the 1890s Henry Morehouse of the American Baptist Home Mission Society served as the only white member of the fifteen-member trustee board of Selma University. He attended the state convention regularly and presented addresses and sermons at those meetings. The convention passed resolutions supporting the all-black National Baptist Convention Publishing Board but also resolved to support the all-white American Baptist Publication Society.

This dualistic support for all-black organizations and cooperation with white organizations did not please every one. Other issues also generated dissatisfaction: lack of recognition of pastors in rural areas, too much leadership and involvement by nonpastors, domination of the convention by a few people, and inadequate reporting and supervision of money matters. Conflict also arose between educated pastors and those without formal training. Men like Boothe, McAlpine, and McEwen, who supported the northern boards and received salaries from them, were men with formal training. Men who opposed the cooperationists had received little or no formal education. It seems clear that those less formally trained felt they were being overlooked.

Separatist sentiment fostered continual dissatisfaction with control of Selma University. In 1898 a pastor interrupted the convention to ask leaders to respond to the rumor that Selma University was not owned by the convention. His query created quite a stir and led to a resolution asking the board of trustees to petition the state legislature to make "certain enactments to put Selma University on a strong legal basis and give the Negro Baptists of the state full power to control it in all matters pertaining to a full fledged University."[8] Obviously, this action was designed to placate those who felt that the American Baptist Home Mission Society and other northern whites had too much influence over the school.

Other separatists accused the convention of being disloyal to the National Baptist Convention. This action obviously came from those who felt that only the National Baptist Publishing Board should be supported and that equal support should not be given to the American Baptist Publication Society. In 1896 William H. Boyd began to attend annual sessions of the Alabama convention as well as some association sessions. Boyd had started the National Baptist Publishing House over objections and opposition from the American Baptist Publication Society. A forceful speaker and promoter of black self-help, he insisted that blacks should give full and undivided support to their own publishing board. Bitter feelings existed between him and the northern American Baptist Publication Society. Not surprisingly Boyd gained supporters in Alabama. When separatists claimed that the convention failed to support self-help, their argument usually focused on the National Baptist Convention Publishing House. District associations often added to the conflict by supporting one publishing board over the other. For example, at the 1897 Auburn District Association meeting, delegates passed a resolution designating the National Baptist Publishing House as their publishing board. In that same year, the Alabama Midlands Association voted to make the American Baptist Publication Society its official board.

T. W. Walker, pastor of the Shiloh Baptist Church of Birmingham, led the separatist forces. Under his leadership, Shiloh had become the largest church in Birmingham and one of the largest in the state. Highly militant and a strong believer in black pride and self-help, Walker had established several businesses in the Birmingham area. He started an insurance company partly because he did not like that white insurance salesmen failed to call black women by their proper names, addressing them instead by their first names or as "auntie." For Walker, black success was predicated on cooperation among blacks, not cooperation with whites. He believed that all-black enterprises did not receive full support from the convention, and he joined forces with those who felt the convention did not adequately support the National Baptist Convention. In addition, Walker concluded that there was too much interference by the white American Baptist Home Mission Society in the affairs of Selma University. Walker had served on the Selma University board of trustees in the early 1890s but was not reelected later in the decade. In 1898 when separatists formed the New Era State Convention of Alabama, Walker served as its first president.

Alabama now had two conventions. No records of the New Era Convention are extant, but it appears that it did not experience rapid growth. The Colored Baptist State Convention of Alabama continued to grow. After making some attempts at reconciliation shortly after the split, the concern with reconciliation with the New Era Convention waned after 1910. By the first decade of the twentieth century, the Colored Baptist Convention claimed 186,000 members, which was an increase over its 1898 figure when the split occurred. The convention continued to receive support from northern mission boards until the 1930s.

Sociopolitical Concerns

As prominent members of their race, black Baptist ministers and church leaders spoke out on a variety of secular issues. Concerned for the uplift of blacks in

Alabama, black Baptists passed resolutions and formed delegations to petition political authorities on behalf of their people. These resolutions were printed in official minutes, designed to be read in churches, and made available to the public. In the 1893 annual session of the state convention, the secretary noted that three thousand copies of the minutes were to be printed and distributed to all the churches and associations in the state. The remaining ones were to be sold for ten cents each.

No issue concerned black Baptists more than the violence perpetrated against them during the last two decades of the nineteenth century. Whites had used violence to destroy Reconstruction and continued the practice after the end of Republican control in 1874. Lynching constituted the most vicious form of violence: blacks were hanged from trees and their bodies savagely mutilated. Historical investigation suggests several reasons for this form of brutality: economic hard times faced by whites, growing white hatred of blacks, reaction to the Populist revolt, and the desire to protect white womanhood. Another reason was the desire simply to keep blacks in their place. Lynching was often preceded by the accusation that a white woman had been raped, charges that were rarely true. Although white Baptist leaders spoke out against lynching, local authorities frequently abetted the mobs. Lynching, along with other forms of violence, greatly increased in the last two decades of the nineteenth century. In the 1890s, southern white mobs lynched more than 100 blacks per year. In Alabama alone, from 1882 to 1902, 224 people were lynched, 198 of them African Americans.[9] Because they were community leaders, black pastors and religious officials were often the targets of white hate groups.

In their attempts to eliminate lynchings and others forms of violence against blacks, Baptist conventions and associations passed resolutions and other formal actions designed to influence white politicians, sympathetic whites, and law enforcement officials. In 1894 the Alabama Colored Baptist State Convention presented a complaint to Governor Thomas Jones saying that Abram Watkins, one of its members, had been driven from his home and prevented from returning because of threats of violence by whites. Committee members included some of the most prominent men in the convention, namely Robert T. Pollard, William R. Pettiford, William H. McAlpine, and A. N. McEwen. In that same year, the convention endorsed a bill by Governor Thomas Jones in which he asked the Alabama legislature to enact laws against lynching and compel officers of the law to protect prisoners from mob violence. In 1897 Professor P. H. Patterson, a lay leader of the convention and a member of the Dexter Avenue Baptist Church of Montgomery, was gunned down at a meeting of the Montgomery-Antioch District Association Congress. Patterson was militant in his racial views and spoke out against all forms of discrimination. Convention records do not indicate whether a white or black killed him. A convention resolution condemned the killing as a "blazing and a most shameful disgrace upon civilization and upon the race and upon the Baptist denomination in Alabama." Obviously, blacks viewed his murder as a racial act intended to intimidate blacks from speaking out. Another convention resolution in that same year urged blacks to do all within their power to prevent a repetition of such deeds.[10]

During the 1890s at least three associations passed resolutions against lynchings. An 1893 Alabama Association resolution condemned lynching as "a mark of barbarism rather than civilization and called on well-meaning whites to stop it. It further urged blacks not to retaliate with similar violence but to use "the weapons of prayer and the gospel."[11] In 1897 the Autauga Association issued a similar resolution that recognized lynching as a heinous crime against humanity but urged blacks not to retaliate with similar violence. Also in 1897 the Mt. Pilgrim Association stated in its resolution that "lynching produced anarchy and was a crime that could not elevate people." Like the Alabama Association resolution, it urged law enforcement officials "to do all in their power to bring the perpetrators to justice, and encouraged churches to begin a righteous crusade against such crimes."[12]

Embarrassing and humiliating treatment of blacks as railway passengers was another primary concern. In the name of creating order in race relations, the Alabama legislature passed a law requiring separate but equal facilities on railroads. In reality, accommodations were far from equal. Forced to travel in second-class accommodations, blacks were subjected to filthy cars that were not only inundated with smoke but also doubled as toilet rooms and storehouses for white passengers. These horrible conditions were of special concern to pastors who frequently traveled on trains to association meetings, conventions, and revivals. In addition to issuing resolutions against inhumane treatment of blacks on railroads, black Baptist groups formed study commissions. For example, in the 1890s the Montgomery-Antioch Association called for equal treatment on railroads, and in 1896 the Alabama Colored Baptist Convention voted to form a committee to obtain evidence of unequal accommodations for blacks and to present those findings to Alabama railroad commissioners.

A third important concern for black Baptists was public funding for educational and benevolent causes. Bourbon political rule was characterized by a general retrenchment in the state's educational and social responsibilities. Reductions in allocations and limited funding for education and benevolent institutions hit blacks the hardest. Blacks were also concerned that they get their fair share of what was allocated.

The 1896 state convention issued a resolution that called on the state to expand funds allocated for black education. It also called for the legislature to establish a first-rate public university for blacks. Furthermore, it encouraged officials to pass a bill exempting Selma University and Baptist academies located at Courtland, Marion, Eufaula, and Anniston from taxation. At the same time, the convention called upon the state legislature to establish a reform school for boys. This resolution declared that it was impossible to reform juveniles when they were confined to prisons, mines, and convict farms with hardened criminals.

Some associations, realizing the need for benevolent institutions to serve the needs of the young and poor, went beyond resolutions and delegations, and undertook special projects. In its 1889 session, the Auburn District Association voted to establish a home for homeless boys and girls. The next year the association made Opelika the site of the orphanage. In 1897 the Mt. Pilgrim Association discussed the possibility of opening a home for boys in the Birmingham area. The home became a reality when William Pettiford, a former moderator of the association, assisted the women's clubs of Birmingham in establishing not only an orphanage but also a children's hospital and a home for the elderly.

Black Baptists made noble strides in educational and social reform during this period, especially when one considers the hostile forces arrayed against them. They established educational and benevolent institutions to uplift their people. Self-help was a guiding force in this development. So strong was the self-help emphasis that some pastors called for blacks to control their own destiny without any help from whites. The strides that black Baptists made between 1875 and 1900 would not have been possible without strong and vigorous leaders. Spurred by well-grounded theological beliefs that they helped formulate, these leaders guided black Baptist development throughout the state.

5
Theology and Leadership

In 1890 Charles O. Boothe published *Plain Theology for Plain People*, in which he illustrated in intellectual terms the liberation theology of Alabama's black Baptists. Boothe, who helped establish Selma University, held ministerial conferences to train pastors, and founded other educational institutions, epitomized the theological order and organization that black leadership sought to foster in the early years to 1900.

Despite operating, after Reconstruction, in a time of deteriorating race relations, black Baptists in Alabama continued to develop certain theological emphases that provided them a measure of assurance and confidence. Their theology reflected continuity with that developed during slavery and Reconstruction but added a strong sense of biblicism as well. In addition, they added Ethiopianism, which stressed the greatness of black humanity along with a sense of the ultimate triumph of the race in spite of its present oppression. And like white Baptists, blacks believed in Landmarkism, which would have both positive and negative consequences.

Black Baptists were fortunate to have many remarkable leaders during this period, but none were more influential than William H. McAlpine and Charles O. Boothe, who consistently emphasized education, cooperation, discipline, order, and missions. These became the primary goals of Baptist associations and the Alabama Colored Baptist State Convention. Their ideas also influenced many of the theological convictions that sustained black Baptists during this era. Other leaders in the state looked to them for advice and counsel.

Theology

Biblical and theological beliefs among the rank and file of black Baptists showed a strong sense of continuity with the past. As in the slavery and Reconstruction periods, it continued to combine tenets of white evangelicalism and elements of African spiritualism. Exhibited through highly emotional worship, black theology emphasized God's goodness, deliverance, and liberation. Although most ministers had no formal training, they delivered sermons with wild enthusiasm and focused on the biblical stories of Moses and the Exodus, Daniel and the lion's den, and the Hebrew boys and the fiery furnace.

Charles O. Boothe's book *Plain Theology for Plain People,* the only attempt by a nineteenth-century black Alabama Baptist minister to codify a theological treatise, contended that God was found among the lowly, but "hides himself from the proud and self-sufficient man." Although often critical of the emotionalism expressed in black Baptist churches, Boothe supported the folk emphasis of black religion that stressed God's deliverance of the poor and oppressed.[1]

This emphasis on God as liberator was also expressed in the Negro spirituals that continued to be a part of black worship. Mary Ovington, a New York social worker and one of the founders of the NAACP, recalled hearing them as she traveled through rural Alabama at the turn of the century. These spirituals were primarily group songs that emphasized freedom and God's deliverance. "My Lord Delivered Daniel," "Go Down Moses into Egypt Land, Tell Old Pharaoh to Let My People Go, and "Steal Away" were but a few of the spirituals that expressed the themes of deliverance and liberation. Although no longer slaves, blacks realized that they were still not completely free. Through the spirituals they expressed the faith that God would one day bring liberation.

Scripture undergirded this emphasis on hope, freedom, and deliverance. Blacks sought to make biblical truth relevant to their situation, and for them the Bible provided many accounts that identified God as deliverer. The exodus experience continued to be important, and they portrayed it as the central event in the Old Testament. Moreover, Jesus had come to save and deliver, and blacks portrayed Calvary and the suffering of Jesus in graphic terms.

The Bible also provided a normative standard for Christian life and activity. Religious leaders and convention resolutions strongly urged Alabama Baptists to be guided by biblical truth. An 1878 convention resolution insisted that the Bible should be studied because "it reveals life and death, heaven and hell. It reveals God's will to a lost and ruined world—reveals our true apostate state— reveals life and death through Jesus Christ." The resolution further added that "it throws light on the immortality of the soul, which the ancient philosophers could not understand. The Bible," it concluded, "was the only true wisdom." In the 1895 convention William McAlpine encouraged Baptist ministers to "listen to the Bible in worship, prayer, and expository preaching."[2]

Ethiopianism was an intellectual movement that the rank and file did not fully comprehend. It emerged in Alabama through association and convention leaders and influenced the liberation emphasis of black Baptists. Part of millennial ideology, it had been prominent in the theology of several religious groups in the United States from the nation's earliest years. Based on Revelation 20:1–7, millenarianism predicted a thousand-year reign of Christ with the resurrected martyrs while Satan was bound and confined to the abyss. Millennial Ethiopianism, which flourished among many black Christians around the turn of the nineteenth century, predicted a future golden age in which black people around the world would rise to a significant role in history. The elevation of the black race would be accompanied by God's judgment on white society and on Western civilization. Ethiopianism also incorporated a strong identification with Africa and the hope of entering the Promised Land.

Ethiopianism, which covered a variety of themes, actually served as a deterrent to racism. The historian Albert Raboteau claimed that the most quoted verse in black religious history was Psalm 68:31: "Princes shall come out of Egypt: Ethiopia shall soon stretch out her hands unto God." Nineteenth-century black Americans believed that verse, in which Egypt and Ethiopia referred to the African race, helped discredit many pseudoscientific theories of black inferiority. Instead of seeing Ham and his descendants as cursed, an argument used to support racism, Ethiopianism maintained that Psalm 68:31 pointed to the future greatness of the black race. In The *Cushite; or, the Descendants of Ham,* Baptist pastor Rufus Perry complained that the black mummy had been "transformed by the art of Pythagorean metempsychosis into a white mummy with a look of disdain upon its former self." Perry aimed to prove that the ancient Ethiopians and Egyptians were black descendants of Ham. Blacks could therefore point to Ham and his descendants with pride and cherish the hope of returning to racial greatness.[3]

Some black clergymen pointed to the rise of great leaders like Booker T. Washington and Richard Boyd of the National Baptist Publishing Board as evidence of achievements by black Americans in the nineteenth century. The growth of black educational institutions also showed the emergence of the race. Ethiopianism advanced the call for black control of their own institutions. In 1903 Richard Boyd began to manufacture black dolls for the National Baptist

Convention. The convention accepted Boyd's argument that dolls manufactured by whites did not portray the beauty of blackness, and state officials endorsed the project, urging members and churches to purchase the dolls. Black pride and black nationalism went hand in hand with Ethiopianism.

Ethiopianism probably had its greatest effect in the area of foreign missions. Since the elevation of black Americans related closely to the emancipation of Africa, black religious leaders became more conscious of the need to spread Christianity to that continent. In 1880 Alabamians helped form the Foreign Mission Convention with William McAlpine serving as the first president. Other Alabamians would succeed him in that office, namely James Foster and J. Q. A. Wilhite. Some leaders spoke of missions in millennial terms, reminding black Americans that their race had a responsibility to purge African religion of idolatry. White nations had spread the gospel to Africa, but their method lacked the element of peace that exemplified the millennium. That mission, they insisted, must be undertaken by black Christians.

Such missionary work by African Americans inspired indigenous church movements in Africa and opened a channel for a number of Africans to receive their education in U.S. schools and colleges after the Civil War. In the late nineteenth century, several South Africans came to the United States to pursue an education, and many of these students entered advanced degree programs at white universities. Selma University was one of several black schools that enrolled African students in the nineteenth century. Some of the students who studied at black colleges in the United States returned to Africa where they fostered independent church movements and became involved in activities against European colonial regimes.

Ethiopianism also appeared in convention speeches and resolutions. For example, an 1887 resolution urged support for Selma University, stating that this support should continue "until it shall be known to the world that Ethiopia has stretched forth her hands intelligently to God." As late as the 1930s, the editor of the *Baptist Leader,* the official organ of the convention, describing the growth of the black population in East Alabama maintained that "Ethiopia was stretching forth her hand."[4]

Landmarkism, focusing on the nature of the true church, had a significant influence on black Baptists in Alabama as well during this period. Like Ethiopianism, it was communicated to church members by their pastors and convention leaders. The concept originated on the frontier of the South and Midwest in the nineteenth century in competition between Baptists and other religious groups. According to Landmark theologians, the Baptist Church was the only true church because it was the sole religious group that practiced the correct methods of baptism and the Lord's Supper. Of the two church rituals, baptism was the more important. Landmarkism insisted that non-Baptist or pedobaptist organizations were not genuine churches. They had neither the proper "subject" for baptism—a regenerated individual—the proper "mode" of baptism—immersion instead of sprinkling—nor the proper "administer" of baptism—a Baptist minister.

The most influential person to spread the ideas of Landmarkism among northern Baptists and eventually to blacks was James M. Pendleton. Because of his pro-Union views, Pendleton left the South and settled in Upton, Pennsylvania, where he helped establish Crozer Theological Seminary at nearby Chester. Blacks who attended American Baptist schools such as Crozer after emancipation were introduced to Landmarkism.

In contrast to more abstract ideals, Landmarkism's simplicity, its strict and rigid biblicism, appealed to blacks. Though whites initiated the movement, most blacks viewed it not as white theology but as proper Baptist doctrine. National Baptist leaders endorsed it, and Richard Boyd reported that "Negro Baptists, wherever they were allowed, formed churches of their own. However, they were Landmarkist, Simon-pure, regular Baptist." Elias C. Morris, president of the National Baptist Convention, asserted that "it may be seen that the Baptists who were formerly called Ana-Baptists, and in later times Mennonites, were the Waldenses and have long in the history of the church received that origin and as such may be justly termed the only Christian community which has stood since the days of the apostles." In 1890 Edward M. Brawley published the *Black Baptist Pulpit,* a collection of sermons by the best-trained black Baptist scholars and leaders in the nation. Many of the sermons dealt with ecclesiology and were written from a Landmarkist point of view. For example, in a sermon titled "Contending for the Faith," Brawley identified the main tenets of the Baptist faith as believer's baptism, freedom of worship, and a democratic polity. He maintained that since early Baptists had established religious freedom, it was the duty of present Baptists to develop the true meaning of baptism. He believed this effort bore fruit because several pedobaptist congregations were immersing their members, and infant baptism was falling into disuse.[5]

Landmarkism came to black Baptists in Alabama from two major sources. Many white Southern Baptists in Alabama practiced Landmarkism, and black Baptists were exposed to it in the biracial churches during slavery and Reconstruction. Also, some white ministers who held classes for black pastors after slavery taught the Landmarkist view. For example, in 1880 John Jefferson Renfroe, pastor of Talladega's First Baptist Church began a school for black pastors. The group met twice a week to study Pendleton's Christian Doctrine. For many years Renfroe was the pastor of William McAlpine, a leader among black Baptists, and he obviously influenced McAlpine's views. Even more important in the spread of Landmarkism among Alabama black Baptists was the influence of black ministers who came to Alabama after being trained in sectarian northern white seminaries. Edward M. Brawley, a Pendleton Landmarkist and president of Selma University from 1883 to 1885, helped spread Landmarkism throughout the state. His pupil and protégée C. L. Purce, who succeeded him as president of Selma University, was a strong proponent of Landmarkism.

Alabama's convention leaders also strongly advocated the Landmarkist position. In 1887 William McAlpine preached at the Mt. Pilgrim Association in Birmingham. In his sermon on closed communion he insisted that "only Baptists should participate in the Lord's Supper at Baptist churches. People from Pedo-Baptist churches should not participate because they were not from genuine churches that practiced the proper form and method of the Lord's Supper." At the same association meeting, William R. Pettiford reminded the group that if they did not train their people to be true missionary Baptists, they would be trained by other denominations. At the Eufaula Association meeting of 1891 P. S. L. Hutchins read a paper titled "Evils of Pulpit Affiliation with Other Denominations." He argued against any form of affiliation because "Baptist churches were based on the Apostles' doctrine and the true word of God while other denominations were based simply on man's thoughts. To cooperate would give the impression that doctrinal differences were small, an idea that would spawn more Pedo-Baptists." In an 1892 sermon to the Alabama Association, H. W. Deville dealt with "the who, how and why of water baptism," making his case that only the form of baptism practiced by Baptists was legitimate.[6]

Selma University, like State University in Kentucky and most black Baptist colleges, was a hotbed of Landmarkism. At Selma, the theology department assigned Pendleton's book on Christian doctrine as early as 1887, and its use continued into the twentieth century. Although students from other denominations attended the institution, theology professors took a sectarian point of view. Selma's presidents supported this position and theology deans William McAlpine, C. O. Boothe, and A. F. Owens taught Landmarkism with a passion. Consequently, ministers who studied at Selma University left the institution with considerable exposure to Landmarkist principles. In addition, the school's charter stipulated that only Baptists could teach at the institution, another factor that influenced its strong Landmarkist bent.

Landmarkism was, however, exclusive and narrow, and its application made ecumenical and interdenominational activity difficult. Usually, Baptists in Alabama formed their own ministerial groups within cities and towns, and few Baptists affiliated with interdenominational organizations. Furthermore, rural blacks tended to identify with their local church communities. For many, being Baptist or Methodist meant more than being a Negro. More cooperative ventures across denominational lines would have benefited racial progress.

Fortunately for black Baptists, Landmarkism did not proceed to its logical extreme and some cooperation among black denominations and their leaders continued. Black Landmarkism tended to be milder than that developed in the American South among some whites, due primarily to the influence by graduates of northern seminaries. Baptist convention and association meetings in Alabama usually included greetings from other denominations, and in 1873 the state convention met in a Methodist church when First African Baptist Church of Tuscaloosa was undergoing repairs. In some instances, then, race took precedence over Landmarkism.

Liberation theology, with its strong biblicism, was a consistent theme among the rank and file of black Baptists. Landmarkism and Ethiopianism were also prevalent theological positions for blacks in the last years of the late nineteenth century. Simple biblicism and the idea of apostolic succession helped complete the Ethiopian myth—that blacks originated in Egypt and Ethiopia. This cultural identification proved especially significant during a time when social Darwinism was on the rise and the curse of Ham was touted as an explanation for the existence of blacks. Liberation theology, Landmarkism, and Ethiopianism helped counter such racially divisive ideas and gave blacks the strength to endure in spite of difficult times.

Leadership: Charles O. Boothe and William McAlpine

Black Baptists in Alabama made progress in the areas of missions, organization, education, and theology, and most of these advancements may be attributed to strong leadership. The denomination produced many outstanding leaders during its first three decades, and association moderators generally provided a positive force in the local communities where they served. In addition, the presidents of Selma University cast a long shadow over the state in terms of education and leadership development. Presidents of the state convention exerted influence as well, and five strong leaders served in that capacity between 1875 and 1900.

Of the leaders, none were more influential than William H. McAlpine and C. O. Boothe. Their ideas, theology, and initiatives provided direction for black Alabama Baptists in the first three decades of their existence. Others also looked to them for inspiration and leadership. A. F. Owens, in his speech on the history of the state convention at the jubilee session of the convention in 1917, aptly described the leadership and influence of these two men in the early years: "Those were the days of Baptist unity and struggles—days, I might say, when the privacy of leadership of Alabama Colored Baptists was disputed by only two men, W. H. McAlpine and C. O. Boothe. When one of these two men spoke, it was as if it was an oracle from God, with all the other brothers fixing their eyes on them. Both McAlpine and Boothe were self-made men but they were skillful makers, having received their pattern in the mountain of God. From the peak of the mount they saw the days of bondage receding in the distance and the days of a larger freedom for the race approaching and they laid plans from the horoscope of enlightened vision."[7]

For thirty years Boothe and McAlpine presided over convention sessions, led devotion, made reports, chaired committees, and offered advice on key issues that came before the convention. Others looked to them for counsel on important issues. These two men were among the best trained in the convention. In a sermon before the 1877 convention, Mansfield Tyler said that Boothe and McAlpine were two of only three people who could write well enough to take down minutes. They were dedicated to working through the convention to uplift blacks in Alabama. For them education, organization, missions, cooperation, church discipline, and order were of vital importance. Because of their leadership, these concerns became paramount for black Baptists in Alabama.

Charles Octavius Boothe was born a slave, the property of Nathan Howard, on June 13, 1845, in Mobile, Alabama. His great-grandmother was born in Africa, his grandmother in Virginia, and his mother in Georgia. Boothe made no mention of his father, whose identity he probably did not know. His grandfather was pure African, a man who had learned to read the Bible and hymnbook, and who taught others how to sing. One of Boothe's early recollections was of a Baptist church near his home where blacks and whites worshipped in the same building.

As a child, the precocious Boothe learned to read and write from a schoolteacher who lived with his slave master. He was especially interested in reading the Bible and spent many long hours devouring it. As soon as he was able to work, Boothe served as an office boy for Colonel James S. Terrell. He actually read law books in Terrell's office and later remarked, "I think I can say that the Colonel and I actually loved each other."[8]

Although Boothe's slave experience was more privileged than most blacks, he did not view the institution in any positive way. Slavery, Boothe asserted, trained blacks as laborers, not as socially and politically responsible adults. In the area of religion, Boothe believed that slavery had retarded blacks from learning the basics of Christianity and had negative effects on black worship. He referred to slavery as the "dark times" and indicted all of white America for imposing such a terrible institution. Boothe dismissed the notion that slavery constituted a school for blacks that ultimately prepared them for freedom. Slavery, he insisted, had been a brutal and horrible institution.

Boothe was baptized in 1866, and was ordained to the ministry by the St. Louis Street Baptist Church in Mobile, Alabama, in December 1868. For a brief time, he attended Meharry, the medical department of Central Tennessee College. He then served as pastor of the First Baptist Church in Meridian, Mississippi. In 1878 he became the first pastor of Montgomery's Second Colored Baptist Church, today the Dexter Avenue Baptist Church, where he served for a short period. Boothe also pastored the Mt. Canaan Baptist Church of Talladega and the St. Phillips Street Baptist Church of Selma.

In addition to his pastorates, Boothe provided outstanding leadership for the denomination. He was not present at the original meeting of the convention in 1868, but began attending convention meetings in the 1870s and held numerous important posts over the next thirty years. As a convention member and officer, he devoted much of his time to generating support for an educational institution. Along with others, he led the convention in establishing a theological school for training ministers. Boothe served on a committee to create such an institution. When Selma University opened in 1878, he taught in the theological department and served as acting president during the 1901–1902 academic year. To publicize the school, he assisted McAlpine in publishing the *Baptist Pioneer.*

In addition to his success in organization and institutional development, Boothe excelled as a lecturer and theologian. As a missionary sponsored by the state convention or other organizations, he conducted ministerial institutes to train preachers and church leaders in the essentials of Christianity and church management. Usually, each institute convened during a weekend, and a particular church served as the host, inviting Baptist pastors, deacons, and other leaders from adjacent communities. Boothe held ten to twenty institutes a year in addition to his missionary duties that ranged from colportage to regular preaching assignments.

During one institute in North Alabama, Boothe laid the groundwork for a new school—North Alabama Baptist Academy. Boothe was elected principal in 1896 but his missionary activities did not allow him to serve. Professor H. E. Levi became the first principal, and classes began in 1897 at the First Baptist Church of Courtland, Alabama. Although designed primarily as an institution to educate preachers, the school soon added academic courses to its curriculum. Many black ministers and teachers in northern Alabama received their training at the academy. Although Boothe declined to serve as the first principal, he became the school's third principal for a brief period.

To enhance his instruction at the weekend institutes, Boothe published *Plain Theology for Plain People* in which he attempted to simplify the truth of the gospel. Since most of the ministers of his day had little formal education and were bivocational, Boothe tried to avoid complicated jargon and terms. Rather, he sought to explain every doctrine in the simplest way possible. For example, in his discussion of John 4:24—"God is a Spirit," Boothe defined spirit as "not akin to matter" and "matter as akin to those things which may be seen with the eyes or heard with the ears, and handled with the hands."[9] Using the term in this simple manner provided an alternative to the vapid, metaphysical speculations of most biblical commentaries.

Recognized as the most distinguished scholar and theologian of his time among black Baptists, Boothe also authored other books. For example, in 1895 he published the pioneer history of black Baptists in Alabama. In his *Cyclopedia of the Colored Baptists of Alabama* he recorded the names and deeds of convention leaders and traced the convention's progress to 1895. Boothe's history has proved indispensable to all subsequent historical research on the early years of black Alabama Baptists. In 1913 he published a pamphlet taken from a sermon he delivered at the Birmingham Baptist Minister's Conference, "Last Day Challenge in Last Day Voice." Boothe maintained that human perfectibility and justice are not possible in this life but that they will be achieved in a future life where justice, righteousness, and goodness are supreme. In spite of his belief that human perfection was not possible, Boothe continued to build structures and institutions to assist in uplifting blacks in Alabama. His final book, *Biblical*

Systematic Theology, published in 1925, provided an expansion of many of the themes addressed in his first book on theology.

Boothe's work with institutes, his concern for black educational institutions, and his theological publications were designed to help establish order and discipline in black Baptist churches. In particular, he emphasized proper decorum in worship and appropriate behavior of church members within the larger society. In many cases, whites regarded black churches as circuses where blacks confused shouting with spirituality. According to Boothe, improper worship and behavior not only caused the wider society to look down on black religion but also hampered blacks from building up their own institutions. He argued that blacks should lead a "pure and spotless life" in order to show their worthiness as Christians and citizens. Furthermore, he regarded a reduction in shouting and emotional excesses in church services not as a concession to whites, but as a sign of a deepening understanding of God. Therefore, he encouraged black Baptists to find a better expression of that "saving faith . . . that exercise of soul . . . that satisfies the intellect, impresses the sensibilities and bows the will beneath the gospel forms and gospel spirit."[10]

Boothe himself was subjected to the church's mania for discipline. In 1885 a committee recommended expelling him from the convention's fellowship "on account of complications in his marriage relations, his opposition to state work, and on account of his want of loyalty to truth." The committee seemed most concerned about his marriage. Boothe's work with the American Baptist Home Mission Society had caused friction and aroused jealously within the convention, but officials did not move against him until rumors surfaced about trouble in his marriage. The paucity of records obscures the nature of the allegations— whether infidelity, divorce, abandonment, physical abuse. Whatever the charge, Boothe consistently refuted it, but his name is conspicuously absent from the record of the convention in 1885 and 1886. The convention conducted a detailed investigation and restored Boothe to fellowship after charges were dropped in 1887. Boothe apparently suffered no lasting consequences from this conflict. After 1887 he served in many noteworthy capacities within the convention and performed missionary duties for several Baptist agencies. However, this episode clearly demonstrates the obsession with discipline and order that consumed Boothe and other Baptist pioneers.[11]

For some unknown reason Boothe's name appears less and less in convention minutes after 1900. However, he continued to serve as a missionary and teacher. In 1904, while serving as a missionary for the Southern Baptist Convention, he and William R. Pettiford began to train pastors in the basement of Birmingham's Sixteenth Street Baptist Church. Those classes are today considered the beginning of Birmingham Baptist College, later named Birmingham-Easonian Baptist Bible College.

Boothe's labors expanded beyond church and denominational work. Like many black religious leaders, he addressed some of the major secular issues of his day, especially Jim Crow politics and the socioeconomic conditions of blacks. He supported Booker T. Washington's "Petition to the Members of the Alabama Constitutional Convention of 1901." Washington had invited some of the black leaders of Alabama to a meeting in Montgomery to approve a petition to the white constitutional convention that opposed the disfranchisement of blacks in Alabama. Boothe opened the meeting with a prayer and signed his name to the petition.

Maintaining a long relationship with Washington, Boothe wrote a lengthy assessment of the civil condition of African Americans in the South in a letter to Washington and also outlined what needed to be done to better their condition. For him, poverty was the major problem for blacks. To reduce poverty, he advised black leaders to convince landowners that improved conditions for tenants increased the profits for the owner and to persuade northern philanthropists to buy farmland in the South and then sell it to blacks. His last public activity in Alabama involved a study of black convicts in the state in which he described the horrors of the convict lease system. Advancing age, his frustration with disfranchisement, and his lack of success in countering the horrors of the convict lease system caused him to lose heart in efforts to secure cooperation from whites. Although he did not defeat Jim Crow in his lifetime, he did help put in place institutions and theological values that produced leaders in the twentieth century who would eventually destroy legal segregation. He remained an important state and nationally known Baptist leader until his death in Detroit in 1924.

Boothe's accomplishments notwithstanding, no person was accorded more praise, respect, and acclaim among black Baptists in Alabama than William McAlpine. Convention and association records reveal a high degree of respect among black Baptists. In 1893 the Auburn Association designated the proceeds from the Sunday morning worship service to be given to McAlpine to pay for his railroad fare. This gesture was done not as charity but to show appreciation for his service to that year's association meeting and to Alabama Baptists in general. Similar action taken in the Rushing Springs Association of Talladega provided funds for his trip to the Foreign Mission Convention. Whenever McAlpine visited an association, he would be asked to preach or to give words of advice and encouragement. At the jubilee session of the Alabama Convention, one speaker described McAlpine as "intrepid, pugnacious, and uncompromising—the plumed knight of Alabama Baptists."[12]

The high esteem in which McAlpine was held stemmed from his pioneering effort in founding Selma University and his selfless service in establishing other institutions and convention organizations. He also exhibited a deep faith and was known for his stainless moral character. Although not the equal of Boothe as a scholar, theologian, or historian, he was unequaled as an organizer and motivator. In many ways, McAlpine's status among black Baptists compares favorably with that of Hosea Holcombe within the white Alabama Baptist Convention. McAlpine helped establish the major organizations that the convention continues to support. Along with Boothe, McAlpine stressed those things that were to dominate the major efforts of black Baptists in Alabama during his thirty years of active service: order, discipline, self-help, cooperation, and education. In the foundational period of Alabama's black Baptists, he was literally involved in every activity, serving as pastor, association founder, school founder and president, missionary, lecturer, newspaper editor, and National Baptist Convention founder and president.

Born in Buckingham County, Virginia, in 1847, McAlpine and his mother and younger brother were brought to Alabama by a Negro speculator when he was about three years old. The three of them were sold to a Presbyterian minister, Robert McAlpine, who lived in Coosa County. His owner died when he was about eight years old. During the division of his property, McAlpine was separated from his mother and brother and became the property of one of Robert McAlpine's sons, a doctor who lived in Talladega County. The doctor's wife, a northerner, was not pleased with the way southerners taught her children, and she refused to send them to school with their peers. She taught them herself or had a teacher come to their home for private instruction. As the nurse for his master's children, young McAlpine was required to be with them all the time. This proximity afforded him the opportunity to learn to read and write and to gain some knowledge of arithmetic, grammar, and geography. He remained separated from his mother until 1874, a period of nineteen years, and never knew his father.

In addition to serving as nurse, McAlpine waited on table for his master. A frequent guest who greatly influenced McAlpine was the Reverend John Jefferson Renfroe. Renfroe served as pastor of the First Baptist Church, Talladega, from 1858 to 1860, resigning to serve as a chaplain in the Civil War. In that role, he distinguished himself by participating in the great revival that swept through the Confederate ranks, and converted hundreds of soldiers to the Christian faith. After the war, Renfroe resumed his pastorate, serving from 1864 to 1888. He pastored both white and black congregations that met separately. Renfroe baptized hundreds of blacks and often praised his black congregation, urging them to continue to avoid emotional excesses and other bad tendencies. Due largely to Renfroe's influence, McAlpine was converted to Christianity and baptized as a member of the Talladega Baptist Church in 1864. Renfroe, one of the great preachers and leaders among white Baptists in postwar Alabama, did much to influence McAlpine in terms of the ministry and the importance of education.

A few months after his conversion and baptism, McAlpine felt a call to the ministry. However, for some years he refused to accept a license from his church because he believed that a minister should attain thorough preparation. Consequently, he entered Talladega College, supporting himself by working in the morning and evening hours. While at Talladega, McAlpine met Erastus Milo Cravath, and his association with Cravath proved indispensable for his later educational work. An effective school organizer, Cravath directed the Middle West Department of the American Missionary Association (AMA) in Cincinnati. In that capacity, he supervised AMA's education and mission work in Alabama. In 1875 Cravath became president of Fisk University in Nashville, Tennessee, and moved that school toward becoming one of the premier AMA black colleges in the United States. A man of vision, faith, and positive conviction, Cravath was convinced that education held the key to black uplift. Under Cravath's guidance, McAlpine learned to raise funds for educational institutions while a field worker at Talladega College. This experience honed McAlpine's passion for educating the black race.

Licensed in 1869 and ordained in 1871, McAlpine left Talladega College six months before graduation, having been aroused to establish a similar institution for his own denomination. While attending the Colored Baptist Missionary State Convention in Tuscaloosa, Alabama, in November 1873, McAlpine offered a resolution to establish a school for ministers. His proposal gained support from blacks but met resistance from white Baptists. When whites sought to challenge his proposal by asking him what he could do to establish such a school, McAlpine declared that he would go into the field and raise the necessary funds. The force and eloquence of McAlpine's argument convinced the black convention to reject the white Baptists' advice. McAlpine then assumed an important leadership role among the black Baptists of Alabama.

At the 1874 session of the convention, held in Mobile, McAlpine was commissioned to canvass the state for six months in an effort to raise money for the proposed school. Boothe's account of the 1875 convention revealed that "every eye was on McAlpine as the leader." He had raised two hundred dollars above expenses, and that initial success aroused great interest all over the state. Attendance at the 1876 convention was larger than ever and approximately four hundred dollars had been added to the treasury before adjournment. The convention then employed McAlpine to work for a full year on behalf of the school, and five hundred dollars was raised above expenses during this year. When Selma University opened its doors in 1878, no one had done more than McAlpine to make this event possible.

In addition to his fund-raising efforts on behalf of Selma University, McAlpine pastored several churches. In 1871 he became pastor of the Mt. Canaan Baptist Church in Talladega. He served there until 1875 when he gave up the pastorate to spend his time promoting and raising funds for Selma University. In 1880, while serving as pastor of the Berean Baptist Church in Marion, Alabama, McAlpine helped establish the Marion Baptist Academy and served as its first principal. He also pastored the First Colored Baptist Church of Jacksonville, the Mt. Zion Baptist Church in Anniston, and the Tabernacle Baptist Church in Selma. His last pastorate was at the Dexter Avenue Baptist Church in Montgomery. After leaving Dexter Avenue, McAlpine returned to Selma University where he served as dean of theology until his death.

McAlpine was involved in the founding of three associations in Alabama. He guided the establishment of the Snow Creek Association while pastoring the Mt. Zion Church in Anniston. The Mt. Pilgrim Association, which included Birmingham and the surrounding area, was organized in 1874, principally by McAlpine, William Ware and J. R. Capers. McAlpine joined Henry Woods and Isham Robinson in establishing the Rushing Springs Association, which included churches in Talladega and surrounding counties.

McAlpine also edited the state Baptist newspaper, the *Baptist Pioneer*, an endeavor begun in 1878 with the express purpose of promoting Selma University. In this endeavor, he was assisted by C. O. Boothe and John Dozier. The *Baptist*

Pioneer was the first black denominational paper to be published in Alabama. According to Virginia's *Religious Herald,* McAlpine made it the best paper published by a black state convention in the nation.

Largely because of his stature in Alabama, McAlpine emerged as a national leader among black Baptists. On November 24, 1880, 151 delegates representing eleven states met in Montgomery to form the Foreign Mission Convention. A majority of the delegates were from Alabama, representing the state convention, various associations, and numerous churches. McAlpine held a prominent position from the beginning. On the first day he read a welcome statement from Alabama Baptists, its six hundred churches, thirty associations, and large state convention, pledging their support for the new convention's foreign mission goals. On the second day, McAlpine was elected president. Escorted to the president's chair by the Reverends C. H. Carey of Virginia and P. Mathis of Alabama, McAlpine appointed committees, received reports, and led the convention as it made important decisions. Richmond, Virginia, was selected as the location of the executive board of the convention. W. W. Cooley, who had served as a missionary in South Africa and had done much to organize the convention, was employed as missionary and corresponding secretary at a salary of a thousand dollars per year.

From the founding of the Foreign Mission Convention to its merger with two other conventions, McAlpine played a vital role. At the second annual session, at the Mt. Zion Baptist Church in Knoxville, Tennessee, McAlpine reminded the delegates of the convention's mission and expressed a desire that the spirit of Christ would direct their proceedings. McAlpine presided at this session and appointed a committee to elect a new set of officers. At the 1882 convention McAlpine presided until the new president was elected; he was also appointed to the Foreign Mission Board. In 1894, when the three existing national bodies of black Baptists in the United States—Foreign Mission Convention, National Baptist Education Convention, and American National Baptist Convention—met in Montgomery to consider unification, McAlpine was one of nine delegates representing Alabama. When unification was accomplished the next year in Atlanta, McAlpine served on the committee to write a new constitution.

In October 1905 McAlpine attended the twenty-fifth anniversary of the National Baptist Convention in Chicago. He was invited as a special guest because he had helped write the constitution, had served as the first president, had worked closely with the organization for many years, and in 1880 had been elected president of the Foreign Mission Convention, the oldest of the national bodies. Unfortunately, the weather turned extremely cold, and someone accidentally picked up McAlpine's luggage that contained his overcoat. Not having the proper clothes for the weather, he caught a cold that developed into pneumonia, and on November 3, 1905, a few days after he returned home, he died. He was fifty-seven years old.

With McAlpine's death, black Alabama Baptists lost their greatest leader. He, along with men like Boothe, Tyler, Brawley, and Dinkins, had founded and sustained Selma University, organized several Baptist academies, and developed major state and national organizations. These nineteenth-century leaders advocated uplifting the race through trained ministerial leadership, religious order, cooperation with other Baptist groups, self-help, and moral living. A new set of leaders would emerge in the first years of the twentieth century. Inspired by the theological convictions of a previous generation, they would deal with new problems and different circumstances. Disfranchisement, legal segregation, and urbanization would provide challenges, but education, coupled with a strong emphasis on improving economic conditions for blacks, would remain paramount.

3
The Progressive Era, 1900–1917

6
Protest, Growth, and Revivalism

The period from 1900 to 1917 is often referred to as the Progressive Era in the United States. It was a period of political, educational, and social reform. In Alabama Progressives sought to improve education, standardize business and medical practices, institute child labor laws, and promote prohibition. But these reforms in Alabama, as for the nation as a whole, were for whites only. During this time, blacks were subjected to further humiliation and oppression. In 1901 Alabama ratified a new constitution that disfranchised blacks and poor whites; legal segregation emerged along with disfranchisement. Black Baptists joined a chorus of protest, but efforts to overturn either legal segregation or disfranchisement proved unsuccessful.

Armed with their theological conviction of God's regard for the lowly, his power to defeat sin, and the ultimate success of their race, black Baptists went about the business of expanding their convention and attempting ways to uplift blacks in the state. The new 1901 constitution severely curtailed educational funding for African Americans. To meet this crisis, black Baptists responded by forming more academies and working to improve and expand Selma University. Black Baptists expressed themselves on a number of other issues as well. On the eve of the United States' entry into World War I, the convention held its jubilee session in which it celebrated fifty years of progress. Delegates and leaders took pride that their convention was the largest religious body of blacks in the state, but they were equally concerned about circumstances that inhibited uplift for the race.

Disfranchisement, Legal Segregation, and Protest

From Reconstruction to the turn of the twentieth century racial prejudice increased in the South. This rising tide of racism was exacerbated by the Populist movement, an attempt to establish an alliance among blacks and poor whites in order to gain political power. To counter such action southern states instituted specific measures designed to disfranchise blacks. Mississippi led the way in 1890, and Alabama followed suit, calling for a constitutional convention in 1901. The convention proposed that a poll tax, literacy tests, a residency clause, and property requirements be added to voting qualifications for the expressed purpose of denying the ballot to blacks. With Democrats advocating white supremacy and honest elections, state voters ratified the constitution and disfranchised almost all black voters. Before 1901, more than 100,000 blacks were registered to vote; following the constitution's ratification and the institution of the poll tax, all but 3,572 blacks were removed from the voting rolls.

Going hand in hand with disfranchisement was legal segregation. Following the Civil War, the segregation of blacks and whites was a matter of custom. However, urbanization brought blacks and whites into closer contact in housing, jobs, places of amusement, and public transportation. The established order seemed blurred until legal segregation emerged. At the national level, the Supreme Court ruling in *Plessy v. Ferguson* legalized the separate but equal principle. One particular focus was public transportation, and southern states such as Mississippi, Tennessee, and Florida passed laws that required segregation on streetcars. In Alabama, city ordinances and streetcar company regulations provided a substitute for state action. Legal segregation then passed to many other areas, producing a caste system in which blacks and whites lived separate lives. Blacks viewed these laws as humiliating, stigmatizing, and degrading.

Protest against legal segregation in Alabama came in the form of boycotts against streetcar regulations in Montgomery and Mobile. The Montgomery boycott lasted from 1901 to 1902 and resulted in the operating company's suspending enforcement of the segregation laws. In Mobile, the president of the Mobile Light and Railroad Company directed employees to allow passengers to sit where they desired. Black ministers led the boycotts in both cities. The *Mobile Register* reported that the Negroes who initiated boycotts were "backed by the exhortations of their religious leaders."[1] Since Baptists comprised the largest black religious group in these two cities, one may assume that black Baptist pastors were among the leaders. After a brief period, segregation laws were reinstated in both cities and there were no further protests.

The curtailment of continued boycotts in Montgomery and Mobile resulted from several factors including internecine conflict among leaders, the conservative nature of the protests, and financial pressure from white institutions. Chief among the reasons was the awareness of blacks that they could not ultimately win because of the awesome nature of the opposition. The boycotts occurred at a time when southern racism was reaching its peak and was gaining a respectable hearing in the North, including the U.S. Supreme Court. With so much power stacked against them, blacks took solace in having made their point, and reluctantly returned to the segregated streetcars.

After the streetcar boycotts ended, almost no proclamations or resolutions against legal segregation appear in black Baptist associations and conventions. Apparently, Baptist leaders considered other issues more important. De facto segregation in schools, churches, and other public places had developed after the end of the Civil War. Protest against streetcar segregation occurred when the inconvenience of such segregation and the conduct of conductors were considered excessive, prompting blacks to publicly express their disapproval.

Black religious leaders then turned their attention to disfranchisement. Blacks presented four petitions to protest the actions of the 1901 Constitutional Convention, and black ministers were involved in two of them. These petitions were generally mild in nature and conceived in a spirit of reconciliation and humility. The most important concern for many of the petitioners was the preservation of educational opportunities for blacks. Petitioners lobbied against a basis for school appropriations that assigned taxes paid by each race to the schools of that race. Such a policy would have virtually eliminated black schools.

Albert F. Owens, pastor of the St. Anthony Baptist Church in Mobile and former editor of the *Baptist Leader,* was the first to petition the 1901 convention. Owens, who was highly respected among Baptists in Alabama, would later become dean of theology at Selma University. In his petition, Owens appealed to the need for blacks and whites to work together. They were best friends to each other, he insisted, and needed to remain so. He attempted to show that whites should not do anything to create bad relations especially by reducing educational opportunities for blacks in the state.

Owens asked the convention to recognize nine facts: "(1) Negroes and whites were together and here to stay; (2) interests of the two races were inseparable; (3) the intelligent, law-abiding Negro was a patriotic and loyal citizen; (4) the law-abiding Negro had used whatever advantages he had to elevate himself as a citizen; (5) the intelligent and law-abiding Negro sought to aid the sympathetic and fair-minded white neighbor; (6) the feeling of mutual dependence of better classes of the two races was growing stronger; (7) the better class of Negroes strongly wished to join the better class of whites where their interests were similar; (8) Negroes were grateful for all the tax money that had gone to Negro education; (9) the better classes of the two races were closer than ever before."[2]

Another petition came from Booker T. Washington and a committee of fourteen associates. Two of these people were outstanding black Baptist ministers and a third was a prominent black Baptist layman: Charles O. Boothe, William Pettiford, and R. B. Hudson. Boothe was dean of theology at Selma University. Pettiford, former pastor of the Sixteenth Street Baptist Church, was president of the Alabama Penny Bank. Hudson was principal of Clark School in Selma and secretary of the Alabama Colored Baptist State Convention. This petition was presented in the same spirit of humility, and each person represented himself as a good citizen and taxpayer. The petitioners maintained that this was the only way they could address the convention since no blacks represented them. They pleaded for justice, reminding the delegates that blacks had served whites well in Alabama. Since the Negro "is taxed, works the roads, is punished for crime, is called upon to defend his country," the petitioners asked for "some humble share" for the race in choosing those who would rule over them. They noted that the Negro had been disfranchised in Alabama twenty years earlier and they saw no need for additional measures that served no useful purpose other than humiliating the race. Like Owens, they urged the convention to retain educational opportunities for blacks. "An ignorant Negro," they continued, "would only retard the progress of the white race."[3] The petitioners also suggested that disfranchisement would probably result in a black exodus from the state, a circumstance that would hurt whites and the general economy.

A more forceful argument against disfranchisement came from James H. Eason, editor of the *Baptist Leader* and the *Union Leader*. The *Baptist Leader* was the official paper of the Alabama Colored Baptist State Convention, and Eason and other religious leaders published the *Union Leader* independently. In 1900 Eason responded to a call for Negro disfranchisement by the white *Anniston Hot-Blast* by challenging the editor's Christianity. Eason asserted that the editor must not understand Christianity if he accepted black money while calling for the disfranchisement of blacks.

In the *Union Leader,* Eason responded to a call for black disfranchisement in the *Alabama Baptist,* the official publication of the white Alabama Baptist State Convention. Eason expressed shock that a Baptist paper would express such a racist attitude. Such action, Eason insisted, was out of harmony with the spirit of Christianity. Neither the Bible nor the spirit of the gospel endorsed a government under the control of one race at the exclusion of another race. According to Eason, as long as religious journals indulged in drawing color and racial lines, their existence made the Gospel a failure. He concluded that "blacks would not object to white control if it were fair; but when considering the white Alabama government of 1901, both God and the Negro object."[4]

Eason also argued against disfranchisement in an article taken from a speech he made in January 1900. He cited the right to vote as a key factor in promoting black progress since the Civil War. The vote gave blacks a spirit of manhood, a sense of honor, some noble ideas, and lofty sentiments. Moreover, political involvement encouraged blacks to improve themselves socially, morally, and religiously. The franchise also brought them in touch with great people, statesmen, and diplomats, and taught them about government. Like Owens, Eason believed that blacks had been manipulated politically during Reconstruction, but he argued that the good aspects of black suffrage outweighed the bad. He asserted that disfranchisement was unfair and that additional restrictions would work to the detriment of the black race.[5]

The Alabama Colored Baptist State Convention did not issue a formal protest against disfranchisement in 1901. In most convention and association meetings, leaders took the theological view that God would somehow bring good out of this evil that whites had imposed upon them. In his 1901 annual address, President J. Q. A. Wilhite of the Alabama convention spoke briefly on the subject. He maintained that blacks had been loyal in protecting the nation during wartime. Therefore, disfranchisement was wrong. Wilhite urged blacks to remain faithful to God who would yet see that justice prevailed. Wilhite also expressed the same themes the following year. He urged blacks "not to become discouraged but to prepare for the future and to trust God who would bring justice in the end."[6] Moderator A. M. Moore of the Morning Star Association in his annual address in 1906 urged delegates to remain faithful to God and to believe that Jesus would eventually reign supreme. He admitted that it was difficult to wait on the Lord when rights had been taken away, but he assured his audience that "God would settle all inequities and differences that existed in the country."[7]

Writing in the *Union Leader*, Eason took exception to the stance taken by both Wilhite and Moore. He insisted that God helped those who helped themselves, and he urged blacks to raise five to ten thousand dollars to bring a suit against the state of Alabama. He praised the people of Montgomery who were attempting to take legal action that would challenge disfranchisement in the

Supreme Court. However, Baptists made no public effort to follow Eason's advice, and some delegates criticized him for taking too radical a stance.

Blacks in Alabama received no support from white Baptists or other white religious groups in their attempt to overthrow disfranchisement. White Baptists in general and the white Alabama Baptist State Convention in particular supported disfranchisement. While calling on whites to treat blacks kindly, the *Alabama Baptist* nevertheless advocated disfranchisement and segregation of blacks in the state. The paper's editor praised the new constitution for improving funding for public schools, for restricting railroad abuses, and for other reforms. But the most important feature of the document for him, which he insisted should "cause every white man to vote for ratification," was the fact that "it secured once and for all white supremacy." His views were typical of many if not most white Baptists. Writing in 1900 the editor maintained that nothing could raise blacks to the level of whites; therefore, whites were compelled to maintain supremacy over blacks. Blacks were to remain in their separate segregated spheres because God had ordained them to be "a hewer of wood and a drawer of water. Above all, blacks should be removed from Alabama's political process."[8] The ratification of the 1901 Constitution offered white Baptists a solution to the "Negro problem."

Convention Leadership and Expansion

Although failing to prevent disfranchisement, black Baptists continued their convention activities. During this period J. Q. A. Wilhite and James H. Eason served rather lengthy terms as president of the Alabama Colored Baptist State Convention. Although Eason tended to be more militant on race issues and generally more outspoken, both men held similar concerns for the growth and expansion of the convention. By 1917, when the convention met in its jubilee session, it had grown to 280,000 members, 102 associations, and 90 Sunday school conventions. It was the largest organized body of blacks in Alabama. Growth took place not only because of urbanization but also because of the initiatives and policies of Eason and Wilhite.

Born on August 13, 1854, in Louisville, Kentucky, Wilhite was baptized in 1866 and ordained into the gospel ministry in 1878. He attended Roger Williams University in Nashville, Tennessee, and upon graduation he became pastor of the Second Baptist Church of Eufaula. Eminently successful in that role, he became financial agent and treasurer of Selma University. He resigned that position to become pastor of the First Baptist Church of Uniontown; during his tenure the church built a brick edifice. Because of his success in Uniontown, Wilhite became pastor of the Sixth Avenue Baptist Church in Birmingham in 1895, one of the largest congregations in the state. He was elected president of the convention in 1896 and served in that capacity for a decade.

In his 1901 presidential address, Wilhite urged delegates not to be discouraged by disfranchisement but to continue to develop the convention. "Persecution," he insisted, "would not destroy the Negro race, but bring us to greater prosperity and a brighter future."[9] He suggested that the convention's work should be so well organized that Baptists could reach every county in the state. This expansion resulted in several new associations joining the convention during Wilhite's ten-year tenure. Among these were the East Bound Lebanon Association of Pickens County, the Mt. Zion Association of Coosa County, and the Selma Association of Dallas County.

Much of the convention's numerical growth during this period came from the work of the state mission board. In 1904 Wilhite began to revitalize the mission work. He authorized the board to hold quarterly meetings at different places in the state and to take collections for missions at those meetings. In that same year he established a State Missions Day to make Alabama Baptists more aware of their missionary responsibilities. Wilhite's most progressive effort resulted in the reorganization of the board in 1906. He assigned four missionaries responsibility for respective sections of the state: S. L. Martin, C. M. Wells, L. P. Foster, and L. S. Steinbeck. Although poorly paid, these missionaries held institutes, preached revivals, and organized churches and associations. At the 1906 convention Steinbeck reported that he had organized eight associations, one Sunday school convention, and one women's missionary district. The other missionaries submitted similar reports.

Wilhite also evinced a deep concern for foreign missions during his years as president. His emphasis on foreign missions coincided with the new thrust of the National Baptist Convention. Led by Lewis G. Jordan, newly appointed secretary of the Foreign Mission Board, mission stations multiplied; as a result more African students came to the United States for study at black denominational colleges. For example, in 1906 Selma University enrolled three African students: Daniel Malekuba from Central Africa, Robert Sisula from West Africa, and Cibaba Thompson from South Africa. Selma's experience paralleled a trend evident at many black denominational schools during this period.

Wilhite's successor, James H. Eason, was born on October 24, 1866, in Sumterville, Alabama. His parents, who owned their farm, were faithful Christian workers, his father serving as a deacon in the Sumterville Baptist Church. Eason finished the normal course at Selma University graduating in 1885 as the valedictorian of his class. Five years later, he graduated from Richmond Theological Seminary, again at the head of his class, with a bachelor of divinity degree. Many of his instructors considered him one of the ablest young men the seminary had produced. After graduating from Richmond Seminary, Eason returned to the state to begin his teaching career. He became principal of Garfield Academy in Auburn. In 1890 he became an instructor at Selma University where he taught until 1897.

Eason became pastor of the Union Baptist Church in Marion in 1891. Later, he pastored the Galilee Baptist Church in Anniston, increasing the membership from eighty-three to seven hundred and building a new facility for twenty-five thousand dollars. While pastoring in Anniston, he was editor of the *Baptist Leader* and the *Anniston Leader,* a community paper. As editor, he wrote about lynch laws, the Negro problem, and educational issues, gaining the attention of Booker T. Washington and other race leaders. In 1899 he wrote the book *Sanctification vs. Fanaticism,* the first book released by the publishing board of the National Baptist Convention. His work as editor, scholar, and pastor brought him notoriety among the Baptists of Alabama who elected him convention president in 1906.

In his first presidential address, Eason stated as one of his main goals the expansion of the convention and its work. He urged that the work should expand until it had reached every person in the state. "We are," Eason argued, "an agency in the warfare against Satan, there are thousand of souls that must be taken from the devil for Christ, many waste places have yet to be built up, moral reforms, religious developments are still the imperative demand of the world." Eason also maintained that as Baptists "we must expand—expand and live bigger lives—love more, do more, know more, give more, raise more money and spend more, employ more men and pay them better."[10]

During his eleven-year presidency, Eason continued the expansion and growth begun by Wilhite. The convention revised the constitution, adding an evangelistic board whose main task was to enhance the evangelistic work of the convention by providing people to conduct revivals and protracted meetings. Missionary C. M. Wells reported in 1907 that revivals were very well attended and that they created much excitement.

Eason's most important constitutional change established four district conventions of relatively equal territory. These "wings," as they were called, were designed to attract unaffiliated rural churches to the convention. Eason made it clear that these district conventions were not autonomous organizations but would operate under the direction of the state convention. The new constitution stipulated that "the district conventions were subject to the Alabama Colored Baptist State Convention and shall not make any regulations or enact any rules that are not in harmony with the rules of the convention."[11] Officers were to be elected by each wing with ultimate approval granted by the convention.

The first district convention meetings took place in 1908. The Northwest Convention met at Moundville, and W. T. Bibb of Bessemer was elected president. The Southeast Convention met in Montgomery, with P. S. L. Hutchins serving as president. W. S. Stratman, pastor and principal of the Prairie Academy, hosted the Southwest Convention, at his church in Prairie, and J. A. Martin became president. The Northeast Convention, meeting in Gadsden, elected R. N. Hall as president. Each district reported several hundred dollars in contributions, and each registered more than twenty churches.

In spite of the measured success of the district conventions, many pastors resisted the idea. Some believed the wings duplicated state efforts while others criticized wings as creating small power bases. When David V. Jemison succeeded Eason as convention president, he urged pastors to give the wings a chance. The Southwest had done well, raising three hundred dollars at its last meeting, and Jemison was convinced that with toil and time, the work would become even greater.

A lack of money constituted the major problem in advancing the convention's work and growth. Blacks in Alabama were poor and often did not have sufficient resources to finance the work. In addition, the convention had no stewardship program to assist them in judiciously dispensing limited resources. Consequently, mission work always suffered. No funds were available for financing mission stations or assisting rural pastors. During the Wilhite and Eason presidencies, missionaries highlighted these problems in their reports. Missionary salaries often went unpaid or remained in arrears. In addition, the *Baptist Leader* operated with a deficit, and Selma University was forced to borrow money to survive. Eason constantly highlighted this problem in his presidential addresses, declaring in 1909 that the convention needed money if it were to pay four missionaries, seventeen teachers, and operate a paper. He also maintained that "reverence and respect could never come to an organization that did not pay its way."[12] Despite poor stewardship, the work of the convention did proceed and growth was a reality because of the faith and perseverance exhibited by key leaders.

Revivalism

Though Wilhite and Eason fostered systematic expansion efforts through the convention, the regular church revival remained the most successful way of church growth as it had been following slavery. Revivals, or "protracted meetings" as they were sometime called, ordinarily occurred in the fall, after crops were laid by and people had more time on their hands. Methodist revivals often followed the pattern of the traditional camp meetings, away from the church and typically in some nearby retreat. Baptist services were conducted at the local church. They were special services intended to convert both sinners and seekers. These revivals were also social events where people who lived far apart could come together daily. Nothing compared to them in rural Alabama communities as a time of socializing and spiritual renewal.

Revival services usually began on Sunday and continued for a week or two weeks. They might extend beyond two weeks depending on the attendance, the number of conversions, the emotional fervor, and "the presence of the spirit." Curtis Maggard, a former Baptist pastor who was one hundred years old at the time he was interviewed in 1998, testified that he remembered a revival that lasted for one month in 1912 at the First Baptist Church, Lowndesboro, in Lowndes County. He reported that crowds continued to swell, emotionalism was at a peak, and more than a hundred people were converted. The revival ended, Maggard asserted, when the pastor and deacons felt it had peaked.

Revivals tended to be highly spiritual events and often elicited more emotion than regular Sunday worship services. The evangelist was usually a pastor from an adjacent community who was known for his vigorous and emotional preaching. He customarily stayed in the community, and there would be eating on the grounds at the church daily. In some instances, prayer meetings would be held daily at the church in the afternoon to pray for sinners and seekers.

The typical revival service in the Progressive Era began with the deacons leading the congregation in a praise service that consisted of meter hymns and long prayers. The unsaved usually took the front seat, known as the "mourner's bench," at the beginning of the praise service. The mourner's bench was inherited from slave revivals and camp meetings where seekers were asked to sit on special benches or seats in the front so the preacher could preach directly to them. Familiar meter hymns were "When I Can Read My Title Clear" and "A Charge to Keep I Have." Often the prayers were directed toward those who were on the mourner's bench.

The entrance of the pastor with the evangelist signaled the close of the praise service. The choir, if present, rendered a brief song service consisting of spirituals, hymns, and plantation melodies. The pastor then proceeded to "search the house"—scanning the congregation to see who had not been converted. The pastor would then ask all the people who were saved to raise their hands. Anyone who did not respond was asked to take one of the front seats. Then, the pastor would proceed to explain to those on the mourner's bench the requirements for salvation. After a lined hymn, the evangelist came forth to preach. Favorite revival sermons included "The Eagle Stirs Her Nest," "Dry Bones," The Prodigal Son," and "Nicodemus." The evangelist preached with wild enthusiasm and there would often be active response and shouting.

After the sermon came the appeal for sinners to come forth and testify of their conversion. These testimonies were expected to be of elaborate and vivid experiences. Those testifying often told of having a vision of walking across hell on a cotton string and not having the fire burn them because of their newfound faith. Others told of being attacked by Satan and rescued by Christ. Still others testified of becoming ill because of their sorrow for previous sins and recuperating when the grace of God healed them. During these testimonies, the congregation, especially family members, erupted with joy.

If the testimony was convincing, the person was accepted as a candidate for baptism. If not, he was told to continue in prayer. In some cases, candidates were assigned a deacon or older woman to pray and talk with them. Those who refused to come forth and accept Christ were prayed for in the service and also assigned a person to counsel and pray for them. Next came the offering and dismissal until the following night. People often left the meeting singing and praising God.

Meeting the New Education Crisis

Along with expansion and growth, education continued to be a major concern of convention leaders. After emancipation, black Baptists had placed a high priority on education, believing that formal instruction was essential to uplifting blacks in the state. Associations had formed academies and the state convention had founded Selma University, the pride of black Alabama Baptists. Increasingly, however, public education for blacks deteriorated. The Republican government during Reconstruction had started the state's first public school system in 1868. Its state constitution decreed that education funds would be applied according to the number of students for both races. A reversal of policy came in 1875 when the conservative Democratic constitution formally segregated state schools. Faced with a declining per capita appropriation for education and unable in most instances to pass local taxes, white legislators in 1888 decided to divert money allocated for black education to white schools. In 1891 the legislature passed a law apportioning school funds to various school boards. This meant that funding for black education was left to local boards, a condition that generated further discrimination. Discrimination against black education reached a climax with the 1901 constitution. The 1891 provision allowing local school boards to allocate education money was affirmed. In addition, the constitution stated that "no child of either race shall be permitted to attend the school of the other race."[13] The superintendent of education's 1908 report revealed that while blacks made up 44 percent of the state school population they received only 12 percent of school fund allocations. Black teachers were paid considerably less than white teachers; black school buildings were often in deplorable condition; and the school term lasted only a few months. In 1909 the value of school buildings per enrolled student in the Black Belt was about twenty-six dollars for whites and one dollar for blacks. White sessions averaged 151 days; those for blacks, 96.

Justification for the neglect of black schools was based on the assumption that blacks were inferior and paid less taxes. In 1900 the editor of the *Montgomery Advertiser* insisted that "there is something lacking in their brains and in their body." Two years later, the president of the white Girls' Industrial School at Montevallo, F. M. Peterson, referred to blacks as an "ignorant, vicious class we recognize as dangerous." On the issue of taxes, Governor William Samford stated that southern governments were generous with blacks when one considers that "the negro pays a small part of the taxes of Alabama."[14]

Such a lowering of the education bar for blacks created an education crisis for the black community. While black education had always been poorer than that for whites, the shameful proportions it reached after 1901 alarmed blacks. James Eason, in several of his presidential addresses to the convention, expressed his deep concern about such matters. Describing the situation in Alabama, he pointed to the fact that black teachers were quitting because of low pay and poor schoolhouses—in some cases, no schoolhouse at all. Annual sessions were limited to a few months during the year, and black schools had little or no equipment. Such conditions were worse, he said, in county districts where 80 to 85 percent of the inhabitants were black.

Regarding education as absolutely essential for their uplift as a race, blacks took on the challenge. Black Baptist leaders suggested several ways to ameliorate the crisis. One was to inform whites of the error of their ways. In his 1907 presidential address, Eason suggested that Alabama whites possessed some sense of justice and that if they knew the truth, they would respond to the gross injustices suffered by the black population. He also argued that blacks must demonstrate that they did pay taxes. To prove this point, Eason focused on the rents that blacks paid as tenant farmers and sharecroppers. In addition to appealing to well-meaning whites, Eason suggested that black Baptists make voluntary contributions to keep schools open for longer periods. Neither of these suggestions was successful.

Once again, Black Baptists turned to providing education through their local association academies. Black Baptists had formed several academies by 1900; many others were established to deal with the new crisis. Among these were Mt. Pilgrim Academy in Birmingham, Mt. Calvary Academy of Coaling, Lebanon Union Academy of Sylacauga, Mobile Academy, Livingston Academy, Prairie Academy, Bibb County School, Oakridge Normal and Industrial Institute, Dothan Industrial Academy, and Collinsville High School. Most associations supported local institutions, and some supported several academies. For example, in 1903 the Wills Creek Association of Etowah County gave monetary support to four schools: Selma University, Collinsville High School, Camden High School, and Anniston Normal and Industrial College. Other associations provided support to community schools that were not owned by Baptists. In the early twentieth century, the Morning Star Association gave money to support the privately owned Cottage Grove Academy. A contribution of thirty-four dollars allowed Cottage Grove Academy to award two tuition scholarships to people that the association designated.

The push for local academies often received support from convention leaders. In 1901 the convention endorsed academies because of the statewide education crisis. Eason served as dean of theology at Anniston Normal and Industrial College, and Wilhite chaired the trustee board of Birmingham Baptist Academy. Both long-term presidents encouraged the convention to support local academies, and its wings also made monetary contributions. For several years in the early twentieth century the convention took an offering for Anniston Industrial Academy and College. The Northwest Convention gave monetary support in 1912 to both the Lebanon Union Baptist Academy and the Mt. Calvary Academy.

Annual convention and association reports give some idea of the effectiveness of these academies. Some were small and had few students, while others had more substantial enrollments. In 1912 the trustees of the Lebanon Union Baptist Academy reported that the academy had graduated 26 students since its founding in 1903. At that time the academy had four teachers and 5 students had graduated in the last term. The school had raised $750 from all sources for its operation. The Mt. Pilgrim Association in Birmingham was one of the state's largest academies. The trustees reported that the school had 110 students and three teachers. The property was worth $20,000. On the whole, however, these academies struggled financially while serving local educational needs.

Though convention leaders endorsed academies, their support was always couched in terms that avoided interfering with the progress of Selma University. Wilhite in his 1904 presidential address stated that "academies were needed but that they must lay good academic foundations for students and be feeders to Selma University."[15] Two years later, he proposed that a common fund be established to finance the academies, but insisted that each school report to the convention. Eason also agreed with the idea of a common fund.

Controversy over the growing number of academies in Alabama became more heated in 1911 when Selma University was in substantial debt. Convention leaders recognized that the local-sponsored institutions often took precedence over Selma University. In that year the trustees asserted that the great proliferation of academies put Selma University in peril because many local associations gave only to their local school and nothing to Selma. President William M. Gilbert, who became president in 1911, urged leaders to restrict the number of academies to four or five established at convenient locations, with eight or nine associations supporting each school. He asserted that at the present growth rate of academies, Selma University would soon be starved out. William Pettiford, former convention president, initiated a resolution that called for a common fund and educational system from which all schools could operate.

Suggestions from Pettiford, Gilbert, and other leaders in the convention were not heeded, however. The convention simply could not exert control over local associations and schools. In addition, the need for education was so great on the local level that association leaders believed that academies were imperative. Overall, academies continued to proliferate and made a valuable contribution to blacks during a time of great crisis.

Meanwhile, Selma University remained the most challenging educational project. Concerted financial efforts were directed toward its operation and enhancement. During the Progressive Era, the institution reached a peak in terms of students and faculty. On the other hand, the university struggled to maintain itself because of increasing debt.

Four people served as university president during the Progressive Era. C. S. Dinkins became president in 1893. Born in 1856 in Canton, Mississippi, his early life was a struggle. He never knew his father, and his mother died when he was only thirteen. Determined to get an education, he graduated from Roger Williams University in 1877 as valedictorian of his class. In 1881 he graduated from Newton Theological Seminary, making him one of the best trained black ministers of his day. After graduation, he became chair of Greek at State University in Louisville, Kentucky. After serving for several years, he accepted the same position at Selma University. He left Selma University to become principal of the Marion Baptist Academy and later became state missionary under the Baptist Publication Society of New York. When the position of president of Selma University became available after the resignation of C. L. Purce, Dinkins accepted the post.

Under Dinkins, Selma University made steady progress, with enrollment increasing to approximately 400 students. He directed the completion of the South Wing of Susie Stone Hall, and succeeded in getting the American Baptist Home Mission Society to give an annual gift of $1,000. By the time of his untimely death in 1901, Dinkins had raised $1,800 of an estimated $13,000 to build the new chapel.

Charles Boothe became interim president after the death of Dinkins. His report to the American Baptist Home Mission Society stated that 295 students were enrolled, and the school was in great need of a new chapel. Because of the inadequacy of the chapel, he reported that students were being turned away.

In 1901 the trustees elected Robert L. Pollard as president. Pollard served two terms, and the institution reached a peak in terms of attendance and financial stability. The growth peaked in 1908 with 762 students and 62 graduates, the largest class in the school's history. Twenty teachers and five departments served the students and enrollment remained high. Despite a smallpox epidemic in 1909, the school continued to have a large enrollment through 1911.

During Pollard's first tenure the institution generally prospered financially and had an ambitious building program. Dinkins Chapel was completed, and plans were laid for Foster Hall, the female Industrial Arts Building. Electric lights were installed in all buildings, and all mortgages were retired by 1910. Pollard succeeded in getting increased contributions from the American Baptist Home Mission Society, the Southern Baptist Convention, and a $5,000 contribution from the General Education Board to help complete Foster Hall. Foster Hall and Dinkins Chapel were the two brick buildings on campus.

When Pollard resigned in 1911, the trustees elected William M. Gilbert as president. A graduate of Benedict College and Colgate University, Gilbert had pastored in Tennessee, South Carolina, and Florida. In addition, he served as president of Florida Baptist Academy and as general missionary and corresponding secretary of the Baptist State Convention of South Carolina. For one year he was the president of Florida Institute at Live Oaks.

When Gilbert became president, the school faced a new debt of $4,096. Apparently, friction and turmoil caused by Pollard's resignation resulted in reduced revenues. People simply refused to give as they had in the past because of their disappointment over Pollard's departure. Part of the debt represented additional expenses such as placing sewers and bathroom facilities on campus. Financial deficits caused by World War I also increased the debt at Selma University, which rose to $9,815.68 by 1914. Enrollment declined to 240 the following year, and to make ends meet and pay back salaries to teachers, the institution borrowed $6,000 from the Alabama Penny Bank. Gilbert resigned in 1916, and the trustees reelected R. T. Pollard to the presidency.

Other Pressing Concerns

In addition to disfranchisement, expansion, and education, black Baptists in Alabama had a host of other concerns during the Progressive Era. Among denominational issues none was more pressing than restoring the New Era Convention. In 1908 the Alabama Colored Baptist Convention commissioned a committee to discuss restoration with the New Era Convention. President James Eason insisted that the issues that caused the initial separation were dead and that nothing remained to keep the conventions apart. Members of the New Era Convention promised to respond, but did not. In his 1910 presidential address Eason declared that failure to even respond was an insult and he urged the convention to put this matter behind them. "The time has come," he insisted, "for us to be State Convention men or New Era men."[16] The convention followed Eason, and no further attempts were made to merge the two conventions.

Concern for aged and sick ministers was another major issue among black leaders in Alabama, as well as for the National Baptist Convention. In his first presidential address, Eason argued that the convention and black Baptists in general needed to change their policy of working pastors to death and then leaving them without support when they were broken down with old age. His attempt to provide some support for aged pastors was tied to the evangelism board. Members of this board were to collect funds for elderly ministers, but his plan proved ineffective. Although leaders continued to express concern for aged ministers and an interest in improving salaries for pastors, nothing was accomplished. There simply were not enough funds to address this need.

"One Sunday a month" churches or congregations were also a major concern. Most pastors in rural areas served more than one congregation. Consequently, they would come to the community on Saturday night, preach on Sunday, and then leave. Mission reports decried this pattern as highly ineffective, especially since Methodists and other black denominations had fewer itinerant pastors. The mission board suggested establishing a fund to pay rural pastors, because many rural churches simply could not expend additional resources toward full-time pastors. Furthermore, convention members were reluctant to divert funds from Selma University.

Black Baptists, the largest body of blacks in the state, were concerned with sociopolitical issues besides disfranchisement and segregation. During the Progressive Era anti-Negro sentiment was rampant, and blacks were frustrated by claims that they could not make progress. Apologists for white supremacy in the South, like Thomas Dixon Jr. and Philip Bruce, maintained that blacks were brutes, who lacked manners, had bad personal hygiene, and were doomed to a backward existence. Even reformers such as John Phillips, superintendent of Birmingham schools from 1883 to 1921, and Alabama governor William Jelks talked openly of black inferiority and the improbability of progress. Jelks believed that the proper place for blacks was laboring on the farm. Educating the black person, he stated, "had proven to be a curse of the material interests of the South because it had led them off the farm to a life of vagrancy and theft." Phillips informed a gathering of southern educators that blacks were "incapable of initiative and executive power."[17]

To counter this racist perspective black Baptists used speeches and issued resolutions to show that blacks had indeed made progress. The report of the Committee on the State of the Country in the 1912 convention indicated that illiteracy among Alabama blacks had steadily declined since the days of slavery. The report also pointed to the increase in the number of black-owned farms, businesses, and homes as evidence of black progress. Reports from missionaries of the Colored Convention who traveled throughout the state confirmed an increase in black-owned businesses and homes, as well as improved church buildings. In his 1906 presidential address, Wilhite argued that, in spite of the racism of politicians like Governor Vardaman of Mississippi, "blacks, the sons of Ham, had made tremendous progress." He pointed to "new church construction in the amount of $16,099, building schools in the amount of $2,686,233, and owning personal property amounting to approximately five million dollars." In Eason's 1910 report on black progress in the state and nation, he noted that there were 150 black lawyers and that blacks operated 48 banks, owned 372,414 homes, and operated 42.1 percent of the farms in Alabama. Because of this progress, Eason bragged, "the Negro is today the wonder of the world. The degradation in which he was found years ago, has forced the conclusion that if he is not a man, he is something beyond man."[18]

Violence against blacks, such as lynchings and other forms of brutality, had been a persistent problem since emancipation, and black Baptists frequently spoke out against such violence. In 1904 many blacks were injured or killed in a race riot in Atlanta. This event, along with renewed violence in Alabama, evoked a strong response from blacks, including President Wilhite of the Colored Baptist State Convention. Wilhite was most concerned about the lack of action by the police, who looked the other way, sometimes even when blacks were taken from jails and lynched. Nonetheless, he cautioned blacks "not to hate but love." "Blacks," he suggested, "must find some way to reach their white brethren through cool and wise consideration." Wilhite ended his remarks on the renewal of violence against blacks by reminding his hearers of the promise that "princes would come from Egypt and Ethiopia shall rise and stretch forth her hands unto God. There was work to do and the sons of Ham must continue the progress they were achieving."[19] Wilhite's suggestion was similar to those of earlier convention resolutions that urged blacks to love the country, obey laws, and wait for God's salvation.

Initially, the Colored Baptist State Convention had refrained from taking an activist stand in its pronouncements against disfranchisement. However, later in the Progressive Era and beginning with the Eason presidency, statements and resolutions against disfranchisement became more forceful and encouraged direct action. In 1907 the convention went on record as deploring disfranchisement, "an action that was tantamount to a deprivation and denial of citizenship, self-protection, and civic rights." The State of the Country resolution of 1912 deplored the fact that with fifty-six thousand blacks in Montgomery fewer than one hundred could vote. The resolution justifiably called it "taxation without representation" and urged black pastors and leaders to discuss ways through which blacks could regain their rights. Most of all, the resolution urged the formation of suffrage leagues to work for the renewal of voting rights.[20]

Baptist leaders also believed that the criminal element represented a major problem for the race. Speeches at conventions and associations reflected the widespread perception that whites judged blacks as criminals rather than as law-abiding citizens. In 1906 William Pettiford sponsored a resolution that maintained that a small criminal element was giving the race a bad reputation. Pettiford insisted that while black Baptists must deplore all criminality, pastors should seek their reformation by engaging in every opportunity to preach to them. President James Eason believed that Baptists must try to help the criminals. Otherwise, he maintained, their numbers would increase and pull all blacks down.

Some black Baptists, including Pettiford, fortunately, believed that more was needed to rehabilitate criminals than merely preaching or passing resolutions. Most black Baptists, it appears, were not opposed to the social gospel or carrying the gospel beyond the walls of the church. The women's convention continued its prison ministry begun in the 1890s, and some pastors initiated prison ministries as well. Reverend and Mrs. Robert T. Pollard sponsored a rescue mission in Selma, and William Pettiford started a bank in Birmingham to teach the working class and the masses how to properly manage their money. Pettiford and other ministers also started an old folks and orphans home in Birmingham, gaining convention endorsement in 1906.

Always strong advocates of temperance, black Baptists went on record as supporting Prohibition. Black leaders believed that the consumption of alcohol was the major factor in producing black criminals and in weakening the family. The 1907 convention noted that the ban on alcohol in some Alabama counties was a good thing, and Eason maintained that Prohibition was not a political issue but a moral one as well. He urged pastors and church leaders to "work for it, vote for it, and support it."[21]

For black Baptists, wrestling with the social, economic, educational, and political issues that threatened to undermine the achievements blacks had attained since the end of slavery was paramount. Their white Baptist counterparts, meanwhile, were firmly ensconced in the myth of white supremacy. There was no common ground for blacks and whites in efforts to uplift the black population in Alabama—or indeed the rest of the country. Nor did theological questions of the day offer a fruitful field for joint endeavors. White Baptists were embroiled in a struggle over how the Bible should be interpreted. In its simplest terms, whether the literal interpretation of the Bible should stand or whether the Bible should be interpreted in the light of modern biblical criticism. For black Baptists the Bible was the word of God and the standard for life and thought. As Mark Noll has correctly shown, black Baptists perceived truth as narrative theology and in broad and general themes. Exegetical arguments of the modernist-fundamental controversy had no place in their biblical understanding. In his 1912 presidential address, James Eason argued for progressive revelation, maintaining that truth given at one point in the Bible could be greater than at other times. One searches in vain to find statements like this by other black Baptist leaders. The Bible for black Baptists was the Word of God, pure and simple.

One theological issue that did affect Alabama black Baptists was the growth of the Pentecostal movement and its view of perfection. Pentecostals were converting some Baptists to their position. Eason took the lead in refuting this doctrine in his book *Sanctification or Fanaticism*. According to Eason, the Bible teaches that sanctification is a lifelong process. The Christian never reaches a finished state of perfection on earth. Perfection is achieved beyond this life. Therefore, every Christian should strive to be moral but not perfect.

During the Progressive Era Alabama blacks suffered disfranchisement, legal segregation, and many forms of humiliation and violence. Black Baptists, however, did not despair. With renewed faith in the providence and promises of God, they continued to move ahead by expanding their convention, erecting academies, building a greater Selma University, and speaking out on social, economic, educational, and political issues. As new cities emerged and grew, blacks migrated to these urban areas where they encountered new problems. Black Baptist churches attempted to deal with these difficulties and meet the particular needs of urban blacks. As a result, economic self-help became important as a means of uplifting the race, and black Baptist leaders would create economic institutions to augment the religious and educational organizations constructed in earlier times.

7
Urbanization and
Economic Self-Help

Alabama's urban centers grew during the Progressive Era, and other smaller areas developed into cities. By 1910 Birmingham had become the largest city in Alabama, far outstripping Montgomery and Mobile. As blacks migrated from rural to urban areas between 1900 and 1917, their churches grew rapidly. Baptist churches, along with those of other denominations, met many needs for blacks and developed a distinctive church life.

During this period, black Baptist leaders also increasingly stressed the need for establishing economic institutions to promote racial uplift. In urban areas, black pastors supported local businesses and promoted the growth of a black business community. Some pastors founded economic institutions such as banks, insurance companies, and newspapers. Among Alabama Baptists who stressed the need for black economic institutions and self-help, William R. Pettiford of Birmingham, who was strongly influenced by Booker T. Washington, wielded the most influence.

Black Baptists and Urbanization

By the early twentieth century, the black population in Alabama's three largest cities equaled or surpassed white totals. In 1900, Montgomery counted 17,229 blacks out of a total population of 30,346, and black growth continued for the next ten years. In 1910, Mobile had a population of 51,521 of which 22,763 were black, and blacks made up 40.2 percent of the population in Jefferson County, including Birmingham and Bessemer.

As blacks moved into these cities they formed churches. Unlike rural Black Belt churches that typically met one or two Sundays per month, many of these congregations worshipped every Sunday. Large urban churches tended to have full-time pastors who were better trained than their rural counterparts. Leadership in the Alabama Colored Baptist State Convention gravitated to urban pastors during this period. Both long-term presidents during the Progressive Era came from cities: J. Q. A. Wilhite was a pastor in Birmingham, and James Eason pastored in Anniston and later in Birmingham.

The Day Street Baptist Church in Montgomery exemplifies this emerging trend of large city churches and their attempts to minister to the particular needs of blacks in a growing urban area. Montgomery's two oldest churches were the First Baptist Church and Dexter Avenue Baptist Church, but as black numbers increased, many new churches came into existence. The Day Street Baptist Church began in 1884 when two laymen, T. H. Garner and Edward Patterson agreed that Montgomery needed another church. They secured the services of Reverend J. C. Casby, and constructed a frame building. As blacks continued to flock to Montgomery, the Day Street Church grew rapidly. William Madison, a graduate of Selma University, became pastor in 1908 and led the congregation in erecting a new edifice valued at thirty-six thousand dollars. In addition to meeting for worship each Sunday, the Day Street Church developed a Sunday school, a Baptist Young People's Union, a Sunbeam Band, a Dorcas Sewing Circle for girls, and a Cadet Department for boys. The church also provided the cooks, washerwomen, and porters clubs for women and formed an employment bureau that assisted people in finding jobs. Like other urban churches in Alabama, Day Street became an institutional church attempting to deal with both the spiritual and temporal needs of its members and Montgomery's growing number of migrants.

Birmingham provides an even better example of black urban church life in a growing city, and how black Baptists sought to deal with the needs of their constituency. Founded in 1871 when two railroads merged in the southwestern section of the city, Birmingham soon became the industrial city of the New South. Blacks left the rural Black Belt when they received word that wage-paying jobs could be obtained in the city. By 1900, 16,575 blacks had settled in Birmingham out of a total population of 38,415.

Birmingham blacks had established several churches by 1900, but significant growth would take place in the following two decades. The expansion of African American churches between 1900 and 1920 was reflected in the *Birmingham City Directory*. The 1900 directory listed only 28 African American churches. By 1920 this figure had grown to 115 within the city limits. Even taking into account the expansion of the city limits in 1910, which brought in areas like Ensley and Pratt City where churches already existed, African American churches clearly increased rapidly during this period.

Baptist churches accounted for most of the church growth. Of the 115 churches listed, 67 were Baptist. Baptists continued to be the most popular denomination because of the freedom to form churches, emotionalism in worship, and the simple fact that most migrants were Baptist. Frequent congregational splits, usually caused by disagreement over pastoral leadership, also contributed to Baptist church growth. For example, the Broad Street Baptist Church (which began in 1878 as the Spring Street Baptist Church) formed two churches from its membership. In 1902 a dispute over the exclusion of a member charged with misconduct led a group to leave Broad Street and form the Trinity Baptist Church in Smithfield. Twelve years later, a dispute over pastoral leadership led to the formation of the South Elyton Baptist Church. Both Trinity and South Elyton quickly became large and flourishing congregations. Other congregations developed from splits out of the Twenty-third Street Baptist Church between its founding in 1899 and World War I. In 1913 a group left with the pastor when deacons and some members challenged his pastoral authority. Reverend John Hawkins and his supporters formed the Zion Star Baptist Church. Some years later, a dispute arose in the Twenty-third Street Church over the pastorate of the Reverend C. S. Riddick. Riddick and his followers formed the Metropolitan Baptist Church.

Whether small or large, black Baptist churches developed a distinctive institutional life, and Sunday was an all-day affair for members. The urban religious experience mirrored Sundays in the Black Belt where blacks had spent all day at church, even eating on the grounds between worship services. For most churches that same pattern continued in Birmingham. In the typical church, Sunday's activities started at nine thirty with Sunday school followed by the regular worship service that usually began at eleven o'clock. The Baptist Young People's Union met around three in the afternoon, and the evening service usually began at seven. On some Sundays there would be a special 5:00 p.m. service. Sundays at church provided not only a time of worship but also a time for fellowship and socializing. Typically, members worked six days a week and regarded Sunday at church as a welcome break from a weeklong routine of labor.

Generally, the most important Sunday service was at eleven o'clock. The service began with a praise service led by the deacons that usually lasted for at least thirty minutes. The praise service was designed to prepare the worshippers for the main service. Near the end of the praise service the pastor entered with his assistants, and his entrance signaled that the devotion was about to close.

At the end of the praise service the choir took the stand and provided a song service. By 1900 most church choirs sang spirituals, jubilee songs, and hymns. Following the choir's singing, announcements were made and an offering was taken. The pastor commented on the announcements and often gave words of instruction to the congregation. Deacons usually took the offering, and they would discuss on occasion the needs of the church. Following another selection or two by the choir, the pastor delivered a sermon, which usually lasted from thirty minutes to an hour. Sermons were delivered with gusto, and pastors concluded by appealing to sinners to express their faith in Christ and become members of the church. The service ended with a benediction.

The pastor's preaching was the highlight of the worship and formed the center of the church life that blacks developed in Birmingham. Although there were exceptions, preaching was usually done with considerable emotion. The notion of being filled with the spirit continued to be a vital part of the worship experience. Whether they were served by a part-time pastor who worked in industry during the week and preached on Sunday or by a full-time minister in the larger churches, black Baptists with few exceptions expected preaching to be touched by the spirit, and they expected to be caught up in the spirit.

The preacher began his sermon in a conversational tone but steadily moved to a higher pitch, working the congregation into an emotional frenzy. One observer who attended a funeral at the Shiloh Baptist Church noted this pattern in the pastor's sermon. The Reverend T. W. Walker began in a simple and dignified way by reviewing the best traits of the deceased as demonstrated by her relationships with family and friends. He then told of her work in the benevolent society as well as her involvement with many charities. As he continued, Walker spoke more slowly, "his tones became more resonant, and he raised his voice to a higher pitch. He described graphically the soul's departure from the body and its journey to be with God in eternal rest. As mourners began to weep, Walker continued his eulogy, his voice growing even higher as he recounted the deceased's last words and reminded the audience that a day of reckoning would come. By this time, the entire audience was now expressing grief with tears, and moans, and distressing cries."[1]

In most black Baptist churches, the congregation aided the pastor with loud and encouraging responses. Such responses stemmed from camp meeting revivals to which blacks were exposed during slavery and were also a part of the call and response that was characteristic of the preslavery African religious experience. The audience responded with "amen," "all right," "that's right," "come on," "help him Lord," and "preach the word." In turn, the preacher often urged the congregation to continue their responses with interjections such as "Have I got a witness?" and "You ought to say amen."[2]

Whereas in Birmingham many small congregations met in alleys and storefronts, a few large churches, like Day Street in Montgomery, could be classified as institutional churches. The Shiloh Baptist Church constituted the prime institutional example in Birmingham. The Reverend Thomas W. Walker established the church in 1891, and it grew around his charismatic preaching and leadership. Like most of Birmingham's African American churches, it consisted of working-class people: miners, industrial workers, or household servants who worked for wealthy whites. African Americans flocked to hear Walker's unique preaching style. By 1895 Shiloh had become the largest church in the city, "the marvel church of Birmingham."[3]

Sunday always brought a full day of activities and worship at Shiloh. Adapting the Sunday schedule to the needs of its members, Shiloh held its first worship service at six in the morning. This provided members who had to work on Sunday an opportunity to attend worship. The early morning service was followed by Sunday school at nine thirty. Instead of an eleven o'clock worship service, Shiloh held its main worship service at three, a time most convenient for female members who worked as maids or cooks on Sunday mornings but were free to come to Shiloh by midafternoon. The evening service, attended by as many as fifteen hundred people, began at seven thirty and could last until midnight, depending on the enthusiasm of the preacher and the congregation.

In addition to Sunday services, the church had activities throughout the week. The choir practiced, the ushers deliberated, and the missionary society convened. The Baptist Young People's Union met Monday evenings, and members gathered for prayer meeting on Thursday night. On any given afternoon the minister might conduct a baptism, a marriage, or a funeral. Shiloh also had benevolent organizations, including the Christian Relief Society and the Afro-Benefit Association, that met during the week. Besides its religious and benevolent activities, the congregation sponsored social activities such as dinners, banquets, and teas. On these occasions, members wore their best clothes and enjoyed much laughter and fun.

The black church provided many services for those who migrated to Birmingham during the Progressive Era. Perhaps the most immediate need involved socialization and adjustment to urban life. Generally, blacks who moved to Birmingham and other Alabama cities were unfamiliar with urban life.

Their rural upbringing had accustomed them to small communities and intimate personal relationships. In contrast, city life generated anonymity and an impersonal environment. Churches provided a sense of community in this strange new environment that gave former rural dwellers a sense of belonging. Although located in big cities, the urban churches provided a style of worship akin to that of rural areas. Congregations sang well-known hymns; members offered prayers for familiar needs; and ministers preached with characteristic emotion. Through the language and emotionalism of worship, blacks maintained their cultural roots and found a sense of well-being in a new and often hostile environment. In essence, first-generation migrants created the churches to fulfill their own spiritual, social, and psychological needs.

For many African Americans the church became a social center. Congregations provided wholesome activities in communities that neglected African American social and recreational needs. Activities were familiar ones: picnics, teas, fund-raising dinners, banquets, and socials. Churches also functioned as music schools, concert halls, recreation clubs, and sites for political debates and town meetings. For the youth, the church provided Sunday school, organizational meetings, and picnics. Special programs at Christmas and Easter furnished young people ample opportunity to express their talents. And the church was where young and old heard the latest news, visited with friends, and sometimes courted and even met their future mates.

A most important service rendered by the black Baptist church was building self-esteem. Viewed by whites as inferior and hired for only the dirtiest and most unskilled jobs of the iron and steel industry or menial jobs as servants, blacks found little in the wider society of Birmingham that gave them a sense of worth. The church provided one place where they could feel good about themselves. When whites attempted to strip them of their humanity, blacks turned to the church that offered dignity. Called "boy" or "uncle" on the job, black men were referred to as "brother" and "mister" at church. They served as deacons, trustees, stewards, ushers, choir members, and heads of organizations. Similarly, black women might work as maids their entire life, but they maintained self-respect by teaching Sunday school classes or coordinating youth programs. African Americans received respect and were "somebody" in their churches.

The church also provided a place of escape from the hostility and injustice of a city like Birmingham. Placed in a position of powerlessness because of disfranchisement, denied justice from the courts, looked down upon as inferiors, and locked in a world of legal segregation, blacks could find warmth and security in the confines of their churches. They felt free from the white world. They were at liberty to express their deepest thoughts. Although whites often scoffed at their style of worship, blacks found solace in one of the few places that whites would not enter. In Alabama, the church served as their refuge and shelter in a hostile environment.

Black Baptist churches constantly urged moral discipline among the early black migrants into Birmingham. Away from the watchful eye of family and friends, many migrants, a large portion of whom were young men, engaged in gambling, drinking, and prostitution. As a result, many crimes were attributed to blacks. At the lowest economic level, living in crowded quarters, unaccustomed to the temptations of city life, and always under the close scrutiny of police officers, blacks composed about 60 percent of Birmingham's criminals. Thus some churches were founded as a means of countering unlawful and riotous behavior. For example, local blacks addressed the lawlessness of the Lewisburg coal mining camp by starting a church. Two ministers came into the company village, built a brush arbor, and started religious services that resulted in the formation of the Evergreen Baptist Church.

Black Baptists used the threat of expulsion to enforce moral discipline among their members. Imitating their experience in the rural areas, Birmingham's churches expelled members guilty of immoral behavior such as drunkenness, adultery, fighting, fornication, or stealing. Females who became pregnant out of wedlock and church officers who created discord within the congregation also faced expulsion. Churches required expelled people to come before the congregation and ask forgiveness before they could be reinstated as members, a process similar in all denominations during this period. Expulsion provided an effective deterrent to immoral behavior, especially among church members who did not want to be embarrassed and who feared being cast out of God's church.

Drunkenness also came under fire from African American clergy, especially when they witnessed many blacks being victimized by liquor. In their view, the use of alcohol led people, especially men, to neglect their families and to perform poorly on the job. Testifying before the U.S. Senate Committee on Capital and Labor in 1883, the Reverend Isaiah Welch declared that "the prohibition of alcohol would go far to correct various ills among African Americans in Birmingham."[4] Most of the city's black Baptist clergy supported the temperance movement and used their pulpits to promote it. Benjamin F. Riley, former president of Howard College and the most liberal and outspoken white Baptist minister on the race issue, formed Birmingham's Negro Anti-Saloon League to teach blacks the dangers of alcohol. During sessions of the Mt. Pilgrim Association and the Colored Baptist State Convention, Riley addressed the subject, and black leaders applauded his efforts. Sometimes a collection was taken to support his work. Although black ministers were sometimes criticized by white Baptists for being too lenient on the temperance issue, as a group they remained strong in their opposition to alcohol.

Black Baptist ministers also encouraged strict morality in marriage and family life. During slavery, families were often separated by the sale of a spouse. Slave marriages generally had no legal standing. Although many blacks sought to reunite with their mates after emancipation, others formed relationships outside of marriage. Many young men migrating to Birmingham often lived with women without benefit of marriage. Churches frowned upon such arrangements and often expelled the participants. In general, black pastors maintained that the race could never succeed without strong families.

Charles L. Fisher, pastor of the Sixteenth Street Baptist Church from 1898 to 1910 and from 1921 to 1930, emphasized moral discipline. In his *Social Evils*, Fisher discussed six offenses that were destroying black individuals, families, and institutions: wastefulness, lust and sex outside of marriage, dancing, alcohol, the theater, and poverty. For him any action that opposed a biblical command or compromised spiritual edification was wrong.

Basing his first sermon on the familiar parable of the prodigal son, Fisher examined the evil of wastefulness. He said this sin needed attention among blacks because of the tendency to spend money unwisely. He maintained that so many blacks seemed to "throw away in a day what it takes to accumulate in a year." The solution, Fisher suggested, "was to teach thrift in homes, schools, and church."[5]

Fisher used the story of Samson and Delilah to denounce lust and sex outside of marriage. He showed how Samson, a strong man and a child of divine promise, was reduced to a pitiful "dwarf" of a man because he yielded to sexual passion. The moral of the story, Fisher pointed out, was to refrain from being deceived by beauty or controlled by lust. Fisher also considered dancing a cardinal sin because it aroused sensual passions. It did not enhance the "mission of the church and the work of Christ." Fisher declared the ballroom was "the devil's hot house."[6]

Fisher agreed with most pastors that the use of alcohol led to a breakdown in character, home, and government. He suggested that the church teach the biblical doctrine of temperance, defined as "total abstinence from anything that was physically injurious and morally degrading." According to Fisher, when Jesus said, "watch and pray that ye enter not into temptation," he had alcohol in mind. Therefore, Fisher maintained that "training children through Sunday school to abstain and to support temperance societies constituted the most effective means of destroying this menace to the world."[7]

The growing popularity of theater also alarmed and concerned Fisher. In his book, he referred to the theater as "Satan's Reception Room," where the devil promised good, clean fun but instead tempted people with vulgar and degrading entertainment. Immoral displays of feminine figures characterized many dramas, and such plays seemed to be all that the public would support. Hence, Fisher doubted that the theater would correct itself and insisted that the only solution was for people to refrain from attending such plays.

Fisher also considered the evil of poverty, which he attributed to laziness, reduced wages, and encouragement of vagrancy by the upper classes. Poverty, he said, encouraged crime and weakened the government. As a remedy, Fisher proposed that homes and schools cultivate strong work habits and industriousness among children. He concluded this sermon by reminding his readers that "riches, wisdom, and length of days are the heritage of those who work patiently, and wait, and murmur not."[8]

The Black Problem and Economic Self-Help

From the beginning of the black movement away from white churches and the formation of the Alabama Colored Baptist State Convention, self-help had been a major concern. Blacks consistently stressed the formation of churches and schools as a means of racial uplift. During the Progressive Era, the thrust toward economic self-help became paramount. Black Baptists did not eschew petition or protest nor the importance of schools and churches, but leaders increasingly called on Baptists of color to form businesses and to become producers rather than simply consumers.

Several circumstances prompted this new emphasis. Legal disenfranchisement and de jure segregation showed blacks that the federal government was increasingly reluctant to intervene on their behalf. The Supreme Court had turned a deaf ear toward attempts to overturn legal segregation and disfranchisement, and blacks now felt that they were on their own. Segregation laws had produced a caste system, and blacks remained trapped in their own communities. Black leaders believed that blacks buying from blacks would enhance the African American community.

The National Baptist Convention supported this stance. Elias C. Morris repeatedly stressed the need for economic self-help. In his annual presidential addresses he stated that the black man's only hope was to own businesses and move from consumer to producer. Morris manifested these beliefs in his own life. He organized Arkansas's Negro Business League, became a director of the Mound Bayou Oil Mill project in Louisiana, and served as a director of the Phillips County Land and Investment Company in Arkansas. In addition, he owned mining stock, a seventy-five-acre farm, his own home, and four additional pieces of property.

Booker T. Washington's influence was another reason for the new emphasis on economics. Washington, the great proponent of black business, was a member of the Mt. Olive Baptist Church in Tuskegee. Many ministers and church members were counted among his closest friends and supporters. Elias Morris cooperated with Washington and served as an officer in Washington's Negro Business League. Washington maintained that blacks had made a mistake by seeking political power during Reconstruction. Instead, they should have begun with economic attainment. In this regard, he suggested that the best course for blacks to take in light of disfranchisement and other political restrictions was to develop their economic potential. Such actions included building farms, establishing businesses, and organizing other economic institutions. As blacks developed institutions, character, and self-respect, whites would eventually give them respect and political rights. Although Washington was criticized by some black ministers for being too conservative, his views carried significant weight among many members of the Alabama Colored Baptist State Convention. When the convention met at Tuskegee Institute at Washington's request, although he was not present, the leaders espoused his philosophy, with many urging the convention "to work toward Washington's goal of moving from consumers to producers."[9]

State convention meetings included discussions on black business. In the 1901 convention, William Pettiford discussed the importance of black businesses, and a resolution from the Sunday School convention in the same year called on blacks to become economically self-reliant, to do for themselves. Blacks were urged to "acquire property, build homes and good character, engage in industry, commerce, and agriculture, and be faithful worshippers and servants of Almighty God."[10] Four years later a discussion on "the Negro in business" commended blacks for building and buying homes. The purpose of these resolutions and discussions was to inspire Alabama blacks to unify their strength and efforts so that the business and commercial progress of the race might be elevated.

The business activities of the Alabama Colored Baptist State Convention also showed increasing concern for economic self-help and black economic solidarity. In 1901 the convention voted to put all funds, including donations collected for building the new chapel at Selma University, into the black-owned Alabama Penny Savings Bank of Birmingham. This decision reversed a resolution from the previous year that called for depositing these funds in the white-owned First National Bank of Selma. The 1901 resolution stated that, "because all convention money came from blacks and since there was a skillfully-operated and successful bank of their own race, funds should be placed in that institution."[11] Later, the Penny Bank made substantial loans to the convention for Selma University. The bank lent the convention three thousand dollars in 1903 to complete Dinkins Chapel and later made a loan of six thousand dollars to pay teachers' salaries and operating expenses. Convention leaders constantly applauded the bank for teaching black people the art of saving money and urged delegates to buy stock in and make deposits at the bank.

In his 1905 presidential address, J. Q. A. Wilhite forcefully endorsed the move to economic self-help. He asserted that building churches and schools was not enough. "We all cannot be teachers and preachers," he maintained. "When black children come out of schools they need places of employment. How many places of employment were open to them? Black Baptists had not taken this into serious consideration." Wilhite argued that blacks were moving too slowly into business and urged pastors to encourage their people to build businesses. Furthermore, he maintained that "if blacks built more businesses, churches and schools would prosper as well."[12]

In his 1909 presidential address, James H. Eason was equally forceful in his emphasis on the need for increased black economic self-help. Eason suggested that blacks were in a state of crisis. Whites were taking jobs that were once reserved for blacks; for example, blacks had once enjoyed an exclusive monopoly in barbering but no longer. Blacks could not vote. Whites were not giving to black causes as they had done in the past. The solution, Eason suggested, was for blacks to operate their own factories. "Negroes," he insisted, "must build their own banks and give the Negro a job. Let us not fret about a Negro not being allowed to run a railroad engine; let us build a road and make him engineer. One good, strong, daily paper like the *Birmingham Age Herald,* operated by Negroes would serve to bring us manhood rights, more than kicking about not being called Mr. and Mrs. in the white dailies."[13]

In association meetings several moderators urged thrift, frugality, and economic self-help. The moderator, R. N. Hall of the Wills Creek Association in Etowah County, was vocal in his concern that blacks develop good economic habits. For him the acquisition of money and property was as important as acquiring an education since wealth brought respect. Hall insisted that every black should own his own home, live in it, and pay taxes on it. No American, he continued, would recognize any man who did not have at least some possessions. He concluded by insisting that "economy, industry, and common sense will be the cause of the Negro obtaining wealth and recognition." In the 1909 session of the Mt. Pilgrim Association of Birmingham, moderator Charles L. Fisher urged delegates to patronize black businesses and to protect one another.[14]

Baptist leaders endorsed the importance of black economic success and entrepreneurship by becoming businessmen and entrepreneurs themselves. In fact, most of the denominational leadership engaged in some kind of business enterprise. James H. Eason, president of the Colored Baptist State Convention, was president of the Mercantile Investment Company and editor of the *Anniston Leader.* J. Q. A. Wilhite served as president of the Birmingham Mutual Burial Association and as a member of the board of directors of the Alabama Penny Bank. R. B. Hudson, secretary of the Colored Baptist Convention, was president of a coal and lumber yard in Selma and served as president of the Negro Business League. A. J. Stokes, pastor of the five-thousand-member First Colored Baptist Church of Montgomery and vice president of the National Baptist Convention, owned several plantations. T. L. Jordan, pastor of the Sixteenth Street Baptist Church, bought shares in the *Negro American* and became an agent for that Birmingham newspaper. Thomas W. Walker, pastor of the Shiloh Baptist Church in Birmingham and president of the New Era Convention of Alabama, operated several businesses including an insurance company, a funeral home, and a coal company.

William R. Pettiford

Among Alabama's black Baptists, the most significant promoter of economic self-help was William Pettiford. Influenced by Booker T. Washington and a substantial supporter of the National Negro Business League, Pettiford was one among many ministers in the South who urged blacks to become producers and owners. He built his reputation over thirty-five years of service to the black Baptists in the state. Having served as teacher and financial agent for Selma University, pastor of the Sixteenth Street Baptist Church in Birmingham and other churches, moderator of the Mt. Pilgrim Association, and state convention president, Pettiford championed economic advancement as a means of achieving black uplift. Leaving the active pastorate in 1900 to become a full-time bank president, he continued to attend sessions of the Alabama Colored Baptist Convention. He helped write resolutions on the importance of economics, lectured on the subject, and provided tangible proof of his convictions through financial support from his bank. His life and work exhibited a concern for elevating blacks through education, morality, protest, and spirituality. But increasingly he insisted that black economic self-help was indispensable to such elevation.

Mirroring the experiences of other African American leaders of his generation, Pettiford rose to prominence from low beginnings. Born of free parents in North Carolina in 1847, he moved to Alabama in 1869 to seek better financial opportunity. With little money but a determination to improve his education, he entered the State Normal School at Marion, now Alabama State University. After seven years of study combined with summer work, he completed his studies. In 1877 Pettiford became a teacher at Selma University and simultaneously entered the theological department of the school, taking courses from President Woodsmall. Three years later, he severed his connection with the school to become pastor of the First Baptist Church of Union Springs, where he also served as principal of the city school for blacks. In 1883 he accepted the pastorate of the First Colored Baptist Church of Birmingham, later named the Sixteenth Street Baptist Church. State Baptist leaders, including Booker T. Washington, urged Pettiford to accept the church, assuring him that he could provide necessary leadership for Birmingham's growing black population.

By 1883 Birmingham had become a thriving industrial community, with a growing black population. Many blacks were former sharecroppers from southern Alabama who moved to Birmingham seeking better economic opportunities. They found jobs, primarily the most menial and dirtiest in the mines and factories. They also experienced discrimination and segregation in a rigid and oppressive caste system that placed blacks at the bottom of the Birmingham community. Despite the hostile environment in the city, blacks continued to move in because it offered a better life than sharecropping in the Black Belt. By 1890 blacks made up 40 percent of the population. With a new and emerging black population, Birmingham provided an opportunity for aggressive black people to achieve a measure of economic self-sufficiency and become leaders within their own communities.

Pettiford spent his first years revitalizing and enhancing the Sixteenth Street Baptist Church. When he became pastor, he joined 150 members who held services in a downtown storeroom. The church had a debt of five hundred dollars. Pettiford directed his first efforts toward canceling the debt and then erecting a building suitable for current needs and future growth. Within a year the church had paid off its debt and started a building fund. Membership exceeded four hundred by 1885, and the congregation constructed the largest and most commodious building in the city. Sixteenth Street Baptist Church served as a center for missions and evangelism, and became known as the "people's church" because the community held so many of its meetings there. Pettiford formed Birmingham's first missionary society, and by 1887 the church was assisting four mission churches in other areas of the city and county.

As pastor and religious leader, Pettiford emphasized the importance of discipline and morality as essentials in uplifting blacks. Like other pastors in Birmingham, he had members expelled because of immoral behavior such as drunkenness, adultery, and fighting. Building strong families was very important to Pettiford. In an effort to strengthen the consciousness of African Americans about the sacredness of marriage, to advise them on the principles of choosing a mate, and to show them how to have successful marriages, Pettiford wrote *Divinity in Wedlock* in 1890. Pettiford believed that marriage was ordained by God and that God instituted it for the general happiness of mankind as well as to bring children into the world. Dissolving a marriage without regard for the divine law of God was to commit adultery, and bringing children into the world outside of marriage was to commit fornication. In selecting a mate, Pettiford counseled, a person should avoid becoming a drunkard, a loafer, or someone too old or too young. Moreover, one ought never marry for beauty or in haste. Pettiford believed that a Christian should never marry a nonbeliever, and he urged people to marry only those of their religious faith. Giving special advice to young men, he suggested that they should have three things before marriage: money, education, and a home. According to Pettiford, a successful marriage depended on love, respect, honesty, good manners, kindness, and a sound economic base.

Pettiford's concern with discipline prompted him to work toward developing better work habits among blacks in Birmingham. Coming from sharecropping backgrounds, most blacks were accustomed to hard work, but they typically did not work around the clock, or on weekends, and holidays. As a result, industrialists complained about the irregularity of African American labor. Realizing the need for discipline, Pettiford conducted classes and held conferences to stress the need for regularity and for faithfulness to employers. At a speech delivered at the Belle Ellen mining camp, he cautioned workers never to leave a job without having someone to take their place. Such action, Pettiford maintained, would produce a bad reputation and reduce their chances for advancement. Speaking to the Birmingham Negro Business League in 1902, Pettiford proclaimed that "the Negro's future was in his own hands. By becoming conscientious workers, blacks would make a place for themselves in the nation's economy."[15] Pettiford joined Booker T. Washington and others in advocating that the black man's best hope lay in joining forces with business and industry rather than in labor agitation and strikes.

Because of his success as a pastor and his reputation as a strong moralist, Pettiford became one of the state's most outstanding and respected religious leaders. His fellow pastors elected him president of the Ministerial Association of Birmingham, and he became moderator of the Mt. Pilgrim Baptist District Association, the largest organization of churches in the Birmingham area in 1887. In this position, he established congregations in previously unchurched areas of Birmingham. He became president of the Alabama Baptist State Convention in 1889 and assumed the office of financial secretary in 1892.

Taking his position as a leader seriously, Pettiford's concerns expanded beyond religion to include benevolence, education, and business. The Representative Council was the major avenue for his leadership in these areas. Formed by him in the 1880s, the council consisted of delegates from Sunday schools, social clubs, conventions, societies, lodges, and business organizations. Its stated purpose was to reach blacks "by furnishing them with information of self-help" and "to study the condition of Negroes in Birmingham with a view [to] finding remedies and the best method of applying them." Pettiford succeeded in organizing chapters throughout the city. The Representative Council consisted of three departments: missionary, educational, and business. The business department was designed to establish and enhance African American businesses in the community. The educational department sought to build needed educational institutions, literary societies, and homes for disadvantaged people. The missionary department focused primarily on starting churches where none existed. Through the Representative Council and with the support of various women's clubs, Pettiford succeeded in forming benevolent organizations such as the

Children's Hospital and the Old Folks Home. Council and club women assisted in those projects, and Pettiford provided leadership and inspiration.[16]

Pettiford demonstrated educational leadership by establishing the first African American high school in Birmingham. In 1899 he and Mrs. B. H. Hudson led a group of African American citizens in requesting such a school. With assistance and support from Samuel Ullman, chairman of the Birmingham Board of Education, and J. Herbert Phillips, superintendent of schools, in 1900 the board established Industrial High School, one of the first high schools for blacks in the South. The board appointed Arthur Harold Parker, a protégée of Pettiford, as the principal and only teacher of the new school. Classes began in September 1900, and eighteen students occupied one room on the second floor of the Cameron Building. Pettiford attended the formal opening and continued to support the school, especially in its early years. Industrial High School held its first graduation at the Sixteenth Street Baptist Church in 1904.

Pettiford's most ambitious project was establishing the Alabama Penny Savings Bank. Inspiration came from many sources, but his experience as financial agent for Selma University and his growing friendship with Booker T. Washington underlined for him the importance of thrift and economic self-help. Pettiford said that much of the impetus for starting the bank stemmed from an incident in 1890. While riding a streetcar one Friday night, he observed an African American woman drinking whisky after receiving her weekly pay. That experience led him to think about some kind of business where blacks could save their money rather than wasting it on alcohol or other foolish endeavors. His inspiration also came in part from William Washington Browne, president of the Savings Bank of the Grand Fountain United Order of True Reformers of Richmond, Virginia, who expressed an interest in opening a branch of his bank in Birmingham. Pettiford and the local black business elite took the initiative to establish their own bank after deciding that they could do a better job than someone from outside the community.

To ensure acceptance of the bank, Pettiford and others engaged in three months of agitation, speeches, and advertising. Some blacks distrusted black-operated banks because of the failure of the Freedmen's Bureau Bank. William Pettiford led a cadre of leaders determined to ensure the project's success. Among those involved were several ministers who had already become involved in successful business ventures. Among these were Reverend J. I. Jackson, a local pastor; Reverend J. Q. A. Wilhite, president of the Birmingham Mutual

Burial Association and pastor of the Sixth Avenue Baptist Church; and Reverend Thomas W. Walker, pastor of the Shiloh Baptist Church and founder of several businesses.

Pettiford accepted the position of president of the bank with some reservations. He had undertaken the formation of the bank as a missionary project that he saw as an extension of his pastoral duties. When asked at an early meeting of the directors to assume the presidency, he declined. The directors threw down the ultimatum: "You'll be president or there will be no bank. Your name is necessary for confidence." Pettiford consented to serve for one year while continuing his pastoral duties. At the end of the one year, the confidence argument and the ultimatum again confronted him. After serving for four years on a one-year basis, Pettiford resigned his pastorate. "Though I'll have you understand," he told the board of directors, "I'm still a preacher."[17] In 1893 he became the full-fledged president of the Alabama Penny Savings Bank, an office he held for twenty-three years. Throughout those years, Pettiford continued to preach in churches and at denominational meetings, and for a brief period he assumed the pastorate of the Tabernacle Baptist Church.

The Alabama Penny Savings Company achieved immediate success. The bank opened its doors on October 15, 1890. It received on deposit that day $555, which, along with the $2,000 already paid in from the sale of stock, constituted its working capital. The bank was not incorporated until 1895 because under Alabama laws of the 1890s capital of $25,000 was needed. During the bank's first decade, Pettiford engineered many real estate transactions that proved highly lucrative for the bank. In 1896 bank officials bought a building for $6,500 and sold it one year later for $20,000. Pettiford and the directors then bought a house for $18,000 that they sold several years later for $35,000. During its lifetime the Penny Bank may have had as many as ten thousand depositors in its main bank in Birmingham and branches.

The cultivation of members of the white power structure accounted in part for Pettiford's success. Like Booker T. Washington, Pettiford believed in self-help and racial solidarity. Because he also agreed with Washington's emphasis on developing partnerships with powerful whites, Pettiford established working relationships with other banks. Needing someone to train his workers in bookkeeping and banking procedures, because no Birmingham institution provided such training for blacks, Pettiford obtained assistance from the city's white financial institutions. Help from the Steiner Brothers Bank appears to have been a major factor in the Penny Bank's ability to survive the economic crisis of 1893, when even some white banks failed because many depositors withdrew their savings.

Pettiford's position as president of the Penny Bank strengthened his belief that thrift, frugality, and economic self-help were essential for African American uplift. In an article written in 1901 titled "How to Help the Negro to Help Himself," Pettiford suggested to white philanthropists that the best way to help blacks was through assisting them in establishing banks and financial institutions that taught thrift, frugality, and industry. While serving both as pastor of Sixteenth Street Baptist Church and president of the bank from 1890 to 1893, Pettiford frequently called the church together to discuss practical concerns of thrift and economic solidarity. He became increasingly convinced that economic solidarity was essential to establish a financial base for black uplift. In 1895 he published *God's Revenue System* in which he gave a biblical basis for this belief. When he became full-time bank president in 1893, Pettiford sought to spread his message of economic liberation. His addresses at various Negro Business League meetings, religious gatherings, and conferences on the Negro held annually at Hampton Institute in Virginia revealed his philosophy of economic liberation. In a 1903 address, "The Importance of Business to the Negro," he emphasized that "no substantial progress can come to any race unless the race is developed in a very large degree along business lines. . . . The substantial progress of an individual, a race, or a nation is measured by its ability to rise from the position of earning wages to that of profitably directing its own business." He also determined that blacks owning their own businesses was not enough. They also had to commit to patronizing black-owned businesses. These views reflected his recognition of the benefits of a self-imposed segregated economy, an idea that other leaders of his time grappled with as well. "The colored wage-earner," Pettiford insisted, "must be prevailed upon to spend his earnings so that a portion of the same may be retained by his people. Any class or race of people who fail to get this idea clearly in their minds and act upon it are past redemption."[18]

Pettiford's philosophy of economic liberation included strong advocacy for home ownership. At several meetings, he revealed both his commitment to help blacks own their own homes through the bank's lending policies and the extensive benefits to the black community engaged in property ownership. In an address to the Sixth Annual Convention of the Negro Business League, Pettiford proclaimed that one of the central features of the Alabama Penny Bank was to teach the art of saving money and of purchasing homes. He reported that of the bank's eight thousand depositors more than a thousand had purchased their own homes. At the Thirteenth Annual Convention, he stated that the very presence of an African American bank in a community provides Negroes a better chance to own their own homes. He further insisted that the presence of black banks had saved thousands of Negro-owned homes from foreclosure.

Pettiford spread his missionary gospel of economic liberation to other sections of the state and nation. He established branches of the Alabama Penny Savings Bank in Selma, Anniston, and Montgomery. Pettiford also helped organize the National Negro Banker's Association and served as the first president until his death. As part of Booker T. Washington's Business League, the organization's stated purpose was "to foster and encourage the establishment of banks among our people and to look after the interest and welfare of those already organized."[19] As president of the National Negro Banker's Association and because of the success of the Alabama Penny Bank, Pettiford traveled to such places as Mobile; Atlanta; Paris, Texas; and Norfolk, Virginia, to assist in the establishment of black banks. Pettiford became the nation's leading figure in the African American bank movement.

In 1913 the Penny Bank built its own building on Eighteenth Street in Birmingham's thriving black business district. The five-story building housed other black businesses on its upper floors. Of its sixty-four rooms, black businesses occupied all of them except one, paying a total of eight thousand dollars in rent to the Penny Bank. The architect Wallace A. Rayfield, who designed many churches in Birmingham, had his office there, and the *Birmingham Reporter,* the *Birmingham Messenger,* and the *Voice of the People,* all African American newspapers, were housed there as well. The building represented a tangible demonstration of Pettiford's philosophy of self-help and economic solidarity: African Americans cooperating to assist other African Americans.

By the time of Pettiford's death in 1914, the Alabama Penny Savings Bank was the largest and strongest African American bank in the nation, with capitalization at one hundred thousand dollars and annual business revenue exceeding five hundred thousand. In 1915 the bank merged with another black-owned bank and became the Alabama Penny–Prudential Savings Bank, with J. O. Diffay as acting president.

William Pettiford, along with other Baptist leaders and urban pastors, stressed economic self-help for blacks during the Progressive Era. His standing as president of the Penny Bank and former convention president, plus his speeches and his participation in state Baptist associations and conventions, gave him a platform from which to exert considerable influence among black Baptists. The large number of pastors serving on the board of directors of the Penny Bank and its branches attests to Pettiford's wide influence among Alabama Baptists. As World War I began in Europe, blacks supported American participation. After the war, there would be attempts to keep alive the educational and business institutions that had been formed in the past while continuing to speak for racial justice.

1. C. O. Boothe, author of the *Cyclopedia of the Colored Baptists of Alabama* and one of the founders of Selma University and Birmingham-Easonian Baptist Bible College. From C. O. Boothe, *Cyclopedia of the Colored Baptists of Alabama* (Birmingham: Alabama Publishing, 1895).

2. Rev. L. S. Steinback, pastor of the First African Baptist Church in Tuscaloosa, Alabama, conducts a river baptism. From C. O. Boothe, *Cyclopedia of the Colored Baptists of Alabama* (Birmingham: Alabama Publishing, 1895).

3. St. Louis Street Baptist Church in Mobile, Alabama. From C. O. Boothe, *Cyclopedia of the Colored Baptists of Alabama* (Birmingham: Alabama Publishing, 1895).

4. The original Stone Hall on the campus of Selma University. From C. O. Boothe, *Cyclopedia of the Colored Baptists of Alabama* (Birmingham: Alabama Publishing, 1895).

5. Dr. William R. Pettiford, pastor of the Sixteenth Street Baptist Church, Birmingham, Alabama, and president of the Alabama Penny Savings Bank. From C. O. Boothe, *Cyclopedia of the Colored Baptists of Alabama* (Birmingham: Alabama Publishing, 1895).

6. Mrs. Dinah Smith Jordan, of the Women's Missionary Society of the Sixteenth Street Baptist Church. From C. O. Boothe, *Cyclopedia of the Colored Baptists of Alabama* (Birmingham: Alabama Publishing, 1895).

7. Mrs. Rebecca Pitts, of the Alabama Baptist Women's State Convention. From C. O. Boothe, *Cyclopedia of the Colored Baptists of Alabama* (Birmingham: Alabama Publishing, 1895).

8. A portion of the Birmingham-Easonian Baptist Bible College faculty in 2004. The author is third from the left. From Wilson Fallin Jr., *History of Birmingham-Easonian Baptist Bible College* (Birmingham: Ebsco Media, 2004).

9. Two former presidents of the Alabama Baptist Women's State Convention, Mrs. Ethel Fallin (*left*) and Mrs. A. M. Wilson. From the private collection of Wilson Fallin Jr.

10. A portion of the delegates to the 1995 Alabama Baptist Women's State Convention. From the private collection of Wilson Fallin Jr.

4
Before and after
World War II, 1917–1954

8
Between the Wars

Some scholars and theologians of the black church portray the years between World War I and World War II as a time of discontinuity. They point to the loss of black nationalism, the quest for the liberation of Africa, and the absence of demands for full freedom in the United States by the black church as signs of its deradicalization and deviance from the past.[1] However, actions by black Baptist leaders and Alabama churches counter this thesis. Despite operating in a time of racial retrenchment and economic hardship, Baptist leaders remained concerned with racial uplift and issued calls for fairness and justice for blacks. As in the past, these ministers urged caution and levelheadedness, and championed self-help, morality, education, and appeals to whites as the best hope for racial advancement. Black Baptist leaders rejected radical methods like communism and advised their parishioners to work within the American capitalistic system.

Ministers continued in their leadership roles, but they were not the only leaders within the black community. The growth of the black middle class, the secularization of education, and the advent of protest increasingly brought laypersons to the forefront in civil rights organizations. Still, black Baptist ministers and lay leaders alike sought above all to preserve the educational, business, and denominational institutions established in earlier years. David V. Jemison and Robert T. Pollard were two influential leaders of this period who emphasized the importance of preservation and continuity. Women continued to comprise the largest number of congregants in black Baptist churches and their efforts in fund-raising for Selma University and missionary programs made them an indispensable part of the convention's work.

A strong emphasis on preserving the past, however, did not prevent new religious forms from entering the black community. Because of middle-class expansion and the growth of black professionals, a few congregations became known in the community as "class" churches, with others known as "mass" churches. In addition, gospel music made its way into black Baptist churches during the Depression and became the favorite of many worshippers.

Loyalty and Hard Times for Blacks

Black Baptist leaders called upon their constituents to support America's participation in World War I. In his 1917 convention address, President David V. Jemison urged blacks to remain loyal in this conflict as they had done in every war throughout the nation's history. He suggested that black loyalty would bring about greater justice. Jemison maintained that through the war, "Ethiopia was stretching forth its hand unto God."[2] Heeding Jemison and other leaders, blacks in Alabama supported the war effort. Blacks served in the armed services and bought and sold war bonds.

Black churches also aided in the war effort. In communities where black soldiers were trained, churches provided assistance and encouragement. The black churches in Montgomery organized the Central Committee of Colored Montgomery Citizens to devise ways to "entertain the colored soldiers stationed in the area." The Dexter Avenue Baptist Church Choir, along with other black churches, created a 250-voice chorus to entertain the troops, with practices and programs held in the Dexter Avenue sanctuary. Dexter Avenue superintendent of the Sunday school J. W. Beverly directed the food conservation program among Montgomery's African American community. In November 1917 the congregation expanded its participation in the war effort to include national as well as state involvement. Kelly Miller, dean of Howard University, organized the Colored Comfort Committee to "aid the dependents of our soldiers and sailors" who were killed or disabled. Victor Hugo Tulane, a member of Dexter Avenue Baptist Church, was in charge of Montgomery's chapter, and Dexter Avenue scheduled programs to raise money for this cause.

Having proved their loyalty to the nation, blacks in Alabama and throughout the nation expected to be rewarded with greater rights. They were not. Although the war was fought overseas in the name of greater democracy, the forces of bigotry, nativism, and exclusion flourished at home. In Alabama this meant blacks remained the victims of a rigid caste system that promoted segregation and denied them their legitimate rights. Blacks were rendered politically impotent through a variety of methods including white primaries, poll taxes, grandfather clauses, understanding clauses, literacy tests, and property requirements. Although lynchings occurred less frequently, blacks fell victim to a campaign of violence and intimidation designed to preserve white supremacy. The Ku Klux Klan, for example, used clandestine and extra legal methods to "keep blacks in their place." Thus, race continued to dominate state politics and political leaders maintained a consensus for white supremacy.

Alabama's education system provides the clearest example of the discrimination practiced against blacks. A 1918 study indicated that the black illiteracy rate was 31.3 percent, a figure that grew to 39 percent by 1920. White teachers received better pay than black teachers. In 1922 white teachers earned more than six hundred dollars annually, while black educators earned less than three hundred. The difference in state appropriations for white and black schools was particularly glaring. In 1924 blacks comprised 40 percent of the population, but Alabama spent only $1.4 million on black schools compared with $13.1 million for white schools. The gap was closed slightly during the 1930s due to concerted black efforts and northern philanthropy, but black education continued to lag far behind that of whites. As Robert Sherer, James Anderson, and others have suggested, "the poor support given black education was designed keep blacks in a web of subordination."[3]

The Great Depression also made life harder for blacks and worked against positive change and greater justice. The Depression years were hard on everybody in Alabama, but especially on blacks. Between 1930 and 1940 unemployment rates were 5.6 percent for whites and 13.6 percent for blacks. In urban areas like Birmingham, blacks were hit unusually hard. Already occupying the dirtiest and lowest-paying jobs, they were often the first group targeted for layoffs. Black unemployment in Birmingham reached as high as 75 percent. Many African American women were unemployed because of reduced demands for domestic work. Shackled with the burden of raising children and limited by poor public and private relief, their lives were exceptionally hard. As a result, African Americans turned to all sorts of survival techniques in the city. Drawing on their rural experience, many planted vegetable gardens ranging in size from small plots to forty-acre farms. African Americans planted gardens on property owned by coal and ore mines, in back alleys, and in vacant lots of industrial towns all over the area. Many raised pigs and cows in the city. Others did odd jobs for food, gathered grocery store throwaways, sold peanuts on the streets, and hauled and sold coal obtained from mines or railroads. In a desperate effort to obtain fuel, some blacks tore down vacant houses. To prevent houses from being demolished for firewood, real estate companies employed men to stay in empty houses.

A Call for Fairness and Justice

Black Baptist leaders in Alabama issued a call for fairness and justice. Although they refrained from aggressive means to overthrow the Jim Crow system, they nevertheless protested against its abuses and injustices. Urging caution and discretion, black leaders took measures that would not unduly offend whites. In his address before the Alabama Colored Baptist Convention in 1919, C. T. Hayes, a convention leader from Dothan, stated that "[all the] blacks of Alabama wanted was racial equality rather than social equality."[4] Most Baptist leaders made a similar distinction.

Through his speeches as president of the Alabama Colored Baptist State convention, President David V. Jemison consistently called for fairness and justice. Some of his speeches provide good examples of the black Baptists' stance on civil and political rights. In his 1921 address Jemison called for fairness in the courts. He made it clear that he opposed crime, but he asserted that "black crime was exaggerated because of injustices in the courts. Blacks did not receive fair trials, and that fact accounted for their disproportionate numbers in penal institutions." In addition, Jemison maintained that "white policemen had been so unfair to blacks and thereby had lost respect in the black community." He insisted further that "getting equal justice for blacks within the legal system and courts of Alabama was paramount."[5]

In his address to the 1927 convention, Jemison focused on "what the Negro wants." He agreed with most of his constituents that blacks should be concerned with political and economic rights, not social equality. He insisted that blacks should have the same legal rights as other Americans. According to Jemison "blacks wanted better schools, justice in the courts, the cessation of lynchings, adequate facilities and respect for black women by the Railroad Commission, industrial opportunity based on merit, and a better image in the press." Three years later, Jemison noted that blacks were discontent. Injustice in the courts and exploitation by farm owners contributed to their frustration. To ease the black man's discontent Jemison suggested that six things needed to be done. Living conditions needed to be fair and decent. Transportation accommodations needed to be equal with those of whites. Blacks should be provided with adequate educational facilities. Blacks needed legal protection when buying and selling. The life and property of blacks in Alabama deserved protection from lawlessness. Finally, blacks were entitled to justice in the courts.[6]

The 1935 State of the Country report of the Alabama Colored Baptist State

Convention mirrored President Jemison's call for justice. The resolution called for blacks to be given the ballot in order to assure proper legal protection. Addressing the issue of lynching, the resolution regretted that such acts still persisted in the nation. It called on all the churches to work to discourage and break down "mobocracy on our American soil."[7]

Jemison's call for fairness extended beyond Alabama and often became a part of his addresses before the National Baptist Convention, USA. In these national addresses he stressed familiar themes, namely the need for justice in the courts, equal transportation, and educational opportunities. In his 1943 speech before the National Baptist Convention, Jemison also dealt with race riots, which had occurred during World War I and were recurring during World War II. Jemison asserted that these riots reflected the continued hostility of lower-class whites toward blacks and the widely held belief that blacks were inferior. Such attitudes encouraged violence against blacks and prevented anti-lynching laws from being passed. Jemison called on white and black churches to take the lead in reform measures. He asserted that the church was the place called by God to teach fairness, honesty, and justice, "with equal rights for all and special privileges to none."[8]

Like other leaders of his day, Jemison believed that, despite the unfair treatment of blacks, there was goodness and fairness in "the better class of whites." He believed that these people knew in their hearts that blacks deserved fairness and justice. Therefore, he urged blacks to avoid trouble and not to provoke riots. Rather, they should be cautious, use common sense, and thereby convince the better class of whites to cooperate with them in providing fair and equitable treatment.

A man of genuine piety who, like other black clergymen, believed in the ultimate triumph of right, Jemison counseled blacks to develop their faith in God. He further insisted that God was with black people in their quest for equal rights. His address to the 1925 Alabama Colored Baptist Convention forcefully pointed to his belief in the ultimate triumph of blacks over racism. In conclusion, he urged blacks "to stand still, stand prepared, provoke no riot, just let God do his work. He may permit a few riots in order to force the Negroes closer together. Riots do not mean that we shall be defeated, if we trust him. Let us learn the lesson that He is teaching us." For Jemison, God's lesson was that through faith and patience, victory over racism would come.[9]

In some instances black Baptist ministers and leaders went beyond convention and association resolutions and petitioned the government for justice. In

1923 the African American community protested the zoning ordinance that mandated segregated housing in Birmingham. Those attending the meeting decided to send a petition to the city council. Among the signers were two outstanding Baptist pastors and leaders: R. N. Hall, president of the Baptist Minister's Conference, and C. L. Fisher, pastor of the Sixteenth Street Baptist Church.

The calls for fair play and justice among black Baptist leaders did not lead them to embrace radical social and economic movements, like communism, that sought inroads into the black community, especially during the Depression. Stressing the economic exploitation of workers by capitalists and the need for a new economic order, the Communist Party attracted a few hundred blacks to its membership in Alabama. Because of the party's stand on racial equality, it found attracting whites very difficult. Therefore, the organization focused much of its attention on the black community. In rural Alabama the communists were successful in organizing a sharecroppers movement, but violence by local authorities took most of the initiative away from the rural movement. Limited efforts were made in Mobile and Montgomery, but the communist movement had its greatest appeal in Birmingham because of publicity from the Scottsboro Boys trials, economic devastation among industrial workers, and effective leadership by charismatic figures like Hosea Hudson, who galvanized other black industrial workers.

With only a few possible exceptions black Baptist ministers and leaders opposed the Party as too idealistic and impractical. For them the Party's lack of recognition of the color line gave it little chance of success in the South. Some pastors joined Oscar Adams, editor of the *Birmingham Reporter*, in maintaining that communism among blacks constituted the emotional response of an ignorant and uninformed people that could only lead to violence and bloodshed. Other pastors agreed with the 1931 report of the Commission on Interracial Cooperation that the Party was manipulating blacks for its own ends. These pastors, including Reverends M. Sears and John Goodgame, insisted that blacks and whites were too interlinked for the races to pull apart from one another. They called for cooperation between the races as well as for fair law enforcement. Still other pastors opposed communism because of its atheistic doctrine, and some opposed it simply because of negative newspaper reports and other unfavorable publicity.

Self-help, rather than radicalism or revolution, continued to be an important part of the ideology of black Baptist ministers and other black leaders, and that was reflected in their sermons and other writing. For example, Charles L. Fisher, who served as pastor of the Sixteenth Street Baptist Church in Birmingham, as well as dean of theology and chairman of the trustee board at Selma University during the interwar period, preached on things that black Baptists had to be thankful for. He thanked God for the black Baptist leaders of the past like McAlpine, Boothe, Pettiford, and Booker T. Washington. All these men, claimed Fisher, laid the foundation for great institutions, but Washington was the greatest man of his time, either black or white. According to Fisher, the spirit of self-help constituted the greatest contribution these men made to fellow Baptists. "Because of their self-help emphasis, blacks often provided for themselves when they could not get their equal share of taxes for things like education."[10]

However, Fisher's gratitude for self-help did not prohibit him from demanding fairness from government. Fisher joined Jemison and others in calling on the government of Alabama to let all qualified voters, blacks as well as whites, cast their ballots. John Goodgame, treasurer of the Alabama Colored Baptist State Convention, called on blacks to develop self-help habits that would advance the race. He admitted that blacks were living in an age of prejudice and discrimination. He pointed to job discrimination, lack of funds for schools, lynchings, police brutality, and the growth of the Ku Klux Klan as evidence of this renewed hostility. Goodgame urged blacks "to develop strong values: frugality, religion, education, and racial solidarity. With these virtues blacks would excel in spite of the times."[11]

Though clergymen sponsored resolutions at association and convention meetings, called for self-help and fairness, and signed petitions, they were not the major activists in Alabama during this period. Laymen who lived in urban areas became the major civil rights leaders among blacks. They formed organizations that were more aggressive in obtaining first-class citizenship. One such group, the NAACP, was founded in 1909. It rejected the accommodationism of Booker T. Washington and sought to use legal means to gain full rights for blacks. Laymen rather than ministers took the lead in forming local NAACP chapters in urban areas. In Birmingham, a local physician, Charles A. J. McPherson, was the leading figure in founding an NAACP chapter in 1916. In both Montgomery and Mobile, postal clerks provided early leadership. John LeFlore was president of the NAACP in Mobile during most of the 1920s, and a chapter was founded in 1919 in Montgomery with J. H. Fegain serving as its first president.

Throughout the 1930s laymen continued to provide most of the civil rights leadership across the state. A group of laymen formed a political organization devoted to restoring political rights for blacks. A few of the most prominent political leaders were Charles Gomillion of Tuskegee; Edgar D. Nixon, Rufus Lewis, and James E. Pierce of Montgomery; and Arthur Shores, Emory Jackson, and E. Paul Jones of Birmingham. These men proved more aggressive than earlier leadership and worked well as a cohesive unit. They were not revolutionaries, but they did challenge the political system more assertively. Working within the Alabama Democratic Party, they formed their own wing, the Alabama Progressive Democratic Association, and began to run for office. As early as 1942 Birmingham attorney Arthur Shores announced his candidacy to become a member of the House of Representatives from Jefferson County.

A major factor that contributed to the rise of lay leadership stemmed from the effect of harsh economic conditions on black churches and pastors. Urban black ministers who provided leadership in the convention and the community were economically strapped. For example, Montgomery's Dexter Avenue Baptist Church experienced serious financial difficulty during the Great Depression and was forced to cut the salaries of the staff and pastor. In 1931 Dexter Avenue paid only one-third of the pastor's salary, and Reverend F. D. Jacobs, who had been a leader in the community, was forced to move to another state. The Sixteenth Street Baptist Church of Birmingham also experienced financial difficulties during the 1930s. The church operated at a deficit during much of this period, and lack of funds created tension among its members. As a result, the church was not successful in calling a pastor between 1930 and 1932. During the tenure of Reverend David F. Thompson, 1932 to 1943, the congregation continued to experience financial difficulties. In order to prevent foreclosure on its building, Sixteenth Street was forced to borrow money. The church cut staff in order to save $250 per month. To make ends meet on a limited salary for his large family, which included five children, Reverend Thompson rented a bedroom in the parsonage, conducted services at various funeral homes, and preached revivals at other churches. These outside activities sparked opposition from some members of the church and Reverend Thompson's pastorate was filled with acrimony. Not all ministers faced the same degree of financial difficulty as Jacobs and Thompson, but almost all experienced some hardship, especially full-time pastors of large churches who had traditionally provided community leadership. Often their poor economic situation prevented them from providing effective community leadership and hampered the overall outreach of their congregations.

The increasing influence of lay leadership did not necessarily mean the church was less important in the community, but it did mark the growth of a black middle class. Black colleges had begun to produce not only ministers but also well-trained doctors, lawyers, newspaper editors, and businessmen who enjoyed economic independence and could act on behalf of the race. This was also the period of the Harlem Renaissance, which stressed the emergence of the "new Negro." He was militant, proud of his heritage, and aggressive in his demands for full rights. A cultural movement led by artists, novelists, poets, and scholars, the Harlem Renaissance spread across the nation and rallied laymen in asserting their rights. Moreover, black college students began to demand more liberal arts courses as well as black control of their institutions. In Alabama, blacks succeeded, in spite of protests from the Ku Klux Klan and Alabama political officials, in getting the Tuskegee Veterans Hospital manned by black doctors. Blacks in general, but especially black middle-class professionals in particular, absorbed the new militant spirit of the times. Believing that their ministers and churches were too passive, some of these activists asserted their leadership and began agitating for full civil and political rights.

Many of these laymen who became political and civil rights leaders were active churchmen who worked with pastors in their respective communities. In fact, the founding and progress of the NAACP was made possible in large part due to the support of pastors and churches. Moreover, church buildings remained the primary meeting places for the organization. Montgomery's NAACP chapter was organized in a Congregational church, and most of its early meetings took place at Dexter Avenue Baptist Church. In 1918 the NAACP and the Minister's Alliance of Montgomery called a meeting of state leaders at Dexter Avenue to map a strategy for attaining greater black rights. That group petitioned the state legislature to do more for public education, to improve conditions on trains, to deter lynchings, and to give blacks the right to vote. Later that year, Pastor Peter Callahan of Dexter Avenue led a discussion at the NAACP meeting concerning getting more African Americans to vote. He helped create a pamphlet on the subject and distributed five thousand copies throughout the state. Although some professional blacks criticized pastors, their increasing role in political leadership reflected the coming of age of laymen rather than a decline of the church. In reality, pastors and lay leaders generally worked together to foster black rights.

Growth, Continuity, and the Leadership of D. V. Jemison

Despite dashed hopes, economic insecurity, and migration, black Baptist churches continued to increase in the state, and pastors demonstrated a strong sense of continuity with the past. In 1929 the Alabama State Convention reported that black Baptists had grown to include 109 associations and 2,111 churches. In 1935 the convention's statistician reported that there were 117 associations, 2,550 churches, and 371,964 Baptists affiliated with the convention. Although these figures may have been exaggerated, black Baptist churches certainly grew—and they continued to satisfy important needs for Alabama blacks. In addition to serving as worship centers, churches were social centers and meeting places. In a society that continued to look down on blacks and to deny them legal and social equality, churches provided blacks the opportunity to use their talents and to build self-esteem.

Most growth among black Baptists during this period was in urban areas. Many rural blacks left the state and moved north, thereby limiting the number of churches in black communities of rural Alabama. Others left their farms and made their way to urban areas like Birmingham. Even though conditions in the city were far from ideal, they were generally much better than life for tenant farmers. In Birmingham, blacks found steady jobs in furnaces and mines. Even as some Birmingham residents moved northward, others from rural areas took their places. Overall, Birmingham's black population remained steady at approximately 40 percent of the population.

As these new residents made their way into Birmingham, they formed new congregations. Most preferred smaller churches to the larger, more established institutions. Migrants were often poorer members of the established churches, had less education, and wore simpler clothes. Many doubted they would ever be recognized or allowed to assume a position of leadership in large churches, so they formed smaller congregations that reminded them of rural churches they had left. One group of migrants from the Black Belt established the Twenty-third Street Baptist Church of Ensley in the home of Mrs. Nora Moore. Mrs. Moore and others in the Ensley community expressed their need for a church of the "poorer classes where they could worship and where there would be fewer calls for money than in the larger, more established churches."[12] Another group started the New Kingdom Baptist Church in North Birmingham in 1935, stating that they felt discriminated against in the larger churches.

Split congregations also accounted for black Baptist growth before World War II. Almost without exception, schisms occurred over issues of pastoral leadership. With few places to exercise leadership, members anxious for recognition and power often questioned the pastor's authority. This discord frequently resulted in bitter internecine conflict and ultimately led to splits. Birmingham churches followed this general pattern. For example, in 1924 a group broke away from the Lively Hope Baptist Church to organize the Peace Baptist Church of Pratt City. In 1926 members left the New Canaan Baptist Church to form the Pleasant Hill Baptist Church of Ensley. In 1931 the Reverend J. A. Martin, pastor of the Jackson Street Baptist Church of Woodlawn, led seventy members in forming the First Baptist Church of Woodlawn after a group of deacons questioned his authority. Members from the Zion Baptist Church of Titusville broke from the Goldwire Baptist Church in 1936 over the issue of whether to call another pastor when the current pastor became ill. According to a Works Progress Association survey of black churches in Birmingham and Jefferson County, approximately sixty-two black Baptist churches were formed between 1920 and 1939.

Meanwhile, black Baptist leaders fought to preserve the past and continue supporting the institutions that had been formed in previous years. Pastors sought to maintain and support African American businesses in several ways. The Reverend Robert Richardson, pastor of the Harmony Street Baptist Church, was insured with an African American company and on the board of directors of the Jefferson County Burial Society. Reverend William Boyd of the Trinity Baptist Church had his health and burial insurance with an African American company. Besides setting personal examples, these pastors promoted African American businesses from their pulpits and on special speaking occasions. In his 1923 emancipation address to the citizens of Birmingham, N. H. Newsome, a local pastor, stated that blacks in Birmingham spent a million dollars a year. That money, he said, should be spent with Negro businesses, which would further help to emancipate African Americans from their poor economic plight. Ministers also sponsored resolutions in support of black businesses. In 1930, at a meeting of the Jefferson County Burial Society, two outstanding black Baptist ministers, Charles L. Fisher, pastor of the Sixteenth Street Baptist Church, and William Atmore, moderator of the Mt. Pilgrim Association, sponsored a resolution encouraging black ministers to support black businesses.

Attempts by black Baptist pastors to preserve educational institutions met with mixed results. During the 1930s many Baptist academies closed because of lack of funds and an improvement of public education. Some academies became county schools and were brought under the auspices of public education agencies, whereas others simply ceased to exist. In many instances, no attempt was made to keep these schools open because the state and county had provided public schools for blacks. Nonetheless support for black public education lagged behind that provided for white students.

Birmingham Baptist College was forced to close because of a lack of financial support. The school could not pay its teachers, and it failed to reduce a mortgage indebtedness of twenty-three thousand dollars. The trustees leased the school's buildings to the County Board of Education for the operation of Powderly High School. Former faculty members held classes in churches in an attempt to keep school spirit alive. The Baptists of Birmingham liquidated the mortgage in 1936, and the institution reopened three years later with J. H. Wrenn as president and T. D. Bussey as his assistant.

The greatest educational struggle for black Baptists continued to be Selma University. The school met a great need for blacks, especially those living in the Black Belt. Under the leadership of Robert Pollard the school maintained an enrollment of 500 to 700 students. However, during the 1930s Selma University's enrollment dropped and it was heavily in debt. In 1930 President Robert Ryan reported that enrollment had dropped to 291 and that the institution was fifty thousand dollars in debt. Teachers had not been paid, and trustees were forced to reduce most of their salaries. Ryan lamented that if something were not done soon Selma University would have to close. He suggested that one solution was for the university to merge with Birmingham Baptist College. But trustees sold school land to pay major creditors and the institution survived.

As local churches and educational institutions struggled, David V. Jemison, who served as president of the Alabama Baptist State Convention during this entire period, provided key leadership. A native of Alabama, Jemison spent his entire adult life in service to Alabama Baptist churches and in denominational work. He was born in Perry County in 1875 to Perry and Tyresa Jemison of Marion. His father had been a slave, but during Reconstruction he bought the plantation where he had once worked. Jemison grew up there and attended the common school for blacks in Perry County. He entered Selma University and graduated from the high school department in 1899. While at Selma, he pastored the El Bethel Baptist Church as well as Marion's Mt. Olive Baptist Church. Not satisfied with his education, he completed a theology program in 1905 and received a bachelor of divinity degree. He became principal of the Marion Baptist Academy for two years, and Selma University would later honor him with two honorary doctoral degrees.

On January 1, 1903, Jemison accepted the pastorate of the Tabernacle Baptist Church in Selma. Upon his arrival, he found there a membership of eighty-eight conscientious members who worshipped in a small frame building. Under his leadership, the frame building was replaced with a brick structure that cost seventy-five thousand dollars, with a seating capacity of eleven hundred. Because of Jemison's success as a pastor and his faithfulness to the Baptist work, his status grew within the denomination. He was elected moderator of the New Cahaba Association and president of the Southwest District Convention. In 1916, at the First African Baptist Church of Montgomery, Jemison was elected president of the Alabama Colored Baptist State Convention, a position he retained until 1953. In that capacity, Jemison not only called for fairness and justice for blacks but also challenged black Baptists to build a greater convention and preserve the gains of the past. In doing so, Jemison emphasized the role of the minister as leader, the crucial influence of the church, and the need to maintain Selma University.

In convention addresses Jemison called on ministers to maintain their leadership roles. The minister, he stated, must lead the church because he had been called and ordained by God. Jemison also believed that black Baptist pastors had a special responsibility to their congregations since the church was the foundational institution among black people. For him the black pastor was important because he led his people into certain beliefs and actions, while the white preachers usually followed the views and actions of their congregations. Therefore, Jemison insisted, "pastors must be prepared to assume burdens and responsibilities, know and preach the Bible, and remain truthful and bold in their witness."[13]

According to Jemison, pastors should lead in the community as well as the church. He decried those who worked to diminish the leadership role of pastors and urged ministers not to give up their responsibility. Any community, he argued, would be in bad shape if leadership were taken out of the preacher's hands and placed in the hands of selfish men. Jemison believed that something was amiss in communities where pastors were not leaders. In promoting pastoral leadership, Jemison did not oppose lay leadership, and as convention president he strove to establish a layman's convention against strong opposition from pastors. He believed that clergy and laity should work together to build a stronger church. However, lay leadership could not take the place of a pastor. And he exhorted pastoral leaders to be unselfish and truthful because selfish leaders could ruin a church and a nation.

For Jemison the church was the most important institution. He defined it as "the spirit of Christ organized for service." While Jemison lamented the loss of ministerial leadership, he also felt that the church had lost the influence and power that it once possessed. Consequently, he emphasized that the church must recapture the power it once had. One of his favorite passages was Acts 1:8—"Ye shall receive power, after that the Holy Ghost is come upon you." Jemison maintained that the present church needed to get back to the power of the early church. To do so, several steps were necessary. Among these was a revival of the Holy Spirit, prayer, and grace. Moreover, the church, he suggested, must also become bold in its witness and lift up the cross of Jesus Christ. In his 1934 presidential address to the National Baptist Convention, Jemison insisted that the race problem could not be solved without the church taking the lead.

Jemison's major task as president of the state convention focused on the preservation of Selma University. As a result, most of his energy was spent in urging its support. Over and over again, he emphasized that the convention must not lose this educational enterprise bequeathed by the convention fathers. Jemison also valued Selma University because it provided Christian education. Too often, Jemison noted, "public schools became anti-religious whether intentionally or not. By neglecting religion, those schools only provided a partial education." He believed that Christian schools like Selma University helped students grow into law-abiding citizens with reverence for authority and respect for the rights of others. According to Jemison, "a non-Christian education resulted in a person with an educated head with an unregenerate heart, and that combination made an individual a clever devil." Jemison stressed the need for black Baptists to gain a Christian education, and in his 1929 presidential address identified five reasons parents should send their children to Selma University: (1) Selma was their school, controlled by them. (2) Every person should support his own; not to do so makes a person worse than an unbeliever. (3) It was a Christian institution. (4) It promoted loyalty to the Baptist Church. (5) It would help children remain true to biblical truths and Baptist doctrines.[14]

Robert T. Pollard and Selma University

Just as David Jemison directed the state convention for more than thirty years, Robert T. Pollard exerted considerable influence as president of Selma University during the first four decades of the twentieth century. From 1902, the year he began his first term as president to his death in 1938, he cast a broad shadow over black Baptists throughout the state. In the mold of McAlpine, Boothe, and Pettiford, Pollard served in many positions. He was pastor, missionary, moderator, convention officer, and school president. From these leadership positions he championed the major emphases of black Baptists: order, education, self-help, racial pride, fair play and justice, a trained ministry, and an effective church and denomination. As president of Selma University, he inspired and helped train many people who would become leaders among Alabama's black Baptists in the twentieth century. During his second presidential term, 1916 to 1930, the institution reached its peak despite its struggles.

Pollard was born on October 4, 1860, at Gainesville, Alabama, the fifth of fourteen children of Reverend R. T. Pollard Sr. and Mary Pollard. At the age of ten he went with his family to live in Jasper County, Mississippi, where his father rented a small farm twenty miles southwest of Meridian. Pollard Sr. entered the gospel ministry, and after arriving at his new home in Mississippi began to do missionary work among his new neighbors. He soon organized the Mt. Pleasant Baptist Church, and at thirteen, Robert Pollard Jr. was converted and baptized.

Although Pollard Sr. did not attend school, he desired greatly that his children receive an education. He taught his children to read, and Robert could do so by the age of twelve. Pollard Sr. provided for the education of his children and others in the community by forming the Twistwood School in Enterprise, Mississippi. Young Pollard became active in church during this period and soon was performing duties as both church clerk and Sunday school teacher. At sixteen he felt the call to preach and became known in Mississippi as the boy preacher. Three years later his father gave him five acres of land and a pony, intending that he farm the land in order to earn money to further his education, which is what Pollard did. After farming for a brief period, Pollard Jr. sold his cotton and pony, and began searching for a suitable school.

In 1880 Pollard entered school at Meridian, Mississippi, and entered a new phase in his life. He studied arithmetic, algebra, English grammar, and Latin for more than two years. Then he entered the Alabama Baptist Normal and Theological School (now Selma University), and graduated as valedictorian two years later. Following graduation, Pollard was appointed by the Home Mission Board of the Southern Baptist Convention to teach Bible at his alma mater. He was the first black person appointed by that missionary agency. Having a nearly insatiable desire for learning, Pollard enrolled in the college department in the fall of 1884, supporting himself through teaching and other employment. He was ordained to the gospel ministry in March 1885 and accepted the call to pastor the Vilula and Union Baptist Churches, both near Marion. Pollard graduated from Selma's college department in 1886.

For the next eighteen years Pollard pastored several churches and engaged in a variety of denominational and missionary tasks, including serving as general missionary for the American Baptist Publication Society. In addition, he had two tenures as pastor of the Dexter Avenue Baptist Church. During his first term Pollard did much to enhance the church's spiritual growth, including organizing the Baptist Young People's Union. In 1894 and 1895 he represented the church in the Alabama Colored Baptist Convention. Pollard also pastored churches in Union Springs and Selma.

Pollard served as moderator of two associations. While pastor in Dallas County, he was moderator of the New Cahaba Association. During his years of pastorate in Montgomery at Dexter Avenue, Pollard became moderator of the Montgomery-Antioch Association. This was a new association, formed by consent of the Alabama Association, that included several churches in eastern Montgomery. The Montgomery churches felt they could be more effective in their urban mission efforts if they had their own association. As moderator, Pollard helped ensure a smooth and peaceful transition. He reminded delegates at the association's first meeting that they were making history and should conduct themselves as servants of God. During his two years as moderator, 1894–95, the association formed a Sunday school convention, gave financial support to Selma University, urged the support of black businesses, appointed a missionary, and promoted Baptist doctrine. In its quest for proper doctrine the association and Moderator Pollard often took a Landmarkist position. For example, when one church accepted a former Baptist who had joined a Methodist church into its membership, the association ruled that the returning member must be rebaptized by a Baptist minister.

Because of his effective work as pastor, moderator, and missionary, Pollard became secretary of the Alabama Colored Baptist State Convention. He held this position from 1887 to 1896. For two of the years, he was editor of the convention's *Baptist Leader*. While serving as secretary of the convention, Pollard resigned his pastorate of the Dexter Avenue Baptist Church to become general missionary under a cooperative agreement between the American Baptist Home Missionary Society and the Board of Missions of the Southern Baptist Convention. In that position, Pollard was responsible for the entire state but particularly the Montgomery District. Pollard conducted New Era Institutes, reporting to the *Home Mission Monthly,* journal of the American Baptist Convention, that he conducted a New Era Institute in March 1896 in Clanton, Alabama, where the average attendance for three days was 130 people. In 1897 Pollard became pastor of the First African Baptist Church in Eufaula.

In 1902 Pollard was elected president of Selma University, becoming the first Selma graduate to assume that position. Under his leadership the school prospered, with enrollment reaching seven hundred. Two brick buildings—Dinkins Hall and Foster Hall—were added to the campus, giving the school three brick buildings. The debt on the institution was also liquidated. In 1905 Pollard attended the organizational meeting of the Baptist World Alliance in London, England. He was not a mere spectator but contributed substantially to the organization's success. Moreover, his activities brought him in contact with leading Baptist figures from across the United States. His fame and prestige grew in Alabama as the university prospered and paid many of its lingering debts. Unfortunately, undisclosed differences with trustees at Selma University caused Pollard to resign from the presidency in 1911.

After leaving the presidency of Selma University, Pollard conducted institutes for the Home Mission Board of the Southern Baptist Convention as well as other mission agencies. In 1914 he became president of Florida Memorial College, the denominational school of the Florida Colored Baptist State Convention. As debts rose once again at Selma University, Pollard was urged by the Colored Baptist State Convention of Alabama to return as president of the institution. Apparently, previous conflicts that had caused him to leave Selma University had been resolved. Pollard resigned from Florida Memorial and returned to Selma as school president in 1916.

Pollard's second term as president, 1916 to 1930, was in many ways more successful than his first. During his second tenure, Dinkins Chapel, which he had built during his first term, burned. Sensing his grief over this loss, students gathered around Pollard to bemoan the failure of the too-little, too-late efforts to extinguish the fire. Their presence drew their beloved president out of his despair and he focused his thoughts on the future. "God will provide," he said, "He always has. We will rebuild the Chapel."[15] Under Pollard's leadership, Dinkins Chapel was rebuilt in 1921 at a cost of sixty-five thousand dollars.

In addition to rebuilding the chapel, Pollard erected a president's home, a teacher's cottage, and a teacher training center. Several lots were purchased across the street from the main campus, and enrollment increased from four hundred to seven hundred students. It would have been higher had there been enough dormitory space for all who wanted to attend. Some parents did not want their children living in the city of Selma.

One reason for Selma's increased enrollment was the expansion of course offerings under Pollard's leadership. In 1921 the institution had nine programs: college, teachers' professional, normal preparatory, college preparatory, theological, music, domestic science, sewing, and business. Though county training schools increased in Alabama during this period, these institutions emphasized industrial education. Selma University was one of the few schools in the Black Belt where blacks could enroll in a liberal arts high school and college program. Pollard reported in 1924 that 595 students of a total enrollment of 631 took some form of literary classes. Four years later, there were 244 high school students, 49 in the college program, and 58 ministerial students. In 1929, Pollard's last year as president, the school reported 228 students in the high school department and 69 in the college program. The institution graduated the largest class in its history that year: 25 from the college program and 42 from the high school.

Selma University's success during Pollard's second term is also attributable to his ability as a fund-raiser. He garnered funds from various foundations and religious groups; some estimates suggest that he raised over $1 million during his years as president. P. L. Lindsey, Pollard's nephew, said that when Pollard talked about Selma University it could bring tears to one's eyes. In addition to raising funds among black Baptist churches, Pollard continued to gain support from philanthropic sources and from white mission boards. He obtained funds from the American Baptist Home Mission Society, the Rosenwald Fund, the General Education Board, the John Slater Fund, the Women's Auxiliary of the American Baptist Home Mission Society, the Home Mission Board of the Southern Baptist Convention, and the National Ministers Institute. Like most black colleges during this period, Selma was always in need of funds and would accept money from any legitimate source. Though Pollard was able to garner donations from conservative boards that stressed industrial education, Selma University retained its focus on training preachers and teachers.

Pressures from institutional expansion, student recruitment, fund-raising, and building construction placed a heavy burden on Pollard. In his 1922 report he addressed the need to create better ways of funding the institution. He reported to the convention that the school was outgrowing its ability to maintain itself at the current funding level. The present system was inadequate because gifts, especially from Baptist churches, were not meeting needs. The school, he asserted, desperately needed an endowment. Selma University competed with state universities with larger budgets, and increasing operating costs were beginning to take their toll. In 1927 the Northwest District State Convention suggested that the state convention provide Pollard with a paid vacation for a month of rest. Pollard's last report, in 1929, revealed the many challenges that faced the institution. He reported an enrollment of 412 students, with 328 in the high school program, 25 in ministerial studies, and 69 in the college program. The school needed money for operational expenses, and teacher's salaries needed to be increased. Of 119 associations in the state, only 65 contributed to Selma University. Some buildings, like Foster Hall, had no heat, and the institution needed additional dormitories. Accreditation requirements also generated pressing needs. Literally exhausted from his years as president, Pollard resigned in 1929. The faculty presented him with a loving cup inscribed with these words of praise: "His wisdom was unfailing, and his industry untiring."

Although lacking the formal education achieved by many of the other presidents of Selma University—namely Brawley, Dinkins, Purce, and Gilbert—Pollard gained a degree of respect among Alabama Baptists that few others attained. His most noble attributes were dedication, honesty, and moral integrity. He was also hardworking and meticulous in business matters. Former students admired him as a thorough and excellent teacher and recalled that he was exceedingly approachable.

Above all, Pollard was motivated by strong values, and he advocated the need for trained minds and an educated ministry in elevating the black race. In a baccalaureate sermon delivered at Selma University titled "Man's Preeminence," Pollard used "how much is a man better than a sheep," as his text. In addressing the graduates, he expressed the things he found most valuable in man. According to Pollard, "man exists as body, mind, and spirit, but the body represents the least important aspect. The soul gains importance because it makes man a moral being and allows him to communicate with God. Of greatest significance, the mind marks the measure of the man. Through the mind, man exercises dominion over God's creation, discovering truth, the secrets of the universe, and possibilities for a better world." Pollard maintained that black uplift depended upon the race developing its mental capacity. In effect, man's true measure rested not in muscle but in intellect. He concluded by urging graduates to develop their minds and spirits. In doing so, "they would ensure that their lives would have purpose."[16]

Pollard also worked for an educated ministry. For him, ministry held the key to black uplift, and a worthy minister exhibited piety, a good name, and sound training. Pollard explained this conviction to the Alabama District Association, using "make full proof of thy ministry" as his text. Pollard laid out principles that would guide him in building Selma University to train men for the ministry. He asserted that "ministerial training constituted the world's highest calling. If people prove themselves unworthy, then God would give His work to others. Just as the doctor or the carpenter required training, so did the minister. That training rested in the Bible and in other good books." The Bible, he maintained, showed the need for training through the preparation of men like Moses, Paul, and the prophets. Moses spent eighty years in preparation for forty years of work, and Paul found it necessary to go to Arabia before going to Rome. Other prophets attended schools where they gained appropriate instruction. Pollard thanked God for theological classes and for Selma University where black ministers could be trained and thereby "make full proof of their ministry."[17]

Some pessimism was evident in 1927 when Pollard proclaimed in his president's report that with the present state of the ministry, "we cannot win." At that point, he believed that ignorance and immorality were still too prevalent in the black community. To counter the negative forces, Pollard encouraged Alabama Baptists to create greater incentives for an educated ministry. He then enumerated three tactics: "(1) churches must insist that ministers go to school; (2) pastors had to support an educated ministry; and (3) Selma University should provide a better education for its ministerial students. The latter must occur even if the school had to sacrifice something else."[18]

After resigning from the presidency, Pollard continued his love and passion for training ministers as dean of theology. He also conducted minister's institutes for Selma University. He taught his last class on Friday, January 14, 1938, suffered a heart attack two days later, and died at 4:45 on Monday morning. He is reputed to have said shortly before his death, "This is the hour and I am ready. I am safe in the Rock that is higher than I." His pastor, David V. Jemison, delivered his eulogy in which he asserted that "Pollard's life stood as a monument to young and old."[19]

Black Baptist Women

Black female Baptist leaders in the state joined the male leadership of the convention to support Selma University. In addition to making annual gifts to the school, Baptist women undertook projects to improve physical facilities and to raise funds for teachers. One of their major projects involved refurbishing Foster Hall. In 1927 President D. V. Jemison reported the women of the Alabama Women's Convention had raised more than six thousand dollars to complete the work on Foster Hall. In addition, he reported that they had paid the mortgage on the president's home.

In the 1930s, when the institution was desperately struggling to survive, women remained very active. In 1931 Baptist women raised funds to install hot water in the president's home. They also supported Selma University president William Dinkins's effort to raise money for the school through an Octagon Soap coupon drive. At the 1931 annual meeting, organizers reported that they had already raised fourteen hundred dollars through this effort.

Providing an instructor for the sewing class was a continuing project of Baptist women during the interwar years. Sewing was one of nine departments in the school. In 1934, 74 girls were enrolled in sewing classes. Within three years, 117 girls were enrolled. Mrs. R. T. Pollard, wife of the former president, was the instructor at that time. Although domestic science did not constitute a major thrust of the institution, black Baptist women realized the value of producing good homemakers.

Black Baptist women supported Selma University because it provided a Christian education. At the Alabama Baptist convention meeting that celebrated the jubilee of Selma University, Mrs. R. J. Fisher, secretary of the women's convention, praised the founders of Selma University as "master builders who laid a foundation that others could build on. They had formed a school that produced thinkers, men and women of good character, and persons with trained minds and regenerate hearts." These qualities were necessary, she believed, for achieving true manhood and womanhood. Fisher further stated that a school like "Selma University deserved to live on because Christian liberal arts colleges glorified God and the church, and produced worthy men and women. She added Selma's seven hundred graduates included great teachers, principals, preachers, doctors, and druggists." At the same celebration, Mrs. C. M. Wells, president of the Southeast District Women's Convention asserted that Selma University's greatest attribute resided in "its uncompromising teaching and doctrine, and in its fearless stand for faith, moral virtue, and righteousness."[20] Every annual session of the women's convention contained a report on Christian education. Some praised Selma for training the mind, the heart, and the hand, and all stressed the university's uniqueness in producing Christian students and teachers.

In addition to supporting Selma University, the women's convention focused on temperance, missions, and Christian training for young people. Annual reports contained strong diatribes against the evils of alcohol and tobacco, and delegates were urged to support prohibition. Temperance advocates identified alcohol as particularly damaging because of its evil effects on the home. The convention formed several young people's groups including the junior missionary societies and the Sunbeams. These groups sent youth delegates to annual convention meetings and to district gatherings. Leaders addressed the young delegates about the value of education and the importance of morality. Missions also received attention, and young people, as well as adults, received instruction on how to form various missionary organizations. Instructors demonstrated the model mission meeting, and President Henrietta Gibbs published mission guides for distribution to the various missionary societies.

Henrietta Gibbs, who served as president for most of the interwar period, established the tone of the convention for thirty-seven years, becoming president in 1922. Born in West Point, Mississippi, of humble, Christian parents, Henrietta married James Gibbs and moved with him to Montgomery where they joined Dexter Avenue Baptist Church. In addition to her work as president of the Women's Convention, Mrs. Gibbs served as president of the Alabama Federation of Colored Women's Clubs, as an official in the Eastern Star of Alabama, and as a trustee of Selma University. She was treasurer of the National Baptist Women's Convention for eleven years. Like other national Baptist women leaders who affiliated with the women's clubs, her dual leadership position provided opportunities to push for increased social services for black youth and greater rights for black women. She approached both causes with a vengeance, and partly through her efforts the city of Montgomery built Loveless School and the state of Alabama provided facilities for black youth at Partlow School. She was also instrumental in founding the State Boys' Industrial Center at Mt. Meigs, and she worked at Julia Tutwiler Prison for Women in Wetumpka.

An outspoken champion of women's right to vote, she is reputed to have been the first black woman to register in Montgomery in 1920.

In addition to her concern for missions, benevolence, social services, and women's rights, President Gibbs worked well with male leadership, despite demanding an active role for women's rights. The Women's Convention remained an auxiliary of the Alabama Baptist State Convention, and both Pollard and Jemison praised her efforts on behalf of Selma University and the state convention. Gibbs accepted their accolades but demanded that women be allowed to manage their own convention and be given a voice in the affairs of Selma University. Male leaders advised and preached to the Women's Convention, but only women served as voting delegates. In 1931, as the only female trustee of the university, Gibbs recommended that the state Baptist convention appoint two other female trustees from the Women's Convention. By 1937 there were three female trustees of Selma University. Obviously the male leaders respected her work and opinions.

Another evidence of Gibbs's leadership and contributions was the growth and expansion of the Women's Convention. In the early 1930s only about 50 societies were represented in the convention. By 1937 the organization counted 310 delegates, 44 district associations, and 96 societies. This growth included new organizations like the Sunbeams, Red Circle, Crusaders, Young Matrons, Royal Ambassadors, Young People, and Ministers' Wives, organizations that came into existence during Gibbs's presidency.

Varieties of Religious Expression

In spite of the strong emphasis among Baptist leaders for continuity and preservation, some changes did occur during this period. In general, black Baptist churches developed greater diversity in membership and in styles of worship. Though most black Baptists worshipped in the same churches they had before World War I, diversity among Baptist churches became more noticeable in the postwar era. Usually, the educational level of the minister and the parishioners was the key.

Some rural churches continued to resemble earlier institutions in both physical appearance and in worship style. For example, in 1934 Charles Johnson, a black sociologist, described a worship service at the Damascus Baptist Church, a rural church in Macon County. The building was a plank boxlike structure with a gabled roof and a small bell tower over the entrance. It had been whitewashed several times, but the ravages of time and the weather had turned the white to gray. Three rows of plain wooden benches faced the rostrum at the end of the room. The pastor sat behind it and three small benches were reserved for the choir. A coal stove stood beside the rostrum. A hat rack and an old clock that did not work completed the decor.

According to Johnson, the service was informal. Worship began with prayers and songs led by deacons. These songs included meter and lined songs, regular hymns, and spirituals. After this portion of the service the pastor came forward to preach. On this occasion, he preached about Paul's conversion on the Damascus road. He began by instructing the youth to get an education like Paul and not "shoot hookie." He then extolled the virtues of living a moral life, urging the congregation to abstain from dancing. The congregation encouraged the preacher in turn, especially as he proceeded to describe Paul's conversion with, "Amen," "Yes, Lord," "Preach it boy," and "Have mercy, Jesus." "Shouting began and the congregation moved literally in a frenzy. The preacher sat down in his chair and continued to preach while seated; this further aroused the congregation. A lined hymn followed the sermon, and then the deacons came forward to take the offering. The service concluded with the pastor giving the benediction.[21]

Not all services in rural areas were as informal and emotional as the Damascus Baptist Church. In the same Macon County community, Johnson described the sixtieth anniversary of the Macedonia Baptist Church. This service was more formal and structured, with a printed program distributed to the congregation. Two members presented papers, one on the history of the church and the other on the vision for the future. After singing, the pastor delivered his sermon. As the pastor preached on the importance of being faithful to the church and to Christ, shouting and some brief moaning erupted but much more restrained than at the Damascus Church. The pastor opened the doors of the church while the congregation sang a meter hymn, and the service concluded with an offering and a benediction.

Although both churches reflected black religious culture through their emotional worship services, the Macedonia Church reflected the impact of education. The Macedonia Church consisted of people who had attained more formal education than the parishioners at the Damascus Church, and they desired greater structure and order. Moreover, the minister at Macedonia had more formal training than the pastor of the Damascus Church. Even so, many Baptist churches, even in rural areas, demanded that their pastor have at least some education.

Benjamin Mays and John Nicholson, in their classic study of the African American church, found that a democratic spirit existed in most urban churches. In Birmingham of the 1920s and 1930s black Baptists of working and professional classes basically worshipped in the same churches. However, some smaller churches attracted almost solely people of the working class, while a few congregations catered almost exclusively to professionals.

According to Robert J. Norrell, some black Birmingham churches worshipped in a style similar to the Damascus Baptist Church. He described churches in the black ghetto called Bear Marsh, a twelve-block area southeast of the center of the city. Eleven small churches existed in this area, with some of them located in alleys where many of the people lived. Several of the congregations had been established by recent migrants who felt uncomfortable in the more formal settings of the larger churches. These churches were made up almost exclusively of working-class blacks. Their worship style was similar to that in small frame-structured, one-Sunday churches in the Black Belt where these migrants had once lived. A typical service was informal, and members were fond of saying "let the spirit have its way." Worship consisted of meter hymns, long prayers, spontaneity, shouting, and emotional preaching. Members responded to the choir's singing and the pastor's preaching with loud "amens" and "shouting." "Whooping" and chanted preaching, in which the preacher pitched his voice in a musical fashion to evoke emotions, remained popular in these churches."[22]

In contrast, the Sixteenth Street Baptist Church was composed almost exclusively of professional and middle-class black Baptists. The pastorate of William Pettiford determined the nature and character of Sixteenth Street Church. He was instrumental in the church getting its first significant building and worked to enlarge the membership. A well-educated minister with an aggressive ministry, Pettiford attracted upwardly mobile blacks and many professionals to Sixteenth Street. By the time Pettiford resigned in 1893, the church had become the leading African American black Baptist church in the city, attracting people of all classes but especially those Baptists who were considered professionals. In 1893, Sixteenth Street claimed 450 members including fraternal and Masonic leaders, teachers, and women's club officials.

Pastors who succeeded Pettiford were also educated. One of the most notable was Reverend Charles L. Fisher, who served two tenures as pastor from 1898 to 1911 and from 1921 to 1930. Fisher was probably the greatest scholar among black clergy in Birmingham at that time, having graduated from Baptist

Union Theological Seminary, now the University of Chicago Divinity School. During his second tenure, membership grew to more than a thousand. Services were spiritual but highly structured. Choirs sang a variety of songs, including anthems, and Fisher preached with scholarly emphasis. Even though some working-class people worshipped there, the church attracted the Baptist elite of the city's black community. When Fisher resigned in 1930, membership decreased due to internecine conflict that caused many members, especially working-class blacks, to leave.

Sixteenth Street continued to attract middle-class and professional blacks in subsequent years. T. C. Windham, one of the wealthiest black contractors in the South, served as chairperson of the trustee board. R. A. Blount, head of Alabama's largest Masonic lodge; P. D. Davis, local civic and business leader; and J. O. Diffay, the city's leading barber, also served on the board. Highly respected women members included Mrs. A. M. Brown and Mrs. L. M. Gaillard, who both served as president of the Women's Federated Clubs of Alabama. Other women of prestigious women's clubs, like the Periclean, Imperial, and Semplis Fidelis attended Sixteenth Street, as well as a host of teachers. Through the years the sons and daughters of Sixteenth Street members received their education from black colleges, with many returning to the city to assume leadership roles at the church. Sixteenth Street Church probably had the largest number of professionals of any African American church in the 1930s, and it developed a reputation for being a "class" church.

The Dexter Avenue Baptist Church of Montgomery was similar to Birmingham's Sixteenth Street Baptist Church in that it was composed primarily of professional blacks. Formed in 1877, Dexter Avenue began when a group of blacks withdrew from the First African Baptist Church and named themselves the Second Colored Baptist Church of Montgomery. The name changed later to Dexter Avenue Baptist Church. The church built a commodious brick structure in 1833 and became a center for many black civic meetings. Dexter Avenue called many of the most educated men in Alabama as pastor—C. O. Boothe, A. F. Owens, A. N. McEwen, and Robert T. Pollard. All these men supported orderly worship and structure. As the Montgomery community grew, upwardly mobile blacks and professionals gravitated to Dexter Avenue, including presidents, faculty, and staff members of Alabama State University. By the 1920s many of the leading educators, and business and civic leaders were members of the Dexter Avenue Baptist Church. It had, like Sixteenth Street in Birmingham, become the "class" Baptist church of the capital city.

New Music Forms

New music forms also entered many of Alabama's black churches during this period. Gospel music emerged during the Depression and challenged the more formal music in many of the larger churches. Some churches such as Sixteenth Street and Sixth Avenue in Birmingham, Dexter Avenue in Montgomery, and First African Baptist Church in Tuscaloosa installed pipe organs. These congregations then began singing more formal music rather than the meter hymns, spirituals, and jubilee songs of earlier years. The newer gospel songs were spontaneous and full of strong emotion. They were songs of faith that rallied the hopes and aspirations of people during the devastating social conditions of the Depression. Rising from urban settings where blacks suffered from poverty and dashed hopes, these songs with their intricate rhythms, strong beats, and alternated scales gave voice to blessings, sorrows, woes, and the joys of the afterlife. Gospel songs tended to be more individualistic and otherworldly than spirituals and jubilee songs, and Jesus rather than the Hebrew children became the dominant theme.

Whereas some pastors discouraged the singing of gospel songs, other forces were at work that helped bring the songs into black Baptist churches in Alabama. First, Pentecostal churches that claimed to represent the true religion of the black man featured gospel songs. As these congregations grew, their worship styles featuring gospel music made inroads into Baptist churches. Second, the 1921 edition of *Gospel Pearls* published by the Sunday School Publishing Board of the National Baptist Convention highlighted the importance of gospel songs. These renditions found a ready market in Alabama and appealed to many black congregations. Third, gospel singers like Sallie Martin, Roberta Martin, Kenneth Morris, and J. M. Gates, presented concerts in cities, increasing the popularity of gospel songs.

The main avenue for gospel singing in Alabama's black Baptist churches was through the emergence of "number two" choirs. At their founding, most churches had formed a choir, but by the 1920s singers in churches began to request an additional choir. In Birmingham the Sixth Avenue Baptist Church, the New Pilgrim Baptist Church, and the Zion Star Baptist Church organized number two choirs in the 1920s and 1930s. In Montgomery the First African Baptist Church started a similar choir during this period, and the Stone Street Baptist Church of Mobile began a number two choir in 1933. Younger adults who preferred to sing with their own age group gravitated to the new gospel singing that was making its way rapidly into the churches. Although both choirs sang gospel hymns, the new number two choirs specialized in the songs from the *Gospel Pearls* and later added the solo-oriented works of Tommy Dorsey and other gospel composers. By World War II, gospel music was well on its way to becoming the most popular choice in Baptist churches. Baptist churches accepted the new music faster than the Methodist churches, which was another reason Baptist churches grew more rapidly.

During the interwar years, both old and new forms of worship were evident in black Baptist churches. Ministers preached on familiar, traditional themes, while gospel music and a variety of religious experiences introduced changes into church services. Baptist leaders worked diligently to preserve Selma University and promote black businesses. World War II proved to be a catalyst for race relations in the nation. Like other black leaders, pastors in Alabama championed a new militancy calling for the end of segregation and full rights for African Americans. In addition, Alabama Baptists became a significant part of black Baptist leadership on a national level.

9
Rising Militancy

World War II gave rise to a new militancy in the African American community. Having experienced a degree of desegregation during the war, African Americans increasingly insisted on full rights and freedoms. While some civil rights historians have focused on the period after *Brown v. Board of Education*, they have obscured the importance of the period immediately after World War II for civil rights advocacy and the critical role of local black leaders. This is particularly true of Alabama. Black Baptist leaders in Alabama became an essential part of this new militancy while continuing as spiritual leaders and preservers of community institutions. Militancy found expression in sermons and addresses, in personal acts of courage, in community and civil rights activities, and in pastoral leadership among various chapters of the NAACP.

The Alabama Baptist State Convention struggled to maintain adequate funding for its departments and auxiliaries. Education remained the convention's major thrust, and the preservation of Selma University was its primary objective. Still, the institution continued to struggle financially, and a dispute arose over the type of education Selma should provide. Although most academies in the state closed, institutions in Birmingham and Montgomery survived and met significant educational needs for blacks in those communities.

Gospel choirs and soloists who had emerged during the Depression era increased in popularity. Gospel music reflected culture and pride and added to the emotional fervor that was important in most black Baptist churches. Congregations in both rural areas and cities were plagued by a number of contentious issues, but churches continued to be the central institution in the black community.

Challenging Jim Crow

While fighting for freedom abroad, blacks became more conscious of their own lack of freedom at home. This awareness led to growing protests in both the North and the South during World War II. Self-criticism revealed northern concerns over past acceptance of certain forms of segregation, and southern blacks began to openly challenge Jim Crow. The March on Washington movement typified this new militancy and heightened sense of race consciousness during the war years. In 1941 A. Philip Randolph called for a march on Washington D.C. to protest job discrimination in the defense industry. His tactic of mass pressure through a demonstration of black power struck a common chord among blacks. Approximately fifty thousand demonstrators pledged to march on Washington on July 1, 1941, but President Franklin Roosevelt's executive order establishing the President's Committee on Fair Employment Practices prompted organizers to cancel.

The formation of the committee reflected growing black political power in the country. During the 1930s blacks accumulated significant voting strength in northern states such as New York, New Jersey, Indiana, and Ohio. Moreover, the black vote had become an important element in the new coalition supporting the national Democratic Party. While blacks became more militant in asserting their political power, whites seemed more tolerant. Ideological confrontations with Adolf Hitler and Fascism in World War II forced many white Americans to see that racism existed in the United States. Many white Americans realized for the first time that white supremacy conflicted with the American ideals of liberty and equality. Recognition of this paradox spawned a climate for racial change during World War II and, to some extent, in the postwar decades. Supreme Court decisions of the 1940s played a role in facilitating tolerance and ushering in a more liberal racial climate. These factors—heightened consciousness among blacks, expanded power of the northern black electorate, and more tolerant attitudes on the Supreme Court and among many white Americans—combined to produce a greater sense of militancy in the black community.

Awakened by this increased militancy on the national level, blacks in Alabama responded more aggressively to discrimination. They protested as never before, and several new organizations emerged to champion black rights. In 1941 blacks formed the Alabama Federation of Colored Civic Leagues. Among other causes this organization championed voter registration efforts and promoted anticrime programs. In 1943 the Jefferson County Progressive Democratic Council was formed as a partisan political organization that supported Democratic Party candidates. Two of the most militant organizations that championed black rights were the United Mine Workers of America and the Communist Party. The NAACP remained the largest and best-known voice for

African Americans in the state, and it championed issues involving voting, job discrimination, and teacher salaries.

Inspired by the unparalleled militancy evident during and after World War II, black pastors and convention leaders gained a greater sense of urgency. Past calls for fair play and gradualism gave way to demands for immediate elimination of inequality. Pastors began to support movements led by laymen to obtain full rights for African Americans. Like laymen, pastors believed that wartime sacrifices and loyalty of blacks entitled them to freedom at home. Too, some black pastors who were graduates of historically black colleges had been exposed to the Social Gospel that stressed church involvement in changing the evils of society. Some of these college-trained pastors moved into Alabama energized to eliminate segregation. Unlike past pastoral leaders who saw no hope of overthrowing segregation because of a hostile national climate, these pastors sensed a more tolerant outlook among many whites that generated optimism in pressing for full freedom. Moreover, parishioners in churches pushed their pastors to stand up for their rights. As leaders enjoyed some freedom of action because of economic support from their churches, many pastors felt an obligation to express the new militancy of their congregations. All these factors contributed to a more militant group of black pastors in Alabama.

The new militancy first appeared during the war. Following the lead of the National Baptist Convention, USA, and other organizations within the state, black Baptist leaders encouraged blacks to support the war. President David V. Jemison insisted that since blacks had been loyal in every war the nation had fought, they should support this war effort as well. He supported a resolution calling for blacks to aid the government in its efforts to save the world from dictatorships. To show support in a tangible way, both the Alabama Baptist Convention and the Alabama Women's Convention bought liberty bonds.

Supporting the war did not keep black Baptists from being critical of the way blacks were being treated. When confronted with a report that declared black men were incompetent to fight in the war, President Henrietta Gibbs of the women's convention countered by arguing that any shortcomings resulted from injustice and lack of opportunity for black youth. She insisted that the United States must offer justice and equality to all its citizens if it were to continue as a great nation. The women's convention also encouraged black women to vote during the war years. Mrs. C. L. Fisher, convention secretary, exhorted black women to recognize the importance of voting in order to increase the number of blacks involved in politics. Gibbs added her endorsement to Fisher's statement, urging the women of the convention to register and vote. State convention president David Jemison contended that black morale was weaker than it had been during World War I because of numerous injustices. He called on the government to abolish legal injustice, to enforce equal accommodation in railroad travel, and to secure equal opportunities for black youth. Like other pastors in the state, Jemison supported a National Baptist Convention resolution that called on President Roosevelt to correct the abuses against black soldiers. The convention called on the president to ensure that an increasing number of blacks would be commissioned as officers and that they would be protected from white mobs and the Ku Klux Klan. The resolution concluded by asserting that "black soldiers were not receiving even the rights of democracy while preparing to fight a war in Europe for democratic ideals."[1]

After the war W. H. Perry, pastor of the Ebenezer Baptist Church of Birmingham, maintained that African Americans should enjoy the same freedom they had fought for in World War II. At a meeting of the Alabama Missionary Baptist State Convention, M. W. Whitt, chairman of the mission board, insisted that all "forms of discrimination, including disfranchisement, should cease." In the same speech, with city officials and several white pastors in the audience, he lashed out against segregated churches. Whitt made it clear that "any church that denied people the right to attend it because of race was not really a Christian church."[2]

Among pastors who took a militant stance, Vernon Johns, pastor of Montgomery's Dexter Avenue Baptist Church was the most outspoken. Born in Virginia in 1892, Johns studied at Virginia College and Seminary and at Virginia Union University. Later, he was a student at Oberlin School of Theology where he received a thorough course in the Social Gospel from Professor Edward Increase Bosworth. Briefly defined, the Social Gospel was the Christian philosophy developed in the late nineteenth century that advocated applying the teachings of Jesus Christ to the problems and evils of society. Initially, proponents addressed social challenges created in the United States by urbanization and industrialization. Johns developed a deep hatred for segregation and racial discrimination.

After pastoring several churches and serving briefly as president of Virginia College and Seminary, Johns became pastor of the Dexter Avenue Baptist Church in 1948. Beginning his ministry as a militant activist, Johns believed that a Christian should live a life of action and that the nation's debt to blacks for historic injustice was long overdue. In addition, he held a strong belief in black economic solidarity and an aversion to class division in the black community, which had caused him in his other pastorates to criticize what he considered the evils of the black middle class.

From the pulpit of Dexter Avenue Baptist Church, Johns preached to inspire his parishioners to fight segregation and discrimination. On at least two occasions, Johns was dragged before the local police for preaching militant sermons. In a sermon titled "Will There Be Segregation in Heaven?" Johns told the story of Dives, the rich man who opened his eyes in hell to see his servant, Lazarus, couched in the bosom of Abraham in heaven. Johns responded to his own query by asserting that "separation would occur, but that disavowed servants would rest in heaven while their evil oppressors were condemned to hell." Another sermon that was even more vexing to the white community came in response to an incident in which white police officers had stopped a black man for speeding and then beat him unconscious. Johns posted the upcoming sermon title on the bulletin board in front of the church: "It Is Safe to Murder Negroes in Montgomery." The Johns family received threatening telephone calls, and a cross was burned in front of the church, but Johns delivered the sermon as planned.[3]

In addition to his militant sermons, Johns also defied Montgomery's segregation laws. On one occasion he took a seat in the "whites only" section of a bus and was instructed to go to the back. The driver refused to move the bus, whereupon Johns demanded his money back. The refund was unprecedented, and Johns then invited the blacks and whites on the bus to follow him in protest. No one did. On another occasion Johns walked into a white restaurant and ordered a sandwich and a drink to take home. His request created a tense atmosphere, but the cook made the sandwich. Johns ordered and drank a glass of water, but he was forced to flee when a gang of whites pushed him from the restaurant.

Most members of the Dexter Avenue Church and blacks throughout Montgomery believed that Johns's methods were dangerous. Johns was also unpopular with many church members because of his outspokenness and a tendency to openly embarrass key members. However, a few members acted on Johns's teachings. In the fall of 1946, a group of Dexter Avenue members led by Dr. Mary Fair Burks, chair of the English Department at Alabama State College, organized the Women's Political Council. In addition to challenging segregation, this organization also sought to register blacks to vote and to improve their overall status. Over time, the group became more militant and formed the backbone for direct action protest that would take place between 1955 and 1960.

Johns's successor, Dr. Martin Luther King Jr., profited greatly from Johns's militancy. Becoming pastor of Dexter Avenue in 1954, King noted an air of indifference toward human rights among professionals in the black community. But Johns had created the beginnings of a social conscience among Dexter Avenue members by keeping incidents of racial discrimination in the forefront. Much of the groundwork for shifting a conservative congregation from complacency to boldness had been laid by Johns before King's arrival.

In Birmingham several pastors exhibited personal courage in their fight against segregation and racial injustice. Reverend James Lowell Ware was considered the "people's pastor" and the "city's most dependable advocate of equality."[4] Born in abject poverty in a sharecropper's cabin near Wetumpka, Ware developed an abhorrence of segregation and injustice against African Americans. After accepting a call to the ministry, he studied for a brief period at Selma University. He pastored several churches in rural Alabama, and then came to Birmingham in 1941 as pastor of the Trinity Baptist Church. He became involved immediately in activities designed to eliminate segregation and racial injustice. In 1949 he became president of the Birmingham Baptist Minister's Conference and later served as president of the Emancipation Proclamation Association. He worked at the state level as secretary of the Alabama Baptist State Convention, but he exerted his greatest influence in Birmingham.

Between 1941 and 1954 Ware objected to Jim Crow showings of the Freedom Train exhibit in Birmingham, protested against unequal salaries for teachers and the relocation of African Americans on Birmingham's Southside to build a hospital complex, and supported efforts to integrate the University of Alabama. Ware presided at mass rallies, made speeches, raised funds, and testified before city and other governmental agencies. In 1952 Ware accompanied Arthurine Lucy and Polly Myers to the University of Alabama. After Lucy's expulsion, he called a mass meeting in support of her readmission. In 1955 Ware delayed a trip to the National Baptist Sunday School and BTU Congress in order to serve as a witness in the NAACP suit to have Lucy readmitted. The suit resulted in a permanent injunction forbidding the university from denying admission to any student because of race.

Reverend Prince Vaughn, pastor of the Tabernacle Baptist Church and an active worker in the NAACP, was one of the black ministers who opposed the relocation of a Birmingham hospital. Because city officials had decided to place the university hospital complex on the Southside, many African Americans would be uprooted. The interracial committee, of which Vaughn was a member, sanctioned the city's decision, but the plan met with general disapproval in the black community. When Vaughn received word of the interracial committee's action, he resigned. In a letter to Bishop C. J. Carpenter, chair of the committee—a letter that Vaughn published in the *Birmingham World*—he listed three reasons for his resignation. He accused the committee of issuing a statement without his knowledge; he argued that the body had been established merely to pacify blacks; and he said members were afraid to express their true feelings. Vaughn's public actions were criticized by many influential whites and some blacks, but his protest highlighted the relocation issue and revealed the timidity of the interracial committee.

Reverend George Rudolph, an associate minister at Birmingham's Sixth Avenue Baptist Church, also exhibited great personal courage during this era. Harboring a deep resentment against segregation, Rudolph was appalled that the Birmingham police department refused to hire black officers, as some cities had done in the South. He led a one-man crusade to reverse that policy. He explained that he was afraid to act alone because he believed that God would protect him. In November 1954 he went to City Hall and made a personal plea to the city council. In June 1955 he returned to the council and renewed his request for hiring African American police officers. A few months later, he went before the city's personnel board to continue his push. Although his efforts were not successful, Rudolph's persistence was symbolic of the new militancy and activism that was emerging within the ministerial community.

In Tuscaloosa, Reverend W. B. Shealey personified the Baptist minister turned social activist. Born in Roanoke, Virginia, in 1908, Shealey was a precocious child whose parents sought to give him every opportunity for an education. After graduating from Randolph County Training School, young Shealey enrolled in Morehouse College. After two years of study there he was compelled to withdraw and secure work. After a short career in teaching, he entered Selma University where he studied as a special student in the College and Theology Departments. In the fall of 1934 he returned to Morehouse College and graduated with an A.B. degree. After pastoring several churches in Alabama, including the Fist Baptist Church of Union Springs and the Union Baptist Church of Gadsden, Shealey enrolled at Andover Newton Seminary in Massachusetts, while pastoring the Shiloh Baptist Church at Newport, Rhode

Island. After graduating from Andover Newton, he became academic dean at the American Baptist Theological Seminary.

While a student at Morehouse, Shealey gained inspiration from president Benjamin Mays. In his Tuesday chapel addresses, Mays urged students to reject all forms of Jim Crow and to develop their minds to the fullest. This instruction complemented Shealey's exposure to the Social Gospel at Andover Newton Seminary, which emphasized the church's role in addressing social problems. When he accepted a call to the First African Baptist Church in Tuscaloosa, Shealey brought these convictions with him.

As pastor of First African, Shealey preached against segregation and discrimination. He became active in the NAACP and in various ministerial organizations. First African became the scene of several NAACP mass meetings, and the church served as headquarters for the 1951 state meeting of the NAACP. Shealey's community messages challenged Tuscaloosa blacks to fight against Jim Crow and other injustices. At a Better Business Program sponsored by Phi Beta Sigma fraternity, Shealey spoke on "the hope of the race." In encouraging blacks to think, he insisted that "blacks could achieve first-class citizenship only through wisdom, clear thinking, and common sense." He also urged his audience to develop economic power and a sense of unity among all classes of the black race.[5]

As time passed, Shealey grew impatient with the slow rate of change in Tuscaloosa. In 1952 he joined the Tuscaloosa Religious Council in demanding that the public safety commissioner add four black policemen to the city's police force. Shealey also cooperated with a group of white professors from the University of Alabama and other black ministers to form an organization known as the Tuscaloosa Improvement Association. Meanwhile, he had alienated some of his parishioners with his refusal to have Sunday funerals at First African Church. Facing rising opposition from whites in the city and conflict within his church, Shealey accepted a pastorate in New Jersey. Shealey's ministry paved the way for his successor, Reverend T. Y. Rogers, who would lead the civil rights movement in Tuscaloosa during the 1960s.

Like individual ministers who became increasingly active in pushing for legal and social reforms, ministerial conferences moved toward a militant stance after World War II. The Tuscaloosa Ministerial Association voted in 1951 to demand that the Interstate Commerce Commission and heads of the Southern and Louisville & Nashville Railroad end segregation. This action came in the wake of a train wreck at Woodstock, Alabama. Because black passengers were confined to segregated cars, in defiance of the Supreme Court's ruling on interstate travel, they sustained 80 percent of the fatalities. The ministerial association referred to the railroad company's refusal to obey the federal mandate as undemocratic and un-American. They pointed out that "black soldiers were dying in Korea; therefore all segments of American society should receive decent and equitable treatment."[6]

The Birmingham Baptist Minister's Conference refused to participate with whites in any segregated activity. Black ministers declined an invitation to join a festival of faith rally at Legion Field in 1947 when they discovered that the meeting would be a segregated affair. Two years later, the conference opposed segregated participation of African Americans in the Christmas Festival Parade. In 1950 the conference opposed African American participation in the Christmas Festival Parade for similar reasons. That same year, black ministers objected to traveling with whites to the National Baptist Convention when members discovered that a curtain would segregate the passengers. In 1953 the group also refused to participate in an Easter egg hunt sponsored by a white company in a segregated park. President J. L. Ware declared that those blacks who supported the event were "tomming for a mess of eggs."[7]

The Birmingham Baptist Minister's Conference also ostracized any of its members who supported segregation. One such group opposed to desegregation was the Southern Negro Improvement Association (SNIA) formed in 1954. Its leaders warned fellow blacks that attempts to force integration would rekindle race hatred and set the race back at least twenty-five years. Instead of agitation, they counseled that African Americans should improve themselves and remain decent; eventually they would receive the rights accorded other citizens. This group included some African American ministers who opposed any mingling of religion with politics. They insisted that pursuing issues like racial equality would diminish their religious influence. One member of the SNIA was Dr. Collier P. Clay, who operated a school to train ministers at the First Baptist Church of Fairfield and was former president of Easonian Baptist Seminary. In January 1955 he delivered a speech in Notasulga in which he endorsed segregation. When news of Clay's speech reached Birmingham, members of the Birmingham Baptist Minister's Conference responded with a barrage of criticism. The conference set a date for dealing with Clay and other ministers who belonged to the SNIA. In February 1955 the conference voted sixty-three to two to expel Clay and Reverend C. J. Glaze, another member of the association.

Baptist ministers also demonstrated their growing militancy by assuming greater leadership roles in the NAACP. The NAACP's success in desegregating graduate education impressed many pastors. Reverend W. C. Autrey was impressed by the way the NAACP scored victories over southern whites and in 1948 he became a charter member of the Luverne chapter. When he became a pastor in Ozark, he became an active member of the NAACP chapter in that city.

In Tuskegee, black Baptist ministers proved instrumental in getting the NAACP started. In Mobile several prominent black Baptist leaders served on the executive board, including D. V. Jemison, president of the Colored Baptist State Convention, and U. J. Robinson, secretary of the Baptist Convention. Laymen led the Montgomery chapter, but meetings were held in black churches, and pastors sponsored programs in their churches to advance the 1948 membership drive. Reverend J. D. Hunter served as president of the Selma chapter of the NAACP.

In no city in Alabama were Baptist ministers more active in the NAACP than Birmingham. Many laypersons, faced with threats of violence and significant economic pressure after the war, abdicated leadership and left the organization. To fill the void, ministers stepped forward into and assumed greater leadership roles. Four Baptist ministers—J. L. Ware, R. L. Alford, Prince Vaughn, and R. R. Hayden—were elected president of the branch's NAACP after the war, but two did not serve. Reverend J. L. Ware was elected president in December 1954 but in January 1955 announced that he would not continue his duties; he gave no explanation for this decision. The Reverend Prince Vaughn was elected president in December 1954 but resigned after accepting a pastorate in Rockford, Massachusetts, in January 1955. Alford, pastor of the Sardis Baptist Church, was elected president in 1950 and served for two years, and Hayden served one year as president. All four of these pastors were elected to the presidency after 1948, when the group began to decline in membership because of external intimidation and internecine conflict. One underlying motive in electing pastors was to attract members of the working class to the organization. Because pastors typically were close to the people, many believed they could attract new members better than others.

Pastors served in other capacities in the Birmingham NAACP, including membership on the executive board, vice president, and as chairmen of key committees. On many occasions pastors spoke at NAACP programs. In 1947 the Birmingham branch instituted NAACP Sunday in the city's churches to build awareness of the organization and to raise funds. On NAACP Sunday in 1949, at least twenty-six churches collected funds for the local branch. Occasionally, churches in local communities held mass meetings to support the NAACP. For example, in 1951, seven churches of the Enon Ridge community came together to raise funds for the organization's educational efforts.

Alabama Baptist State Convention

Meanwhile, the Alabama Baptist State Convention continued to operate through four boards: executive, missions, publishing, and education. The executive board's primary task was to make operational decisions for the convention between annual meetings. The mission board had a general superintendent and four district workers. All five men were pastors or former pastors who visited churches to report on the work of the convention and to request contributions for the convention's work. The publishing board financed and operated the convention's major paper, the *Baptist Leader*. Editor and publisher of the paper during this period was Reverend W. H. Smith of Birmingham, who was diligent in getting the paper out on a weekly basis. The education board of the convention consisted of the Selma University trustees. After C. L. Fisher's death, M. C. Cleveland of Montgomery became chairman of the board and served in that capacity until 1971. The convention also included a benefits department that gave small stipends to retired or sick pastors.

In addition to its boards, the convention was divided into four districts, or wings: northeast, northwest, southeast, and southwest. Originally the wings maintained contact with rural churches and pastors who did not attend the state convention. By 1939 they had become important for fund-raising. Presidents of the district conventions were also convention vice presidents and charged with the responsibility of promoting the programs of the state convention. The Northeast Convention was the strongest of the wings and reported a total contribution of $256.50 in 1939. R. N. Hall was president of the Northwest Convention; other presidents were P. H. Brown, J. L. Mathis, and R. H. Williams.

The Alabama Colored Baptist State Convention also operated three auxiliary organizations: the Sunday School Congress, the Baptist Training Union Congress, and the Women's Baptist State Convention of Alabama. The Sunday School Congress, led by H. C. Walker of Dothan, promoted Sunday school work in local churches. The Baptist Training Union Congress, under the presidency of W. C. Campbell of Waugh, did not grow as rapidly as the Sunday School Congress because there were fewer Baptist Training Union organizations in local churches. The Women's Convention expanded rapidly under the leadership of Henrietta Gibbs. In 1953 there were 615 delegates enrolled, representing 306 missionary societies and 72 district conventions. This convention included a Young People's Department, Sunbeam Bands, Young Matrons, Crusaders, Young People, Ministers' Wives, and Deacons' Wives.

The women's convention led the way in supporting Selma University. The convention continued to provide a sewing teacher, with Mrs. R. T. Pollard serving in that capacity for thirty years. Mrs. Etta Collins succeeded her in 1948. As early as 1940 women supplied the institution with coal and brought food for the dining hall each year. After each annual convention, the group made a sizable gift to Selma University. In 1946 the women's convention raised $9,040.37, nearly half of which was given to Selma University for operating expenses. In 1954 President Gibbs reported that the convention donated $10,536.76 for that year's operational expenses. In addition, the women's convention retired many institutional debts. In 1942 the convention liquidated an unpaid grocery bill of $2,640.00, and the following year the convention paid two notes on money borrowed for teacher's salaries. In 1953 the women's convention presented a new dining hall to the trustees that they had erected at the cost of $42,418.84. It was a debt-free building, which included all the equipment for the kitchen, dining hall, and lounge. The dining hall was named for President H. M. Gibbs who pioneered the project.

Officers of the convention in 1954 were Henrietta Gibbs, president; E. M. Moton, vice president; C. E. Powell, recording secretary; A. W. Wilson, corresponding secretary; M. B. Gaillard, treasurer; and V. A. McGhee, historian. Auxiliary leaders included Corenne Watts, supervisor of the Junior Missionary Societies; R. L. Perry, supervisor of Sunbeam Bands; Pauline Thomas, supervisor of matrons; Bessie Washington, supervisor of Crusaders; W. A. Jones, supervisor of pastors' wives; and Ella Lamar and Ella Collins, cosupervisors of the deacons' wives. District state presidents were Lola M. Hayes, northeast; Lillie C. Burnett, northwest; A. A. Wright, southwest; and Ruth Walker, southeast.

Selma University and Controversy

Selma University remained the main project of the convention. Black Baptists took pride in their religious institution, one of only a few schools that remained under black Baptist control. The school was consistently in debt and often operated at a deficit. In 1949 the institution owed creditors a total of $81,251.41. At that year's convention, President David V. Jemison encouraged delegates to raise at least $20,000 to stave off even worse financial conditions. In her presidential address one year later, Henrietta Gibbs bemoaned the institution's large debt. Despite its financial woes, Selma University continued to educate hundreds of students, and it remained one of the few schools in the Black Belt where African American students could attain a high school diploma.

William Hovey Dinkins, son of Selma University's fifth president, C. S. Dinkins, served as president for most of the immediate postwar period. Dinkins had spent much of his life at Selma as student, instructor, and academic dean before becoming president in 1932. A fine scholar and schoolmaster, he earned a B.A. degree from Brown University, where he was also a member of Phi Beta Kappa, and a master's degree from Columbia University. Dinkins envisioned Selma as an institution that would meet the educational needs of black students from elementary school through college. From 1932 to 1950 Selma provided four-year programs that included a classical degree, a theological degree, and a regular college degree. The school also offered programs leading to a junior college degree or a high school diploma. In addition, the university operated auxiliary schools at elementary and junior high school levels. Selma University's enrollment remained high during the Dinkins years. In 1939 enrollment was 559; the student body increased to 707 by 1945. In 1949 it was 597. Even as overall enrollment peaked in the mid-1940s, college enrollment remained small. Of the 707 students enrolled in 1945, only 79 participated in college programs.

Selma University found its college program and accreditation falling behind other black Baptist schools. Unlike Selma, other historically black denominational schools had closed their precollege programs in order to concentrate on the college curriculum. The board of trustees and convention leadership agreed that the time had come for Selma University to move in the same direction. In his 1949 address, President David Jemison voiced support for the trustees' initiative to eliminate the elementary and junior high schools. He also strongly supported accreditation efforts, assuring the convention that accreditation would not detract from the school's religious emphasis but make the university better. Jemison forcefully proclaimed that there was "no need to fuss about this because the truth is the truth and it matters not what some may say, Selma University should be accredited."[8]

Dinkins, on the other hand, strongly opposed eliminating the elementary and junior high school programs. In his final report to the convention in 1949, he stated that he could not preside over the dissolution of the school. He pointed out that he and the trustees had agreed to serve all the educational needs of black Baptists. He further maintained that current needs called for the retention of the lower grades. Dinkins informed the convention that he would not stand for reelection when his term expired on June 1, 1950.

Dinkins's resignation and the trustees' decision to maintain only the college, the theology department, and high school programs to serve ministerial students caused a split among black Baptists. Some graduates of Selma University, such as M. W. Whitt, pastor of the Harmony Street Baptist Church in Birmingham, defended Dinkins. Whitt stated that when he came to Selma University he entered the junior high school, and he argued there remained others who needed training below the college level. "The breadth of Selma's programs," Whitt contended, "was what made Selma University both unique and great." Many others echoed Whitt's sentiments and some withheld funds from the institution in protest. In his 1950 address, President D. V. Jemison maintained that Selma University was in crisis, and he urged the delegates to give as much money as possible so the college could operate successfully during the winter months.[9] In 1951 the university began to phase out other programs and emphasize its college curriculum. President C. Lopez McAllister, former dean of theology, presided over the reduction in programs, but he left after a few years because of the institution's continuing financial struggles.

Educational Efforts in Birmingham and Mobile

In addition to supporting Selma University, Baptists in Birmingham and Mobile continued their support of other educational efforts. Baptist academies and institutions in other areas of Alabama were phased out because of a lack of funds and the growth of public schools. Some of these institutions were taken over by the state and eventually became county high schools. However, because of the large number of churches in Birmingham and Mobile, Baptist institutions persisted in those cities.

The most ambitious educational project sponsored by Birmingham Baptists was Birmingham Baptist College. This school traced its origins to 1904, when C. O. Boothe and W. R. Pettiford conducted classes in the basement of the Sixteenth Street Baptist Church. Gradually, the idea of a school to train ministers and Christian leaders began to emerge. In 1913 three associations—Mt. Pilgrim, Bethlehem-Blount Springs, and Peace Baptist—gave up their individual schools and formed Birmingham Baptist College. The state granted a charter in 1913, and an educational association directed and owned the institution.

After moving to several different locations, including East Thomas, the trustees finally settled on its present-day location in Powderly in the southwestern section of Birmingham. J. W. Goodgame, pastor of the Sixth Avenue Baptist Church and chairman of the board of trustees, directed the purchase of ten acres of land. The school's first structure housed a dining hall and library on the first floor, administrative offices and classrooms on the second floor, and dormitory space on the third floor. In the early years three men served as president: J. H. Eason, W. A. Davis, and J. S. Saunders. The school was forced to close during the 1930s. Unable to pay teachers and facing mortgage debt of $23,000, the trustees leased the school's buildings to the Jefferson County Board of Education.

The institution reopened in 1937 in the Sunday school annex of the Sixth Avenue Baptist Church, with J. H. Wrenn serving as dean. During the time the school was closed, Wrenn and his assistant, T. D. Bussey, held classes in various churches. Finally in 1947, Wrenn and Bussey were able to satisfy debtors and classes resumed on the Powderly campus. Wrenn did much to foster a scholarly atmosphere on campus. A graduate of Selma University and State University of Kentucky, he was an excellent Bible teacher and was proficient in Greek and Hebrew. Former students remembered him as the greatest scholar among black Baptists in Birmingham during the interwar years. R. N. Hall, the editor of the *Baptist Leader,* called him one of the greatest scholars in the nation. During Wrenn's tenure the institution remained small, graduating only six ministers in 1939, and they received Bible certificates instead of degrees. Nonetheless the school rendered a valuable service. Many people who became pastors and denominational leaders in the Birmingham area graduated from the Baptist College during this period. In spite of a small student body and limited funding, Wrenn was able to attract excellent and qualified teachers. He and T. D. Bussey were joined in 1940 by W. H. Perry, O. C. Thomas, and J. S. Saunders. Saunders graduated from Birmingham Baptist College, and both Thomas and Perry were graduates of Morehouse College.

When President Wrenn resigned to work at Easonian Seminary, Bussey became president of the college. Born in Camden, Alabama, in 1897, Bussey attended Camden Academy. He moved to Birmingham where he joined the Sixth Avenue Baptist Church. After graduating from Birmingham Baptist College in 1926, Bussey joined the school's faculty. To prepare himself as a teacher, he attended Alabama State University and in 1946 graduated from Miles College with a bachelor of arts degree. Under Bussey's leadership, Birmingham Baptist College expanded. The institution added a night school for ministers, as well as a junior high school, high school, kindergarten, and ministers' wives program. The school continued to grow as churches in Birmingham and the vicinity increasingly called Baptist College graduates as pastors.

Funding for the college came primarily from the Mt. Pilgrim, Peace Baptist, Jefferson County, and Bethlehem Blount Associations. These churches commissioned pastors and mission leaders to form the Educational Association of Birmingham, which was the official owner of the institution. The Educational Association elected a board of trustees that made policy and recommendations for the school and advised on the selection of the president and instructors. William Atmore, moderator of the Mt. Pilgrim Association, served as chairman of the board for many years.

A second school of Bible and theological instruction emerged in Birmingham's black Baptist community. Easonian Baptist Seminary grew from the vision of J. H. Eason who was forced to leave Birmingham Baptist College. Eason argued that the name "Baptist" should be removed from the school's name so it could more easily attract students from other denominations. The trustees refused to make the change and did not renew Eason's contract. Eason responded by forming Easonian Seminary, a school intended as an interdenominational institution. Eason's seminary began in Selma as a correspondence school, but its headquarters moved to Birmingham in 1937. Its first commencement was held at the Thirgood CME Church. Eight graduates received Bible diplomas at the first commencement. Reverend C. J. Baker, pastor of Miller Memorial Presbyterian Church, was on the faculty as well as a cross section of people from other denominations. Shortly after the 1937 commencement, the institution became affiliated with the New Era Progressive State Convention. The convention placed strong emphasis on training for Baptist leadership. Eason became the school's first president, and it was named Easonian Baptist Seminary in his honor.

Like their counterparts in Birmingham, black Baptists in Mobile also established a school; it was named Cedar Grove Academy. The vision for a school that served the educational needs of Mobile's youth began with A. N. McEwen, pastor of the Franklin Street Baptist Church and moderator of the Mobile Sunlight Association. The association purchased seventeen acres of land for a total cost of five hundred dollars. Reverend C. S. English organized the construction of the first building and classes began in 1913. The moderator, E. A. Palmer, was instrumental in paying off the loan and securing the deeds for the land. Palmer, an advocate of young preachers, was convinced that a trained ministry was essential for a vibrant church life. He added ministerial training and organized night classes for ministers. In 1942 the school closed because of lack of funds, and students in the academic department were forced to attend other public and private schools. However, the work among the ministerial students continued because pastors U. J. Robinson and B. B. Williams taught without compensation.

Palmer became convinced that the institution could expand its programs beyond the training of ministers if a more modern building were erected. Envisioning a Christian high school, he began to raise funds for a modern school building. After twenty years of fund-raising, Palmer had acquired forty thousand dollars, and the association gave its permission to build a new brick building. The new structure consisted of eight classrooms and an assembly room, but for the next five years, the school served only the night theological school for ministers and laypersons.

Palmer's vision became a reality in 1958 when Allen Institute, a private school for blacks in Mobile, closed. Charles A. Tunstall, principal of the institute and pastor of the Stone Street Baptist Church, proposed that Cedar Grove Academy be reopened and former students of Allen Institute be offered an opportunity to study there. With strong support from Moderator Palmer, the school opened with Charles Tunstall as principal. His first session opened with five hundred students in twelve grades.

Supremacy of Gospel Music

While black Baptists gave much emphasis to education, nothing was more important in their church worship than gospel music. Its popularity soared after World War II. By the 1940s, it had replaced spirituals and jubilee songs as the most popular music, and gospel choirs and number two choirs proliferated in churches.

Gospel music and spirituals had much in common. Both provided a sense of the immediate and living presence of God, and each style included songs of aspiration and affirmation. But there were important differences as well. Gospel music tended to be otherworldly, proclaiming that this world would have toil and tribulation but that peace would come in heaven. Also, Jesus rather than the Hebrew children was the dominant figure in gospel songs. Another important distinction was that spirituals were almost always performed antiphonally by the entire congregation, whereas gospel music frequently featured soloists and choir singing. It rallied the hopes and aspirations of blacks, especially those in urban areas who were faced with blatant discrimination, dashed hopes, and crushing poverty.

The rising popularity of gospel music in the black community after World War II can be attributed in part to the singer Mahalia Jackson. Born in a three-room shotgun shack in New Orleans, Mahalia early absorbed the music from the Plymouth Rock Baptist Church, local brass bands, Dixieland jazz, and the blues records of Bessie Smith. All these sounds blended into the music she brought to Chicago in 1928. Unappreciated in the larger churches of Chicago, Mahalia began to sing in smaller storefront churches. Discovered by Thomas A. Dorsey, she sang his arrangements for Baptist conventions and the various churches around the country. Her first recording, "God Shall Wipe Away All Tears" was for Decca Records in the mid-1930s. In 1946 she brought gospel music out of the storefront churches and basement congregations by recording "Move Up a Little Higher," which sold more than 8 million records on the Apollo label. Benefiting from post–World War II communications, she became better known as a recording and performing artist. From 1954 to 1955 she hosted her own CBS radio program and television show. Mahalia became an international celebrity and helped prepare the public for later gospel and soul singers.

For black Baptist churches in Alabama, the music department of the National Baptist Convention was also important in shaping the popularity of gospel music. Lucie Campbell, known affectionately as "Miss Lucy" and J. Robert Bradley proved significant in this regard. Miss Lucy headed the music department of the National Baptist Convention in the 1940s and 1950s, and she arranged forty-five published compositions. Among her most famous were "Heavenly Sunshine," "He'll Understand and Say Well Done," "Something Within," and "Touch Me Lord Jesus." Choirs in black Baptist churches throughout the United States began to sing her songs.

J. Robert Bradley was a gospel soloist who popularized the compositions of Lucie Campbell and Thomas Dorsey. Born in 1920 in Memphis, Tennessee, Bradley grew up in abject poverty. Early in his life, he had a strong bass voice and a talent for singing. As a teenager, he sang in the churches of Memphis, and in 1933 Lucie Campbell introduced him to the National Baptist Convention. At thirteen, he became known as the "little boy with the big voice." This title served as a springboard for Bradley's long and fruitful career with black Baptists. He worked for a number of years at the publishing board of the National Baptist Convention and went on goodwill tours sponsored by the convention in order to pay off publishing house debts. The tours spanned the entire United States, and his fame grew as a gospel singer. After returning from studies in Europe, he became the major soloist at all National Baptist Convention meetings, and by the 1950s, he participated in numerous events, including church concerts across the nation. He accompanied well-known evangelists like the Reverend C. A. W. Clarke of Texas, but he spent much of his time in Alabama, especially in Birmingham, where he was always in great demand.[10]

Mable Williams was the premier gospel singer among black Baptists in Alabama. Mable Williams excelled as church musician, pastor's wife, and denominational organist. Born in East Lake, Alabama, in 1902 to William and Drucilla DeVaughn, she was one of eight children. Her father was a steel worker and her mother a housewife. Her industrious father bought his own home and some additional land in the eastern section of Jefferson County. Williams professed faith in Christ at an early age and was baptized by Reverend R. N. Hall of the Mt. Zion Baptist Church. As a young child, she expressed a deep faith in God and was instrumental in bringing her brothers and sisters to Christ. Blessed with a strong soprano voice, Mable began to sing in her church choir. She took music lessons from Georgia Miller and became a pianist at the Mt. Zion Church. After receiving her early educational training at Zion City Elementary and Junior High Schools, Mable enrolled in the high school program at Selma University.

After completing her studies at Selma University, Williams returned home and served as musician for several churches in the Birmingham area, including First Baptist Church, Mountain Park; New Hope Baptist Church; and St. Mark Baptist Church of Avondale. In addition, she performed as guest soloist for many programs sponsored by district associations. During one solo performance at the Mt. Pilgrim Association Institute, she attracted the attention of Reverend E. W. Williams, pastor of the First Baptist Church, Fairfield, Alabama. After a brief courtship, they were married.

As a pastor's wife, Mable helped build First Baptist, Fairfield, into one of the largest churches in the state. She served as the church's organist and minister of music. One choir member remembered her as a hard worker and perfectionist: "When Mable Williams came to rehearsal with a towel, used to wipe her face, choir members knew they were in for a long evening."[11] When First Baptist began to broadcast over radio station WBCO, the singing of Mable Williams did much to draw new members to the church. She also organized a literary guild, taught a Sunday school class, and was active in the missionary society. She had opportunities to become a traveling gospel singer like Bradley and others but chose to remain at First Baptist Church to work with her husband.

In addition to her enormous talent as a soloist and musician, Mable Williams was also well known because she was the wife of E. W. Williams, who was a leader in the Alabama and National Baptist Conventions. She became the organist for the Peace Baptist Association of Birmingham, the Alabama Baptist State Convention, the Alabama Baptist Sunday School and Baptist Training Union Congress, and the National Baptist Convention. In addition, she was selected as organist for the U.S. delegation to the Baptist World Alliance that met in London in 1955. As organist for the National Baptist Convention, she played for Robert Bradley and other groups, performed solos, and popularized songs composed by Lucie Campbell.

Traveling to various denominational meetings throughout Alabama, Williams popularized the gospel music of Dorsey and Campbell. As head musician for Alabama Baptist Convention she often went to cities before convention meetings to organize convention choirs composed of musicians and choir members from local churches. Her fame as a musician grew, and songs that she performed at the Alabama conventions spread to churches across the state.

The key to Mable Williams was deep spirituality and God-given natural ability. Although she received little formal musical training, she had supreme confidence in herself and was a hard worker. She was an accomplished soloist and organist who could lift the spirits of her audience. One of her contemporaries recalled that Williams had "God in her soul and it came out in a powerful way as she played the organ or sang. When she played, audiences shed tears accompanied by shouting and celebration."[12] Others testified that she brought audiences at the National Baptist Convention to near pandemonium. Among her favorite songs were "Amazing Grace," "Precious Lord," "It Pays to Serve Jesus," "Guide Me O Thou Great Jehovah," "At the Cross," "Father I Stretch My Hands to Thee," and "There's Not a Friend Like Jesus."

Rural Church Life and Persistence of Rural Patterns in Urban Churches

In spite of the rising militancy of pastors and the increased movement of blacks to urban areas, black Baptist churches continued to be influenced by rural patterns and faced various problems during this period. Rural churches were limited in their ministries because rural ministers served several congregations, some as many as five. These ministers usually followed a pattern of coming to the community on one Saturday night a month, holding a deacons' meeting or church business meeting, staying in the home of a deacon, and presiding over the Sunday worship service. On other Sundays, the churches conducted Sunday school under the direction of a lay superintendent. Typically, missionary societies met once a month under the leadership of the lay president. These societies provided aid and assistance to the poor, sick, and needy, and sometimes conducted special fund drives for the Alabama Women's State Convention.

The major event in most rural churches was homecoming and the annual revival, which took place during the summer. Homecoming was the time when former members, many of whom had moved to the cities, were invited back for a special service of remembrance. The annual revival that began on Monday night following homecoming activities held special appeal as well. A guest preacher, usually a minister who could preach traditional sermons like the "Prodigal Son" and the "Eagle Stirreth Her Nest" and also had the ability to stir the congregation emotionally, was invited. The visiting minister stayed with a family in the community, and members ate meals on the church grounds. The Sunday after homecoming and revival was the day of baptism, when candidates were led to the local creek with singing and fanfare to be immersed.

In general, two types of rural pastors existed in Alabama during this period: the professor-pastor and the farmer-pastor. Farmer-pastors were often people of limited training who farmed during the week and traveled to their church on Saturday. Some lived in the same communities as their church members. Professor-pastors were primarily principals or teachers in black schools who preached in churches on Sunday morning. In some cases in the Alabama Black Belt, churches housed the schools where the pastor taught. In Gees Bend, located in Wilcox County, the local Baptist church included a one-room school in the 1940s.

Wilson Fallin Sr., who served several churches in rural Alabama during the 1940s, is a good example of the professor-pastor. Born in 1908 to teachers Bruell and Josie Fallin, Fallin received his early education in the public schools of Coosa County. In 1930, he entered Selma University, completing high school in 1932 and junior college in 1934. In 1937 he was licensed and ordained to the ministry. He entered Alabama State Teacher's College, receiving his bachelor of science degree in 1940.

Fallin combined his work as educator and pastor, serving several rural churches while teaching in public schools from 1938 to 1953. He pastored the

Shiloh Baptist Church of Eclectic; Mt. Zion at Central; Mt. Nebo at Coosa County; and Beulah at Tallassee. Meanwhile, Fallin worked as an instructor at Slater School and Benson Junior High in Alexander City and at Tallassee Junior High School.

Like other professor-pastors, Fallin traveled to his churches on Saturday, held meetings Saturday night, and conducted worship on Sunday. On the Sundays when he was not present, the local superintendent conducted Sunday school and the president of missions presided over the missionary society. Fallin received modest compensation from these churches, and congregations often paid him with food rather than money.

In 1953 Fallin accepted a call to become pastor of the Jerusalem Baptist Church in Bessemer. Jerusalem was a full-time church that met every Sunday, and Fallin, like many others, gave up his four one-Sunday or quarter-time, churches. Jerusalem Baptist paid a regular salary and provided opportunities for expanded ministries that were impossible in the rural setting.

Joe W. McKinney is a good example of a successful pioneer farmer-pastor. Born June 11, 1883, at Cottage Grove in Coosa County, McKinney became a farmer and acquired a plantation consisting of several hundred acres. He was called into the ministry and began pastoring quarter-time churches in the Morning Star District Association. Although unlettered, McKinney had a zeal for the gospel, a free and easy sermon delivery, and a personality that drew people to him. Over time, he pastored almost every church in the Morning Star District and succeeded in raising funds to construct several church buildings. One Baptist minister reported that McKinney had baptized more than 2,000, excluded 250, restored 200, dismissed 250 by letter, received 175 by letter, and ordained 10 ministers and 25 five deacons. He built ten houses of worship and three schools. In addition, he maintained his farm and raised nine children.

Like their rural counterparts, urban pastors were also overwhelmingly bivocational. A 1940 survey revealed that only 365 Southern Baptist churches had full-time pastors in 1940. This figure was probably much lower among black Baptists. Although a few pastors of larger churches were full time, most city pastors in areas like Birmingham, Gadsden, and Anniston could be described as industrial worker–pastors.

William Murray Williams is a classic example of the industrial worker-pastor. Born near Brewton, in 1919, Williams joined the Little Brooklyn Baptist Church when he was nine. His parents were active members of the church, and Williams grew up in a Christian home. In 1942 Williams moved to Birmingham seeking better economic opportunity. He obtained employment at the U.S. Steel plant in Ensley and joined the Twenty-third Street Baptist Church. Williams was later transferred to the Westfield plant and joined the Hopewell Baptist Church. In 1948 he accepted his call to the ministry and enrolled at Birmingham Baptist College. While studying for the ministry, Williams was called to the First Marietta Baptist Church in Escambia County, a church that met only one Sunday a month. The congregation paid him a meager twenty-five dollars, hardly enough to pay for the drive to the church from Birmingham, but Williams stayed there for eight years because of his desire to preach and pastor. Five years later, he was called to the Eastview Baptist Church in Cedartown, Georgia, a congregation that met two Sundays each month. Williams pastored at Eastview for three years, but he assisted at Hopewell Baptist Church. When Hopewell's pastor died, Williams became the pastor.

The Hopewell Baptist Church was similar to other black churches in that a company owned the church building. Industrial operators provided meeting space, utilities, and maintenance for their laborers, but church members were responsible for paying the pastor and any administrative help, such as a secretary. Because Williams had a full-time job and could not conduct weekday or weeknight programs, most church activities took place on Sunday. Usually Sunday school and worship filled the morning and the Baptist Training Union met in the afternoon. Several auxiliaries sponsored afternoon programs once a year: missionary society, ushers, deacons' wives, and choirs. The annual revival and the vacation Bible school were the most important events of the summer season. Williams wasn't a "whopping" preacher, like many in Birmingham, but he sought to deliver sermons with some measurable degree of "fire" and enthusiasm.

In 1964, when U.S. Steel decided to close the Westfield plant, Williams convinced the company to sell the church building to the congregation for a dollar. The church building was then moved to Wylam, and in 1969, a new sanctuary replaced the old church. The new church, which cost one hundred thousand dollars, was financed by Citizen's Federal Savings and Loan Association, a black company directed by millionaire A. G. Gaston, which financed most black churches during the era of segregation. One of Williams's major contributions to his congregation was encouraging them to be self-supporting, rather than depending on outside support. Williams, like many black pastors, also encouraged church members to buy their own homes. Most lived in company housing and paid rent to U.S. Steel. Williams counseled them to become independent through home ownership, and he set the standard by buying a home in Smith-field, one of Birmingham's middle-class black communities.

As black Baptists increasingly migrated from the country to the cities, they brought with them many aspects of their rural church rituals. Emotional worship services were followed by fellowshipping and eating. More than any other event, the annual revival revealed the influence of rural patterns on urban customs. Although agricultural requirements no longer necessitated a late summer revival, most congregations continued the July or August tradition. The guest minister stayed at the home of the pastor or a church member, and individual members or a church group provided his meals. The revival meeting began with a long prayer meeting, and then the choir sang several songs. The pastor read the Scripture and prayed, then invited the unsaved to take the front seat, known traditionally as the mourner's bench. The guest evangelist then preached a long and emotional sermon, and the pastor followed by appealing to the unsaved to come to Christ. Revival week was followed by the Sunday baptismal service, usually at a local creek or river. Whether rural or urban, the revival and baptism were always joyous occasions filled with much singing, rejoicing, and shouting.

But black Baptist city churches faced problems that were unique to the urban setting. These problems increased as more and more blacks moved to industrial areas during World War II. *Baptist Leader* editor W. S. Smith, whose headquarters were in Birmingham, often editorialized about problems facing churches in urban Alabama. Smith assessed correctly that the lack of full-time ministers prohibited churches from fulfilling their potential. Poorly developed stewardship programs were another problem. Smith urged churches to develop ways of raising money other than through dues, the ward system, special programs, cake and pie sales, and annual days. In a 1940 editorial Smith chastised churches that sought to raise money by charging admission fees for glee club concerts and other musicals. To do so, he insisted, "was anti-Biblical and used secular means for financing the church." He urged churches instead to move toward tithing and systematic giving.[13]

Smith also noted that church divisions inhibited black Baptist churches from fulfilling their potential. Congregational splits were often the result of tensions between the pastor and the deacons. In rural areas, deacons were responsible for church business and for making decisions, and the pastor came only on the weekend to preach. With pastors now living in the city near their churches, many ministers viewed themselves as administrators and decision-makers.

This sometimes generated conflict with deacons and trustees, and members often took opposing sides. These differences could lead to schism, with disaffected groups forming their own church, a plight that Smith lamented.

Smith also noted in his editorials another major problem affecting black Baptist churches: the method used in calling pastors. Whereas some churches received advice from association and convention leaders, other congregations made their selection through a preaching contest. The danger of such a process, Smith pointed out, was that pastors were called to churches on the basis of their emotional preaching ability rather than their pastoral skills. In a 1939 article, Smith criticized a church in a Birmingham suburb that brought in eighteen pastoral candidates to preach to the congregation. The selection process, Smith insisted, had become one of politics and chaos, which could potentially divide the church.[14]

The numerous problems and inadequacies facing black Baptist churches did not destroy their power and influence in the community, however. Churches remained the major self-help organizations for blacks during and after World War II. Churches provided meeting places, established social centers, preserved black culture, and sponsored education. And black Baptist pastors increasingly expressed the growing militancy within the community. It is not surprising that when the modern civil rights movement began in Alabama, black Baptist pastors were among its most militant leaders.

5
The Civil Rights Movement and Beyond, 1954–2000

10
Protest and Reorganization

Charles Morgan, a liberal white lawyer from Alabama who served on the board of directors of the Southern Christian Leadership Conference (SCLC), said that the civil rights organization founded by Martin Luther King Jr. could not be judged as other organizations in terms of bureaucratic behavior. "SCLC is not an organization," he told a reporter from the *New York Times*, "it's a church." Ralph Abernathy, its vice president, called SCLC, which sustained the Birmingham and Selma civil rights campaigns, a "faith operation" that depended on Christian inspiration, "you . . . can't always analyze what might happen. You just have to go."[1] The religious dimensions of the civil rights movement of the 1950s and 1960s are irrefutable. The movement was led by black ministers and firmly rooted in the black church.

Black Alabama Baptists played a significant role in the civil rights struggle in their home state and in the United States at large. Black Baptist pastors spearheaded movements in their local communities, and their churches provided funds, charisma, spiritual culture, and protestors for the major campaigns in Alabama. Because of events in Montgomery, Birmingham, and Selma, the 1964 Civil Rights Act and the 1965 Voting Rights Act became law. The movement not only impacted society but also affected black churches in several ways.

Black Baptists' response to the civil rights movement also resulted in the formation of a new national convention: the Progressive National Baptist Convention. Some churches in Alabama left the National Baptist Convention, USA, and joined the newer organization. One Alabama pastor served a two-year term as president, but the number of Alabama churches involved in the new convention remained small.

Though the Alabama Colored Baptist State Convention supported the civil rights movement, its greater effort was reserved for its own internal reorganization. With the death of D. V. Jemison, who served the convention as president for nearly forty years, Uriah Judkins Robinson became president and directed significant convention reconstruction. The state convention established a headquarters on the Selma University campus, and convention leaders proposed a unified plan of financing convention objectives.

The primary impetus behind reorganization was to provide greater funding for education, which remained the major goal of the convention. Birmingham Baptist College and Cedar Grove Academy continued to operate in Birmingham and Mobile, respectively, and each received significant financial support from local churches and associations. Meanwhile, convention leaders and trustees of Selma University sought to move the institution into the mainstream of black colleges by reorganizing it into a junior college with a separate school of religion. Several buildings were also erected on the campus during this period.

Black Baptists and the Civil Rights Movement

The heart of the civil rights movement was a series of local campaigns with national implications. Alabama provided the setting for three of the most important—in Montgomery, Birmingham, and Selma. Although ministers from other denominations participated in the struggle, black Baptist pastors emerged as the primary leaders. Several factors contributed to their leadership role. The sheer number of Baptist congregations offered their pastors great prestige and influence. Furthermore, most black Baptist pastors were free from white economic control since they received their livelihood from their black congregations. In contrast, laypersons were inhibited in their ability to participate or provide leadership because their income was often tied to businesses and other institutions owned or controlled by whites. Pastors of other denominations were frequently hampered by conservative bishops or other church officials while Baptist ministers were responsible only to their local congregations, many of whom appreciated and openly supported the civil rights movement.

Black Baptist theology also supported the involvement of pastors in civil rights work. Drawing strength from the era of slavery in Alabama, the Afro-Baptist faith of black Baptists emphasized the exodus experience and identified with Jesus as liberator. Just as God had delivered the Israelites from bondage in Egypt, he would deliver them from slavery. This belief continued into the civil rights era. For approximately half a million black Baptists in Alabama, the gospel proclaimed freedom, liberty, social justice, and human dignity. Therefore, segregation represented a great evil that needed to be destroyed. White Baptists generally considered blacks as inferior and applauded segregation as a God-ordained institution.

The historian Andrew Manis, in a discussion of the conflicting interpretations of the civil rights movement among black and white Baptists in the South, pointed out that two different civil religions emerged in the mid-1950s. Blacks interpreted the movement in such terms as the biblical exodus, liberation, emancipation, freedom, the fulfillment of the American promise, and the triumph of justice. They proclaimed that God Himself was at work in the civil rights movement, and they defined equality as a God-given and sacred right. White Baptists, with few exceptions, identified the movement with communism, the destruction of individual rights, and the promotion of interracial marriage. Some insisted that God was the original segregator and that integration was against His will. For many white Baptists, preserving the southern way of life offered the only hope for saving America, a way of life that included white dominance over blacks.

The first of three major civil rights campaigns that took place in Alabama occurred in Montgomery. For most historians, the Montgomery bus boycott marks the beginning of the modern civil rights movement. Although other bus boycotts led by black Baptist pastors had taken place in the 1950s in Baton Rouge and Tallahassee, the Montgomery movement attracted national attention. The boycott began on December 1, 1955, when Rosa Parks was arrested for refusing to give up her bus seat to a white man. Although black Baptist pastors would eventually provide key leadership, a group of women initiated the protest. After Park's arrest, Jo Ann Robinson and other women of the Women's Political Council called for a one-day boycott. E. D. Nixon, former president of the Montgomery NAACP and a longtime black activist, organized a meeting of ministers and local community officials. These leaders decided to support the one-day boycott, calling for a mass meeting on Monday night, December 5, to determine whether community sentiment would support extending the boycott. A. W. Wilson, pastor of the Holt Street Baptist Church and vice president of the Alabama Baptist State Convention, offered his church as the meeting place; the facility was ideal because of its size and location. With the success of the one-day boycott, leaders formed the Montgomery Improvement Association (MIA) to continue the boycott. Officers were elected and Martin Luther King Jr. was selected as president.

As the heart and soul of the Montgomery boycott, the MIA held mass meetings on Monday and Thursday nights to keep the people together. Although these gatherings occurred in churches of all denominations, most were held in Baptist churches because they had the largest and most numerous church buildings. The meetings followed a simple pattern: songs, prayer, Scripture reading, opening remarks by the president, collection, reports from various committees, and a pep talk. The latter constituted the main address of the evening, usually by a different minister at each meeting. Often these pep talks resembled the sermons at Baptist revivals. The mass meetings gave people hope and inspiration to continue the movement. Through singing, praying, and preaching the people were reminded that their cause was just and that God was on their side.

In addition to providing meeting places and leadership for the movement, Baptist churches in Montgomery provided financial support. To ensure transportation for blacks throughout the city, pastors urged their members to offer their cars, allowed their churches to become pickup stations, and used church vans and station wagons to transport their members and other people to work. Jo Ann Robinson, president of the Women's Political Council and organizer of the one-day boycott, admitted that black ministers and churches made the boycott a success. "Without their support," she maintained, "things would probably have been different."[2]

As president of the MIA, Martin Luther King Jr., pastor of Dexter Avenue Baptist Church, became the primary leader of the Montgomery movement. His life and his role in directing the MIA have been well documented. Born into a black middle-class family in Atlanta, Georgia, on January 15, 1929, King graduated from Morehouse College at the age of nineteen and received a bachelor of divinity degree from Crozer Theological Seminary in 1951. While at Crozer he became familiar with the nonviolent, passive resistance philosophy of Mahatma Gandhi and concluded that it was the best method for blacks to obtain justice in the United States. After Crozer Seminary, King pursued a Ph.D. in systematic theology at Boston University. In 1955 he returned with his wife to the South to assume the pastorate of Dexter Avenue Baptist Church in Montgomery. King completed his doctoral dissertation, organized a political and social action committee within his congregation, and was elected to the executive board of the local NAACP. King, who had lived in Montgomery for only fifteen months, was considered the best choice to head the MIA because he was not embroiled in the factionalism that divided the city's black leadership. Moreover, he had established a reputation as a well-educated minister with extraordinary oratorical skills. King succeeded in uniting the city's black people into a powerful nonviolent force for social change.

Other Baptist pastors also played key leadership roles in the movement. Several deserve special notice because they served the boycott from beginning to end. A. W. Wilson, pastor of Holt Street Baptist Church, provided his building for the first mass meeting, was selected as the MIA's original parliamentarian, and served as an active member of the negotiating committee that met with city political and business leaders. H. H. Hubbard, pastor of Bethel Baptist Church, was a member of the original executive committee, served as MIA treasurer, and worked with the negotiating committee. Ralph Abernathy, pastor of the First African Baptist Church, became the most active and influential leader next to King. Abernathy called local pastors together for the initial meeting, served as vice president of the MIA, endured arrest and a house bombing, and served on the negotiating committee. He became King's closest friend and later assisted him with the Southern Christian Leadership Conference.

After twelve months of struggle, the Montgomery movement achieved success. On November 13, 1956, the U.S. Supreme Court affirmed the lower federal court ruling that bus segregation in Montgomery was unconstitutional. On December 20, 1956, U.S. marshals officially served the Supreme Court order on Montgomery officials. For the first time in more than a year, blacks returned to the city buses, now on an integrated basis.

The Montgomery bus boycott proved significant to the civil rights movement for several other reasons. It provided a leader—Martin Luther King Jr.—for the overall movement and offered nonviolence as an effective method for resisting the evils of segregation. In addition, the movement awakened the power of the black church as a force for social change and racial justice. Moreover, Montgomery served as a testing ground. The historian J. Mills Thornton has observed that King learned two things from Montgomery: the inflexible nature of segregation and the impossibility of changing it in the absence of outside pressure. The institution of segregation was so much a part of the social relationship between whites and blacks that even modest reform threatened the entire social fabric of the South. Because it was so entrenched, it could not simply be modified; it had to be destroyed. King also perceived that no force or institution within the South could destroy segregation. If segregation was to be eliminated, pressure had to come from outside the South, and the federal government seemed the most likely source. According to Thornton, these two lessons would guide King and the civil rights movement beyond Montgomery.

By 1956 another important civil rights movement had begun in Birmingham, Alabama's largest city. This campaign also garnered national attention and was largely responsible for passage of the 1964 Civil Rights Act. As in Montgomery, it was led and supported by black Baptist pastors and churches. The spark that ignited the movement came from a state order that outlawed the NAACP. Fred Shuttlesworth, pastor of Bethel Baptist Church, was perturbed by the ban. Shortly after coming to Birmingham, he had joined the NAACP and become chairman of its membership committee. He worked hard to enlarge the branch's membership and to create a more broad-based organization. In a major speech before the group, Shuttlesworth called for a program to reach the masses. With the outlawing of the NAACP, he proposed a mass meeting to see if blacks in Birmingham wanted to organize a movement to fight for their rights. He convinced four pastors—N. H. Smith Jr., G. E. Pruitt, T. L. Lane, and R. L. Alford—to join him in the call. Three of these ministers were Baptist pastors; Lane served as pastor of an Independent Methodist church. They scheduled the meeting for June 5, 1956, at Alford's Sardis Baptist Church. Those present voted to form a new organization, the Alabama Christian Movement for Human Rights (ACMHR), and Fred Shuttlesworth was elected president.

Shuttlesworth played the central role and provided critical leadership. He possessed a stubborn will, an indomitable faith, and a sense of divine compulsion and destiny. As pastor he felt that God had called him to be the leader of the church. While pastoring the First Baptist Church in Selma, Shuttlesworth had refused to allow the deacon board to make major decisions without his participation. He succeeded in getting the congregation to stand with him over the objections of the deacons. Shuttlesworth brought the same determination and sense of divine commission to the civil rights movement. In December 1956, less than six months after the formation of the ACMHR, Shuttlesworth's home was bombed. The bomb exploded beneath the room in which he was talking to a deacon. The force of the explosion threw Shuttlesworth into the air and destroyed the box springs of the bed on which he was sitting. Miraculously he escaped unharmed. Shuttlesworth and his followers interpreted his survival as a sign that God had ordained him to lead the movement. "He's all right," shouted a woman from among the crowd of five hundred people who had assembled at his bombed house, and "he is going to be all right." Someone else cried out, "God saved the reverend to lead the movement."[3] Shuttlesworth related on more than one occasion that this event convinced him that God would protect him and give him victory over his fight to eliminate segregation in Birmingham. More than any other single event, the bombing galvanized the movement and provided Shuttlesworth a personal following.

A core of approximately fifteen pastors, mostly Baptist, made up the ACMHR's inner circle. They supported the movement financially and with their physical presence, served on the board of directors, and were dedicated to Shuttlesworth's leadership. Among these were Reverends Edward Gardner, Abraham Woods, Nelson Smith Jr., Calvin Woods, J. S. Phiffer, L. O. Lane, L. J. Rogers, and Herman Stone. They drew strength from Shuttlesworth's courage and believed that he was God's man appointed to destroy segregation in the city. These pastors could identify more readily with the religious militancy of the ACMHR than with the NAACP and other organizations in Birmingham. Like Shuttlesworth, these ministers deeply resented the segregation and oppression of African Americans. Several gained inspiration from the Montgomery movement and believed they could duplicate its success in Birmingham.

In addition to their growing disgust with segregation and their devotion to Shuttlesworth, members of the inner circle had several other things in common. All came from poor economic backgrounds and each had witnessed the oppression of segregation firsthand. Those born in Alabama's Black Belt had grown up in sharecropping families. Second, these pastors enjoyed a sense of freedom that most blacks did not have. Those with secular jobs were not dependent on whites, and Baptist pastors were free from control by bishops and other denominational restrictions. Moreover, most of Shuttlesworth's inner circle pastored small churches and were not the traditional religious leaders of the black community. Most importantly, these pastors had the religious conviction that God would enable them to defeat the sin of segregation, which they saw as the real enemy. These pastors urged their members, most of whom were working-class people, to join the ACMHR. Thus, in Birmingham the pulpit was linked to a religious and popular movement for first-class citizenship.

In almost every way the ACMHR mirrored a black Baptist church. Its leader, Fred Shuttlesworth, was a charismatic pastor who believed God had called him to the task. His followers also believed in his divine calling and showed their esteem for his leadership by standing and applauding as he entered mass meetings. In addition, the ACMHR's board of directors resembled a board of deacons. As in most black churches, the deacons met infrequently, and Shuttlesworth made the important decisions. The group raised funds through its membership dues but, as in Baptist churches, they also collected special offerings at mass meetings and held special fund-raising events such as teas, musicals, and candy and bake sales.

The ACMHR had its own choir and ushers. Twenty-three members founded the original ACMHR choir in July 1960 at the Forty-sixth Street Baptist Church. The choir combined freedom songs with gospel music to produce a charismatic style unique to the civil rights struggle. Gospel music emphasized the organization's cultural and religious ties to the black community. At the mass meetings, singers allowed their emotions to take over, and ushers had to restrain them on many occasions. One choir member remarked that "the choir sings with faith in God, knowing that his power works through their songs and gives them courage to keep singing while struggling for freedom."⁴ One of the choir's favorite songs was "Ninety-nine and a Half Won't Do." Composed by Carlton Reese, the choir's director, the song expressed the need for total commitment to the cause. Other songs such as "God Will Make a Way" expressed absolute faith in God, who would give them power to overcome prosegregation forces in the city.

The ACMHR formed an usher's group shortly after the movement began. In churches, ushering provided an opportunity for members to gain a sense of self-worth and importance. People who worked as maids or janitors in the secular world were prominent and respected individuals when they served as ushers in church. In most black Baptist churches ushers were women, which was true of ACMHR ushers. Coming from various churches but directed by a Baptist minister, Charles Billups, ACMHR ushers met people at the door, welcomed them into the church sanctuary, maintained order, and restrained those who became overly emotional. These ushers gained a measure of self-respect by providing a valuable service and assisting an organization that promoted change for African Americans in Birmingham.

Women were indispensable to the ACMHR. As in African American churches, they made up the majority of the ACMHR membership, 61.7 percent in 1959. Although men made the major decisions, women were the chief fund-raisers. Women almost exclusively directed candy and bake sales, socials, and dinners, and they organized special occasions like the annual anniversary celebration. In addition to serving as ushers, women made up most of the choir. Key women included Lucinda Roby, a school principal, who directed the movement's youth division, and Georgia Price, who assisted her husband in coordinating voting activities. Women serving on advisory and executive boards included Daisy Jeffries, Lola Hendricks, Altha Stallworth, Josephine Jones, Rella Williams, Myrtice Dowdell, and Dester Brooks. Most of these women were members of Baptist churches, and many had been inspired to join the movement because of their pastors.

The influence of the African American church's distinctive culture on the

ACMHR was manifested most vividly in the organization's weekly meetings. Essentially, these gatherings were worship services patterned after those held in Baptist churches. They began with a thirty-minute devotional service consisting of prayers, spirituals, and meter hymns, followed by singing by the ACMHR choir. The presiding officer, usually vice president Edward Gardner, pastor of Mt. Olive Baptist Church, offered brief remarks, before a local pastor delivered a sermon. Following the sermon, President Shuttlesworth issued directions. Next, the ushers collected an offering. In general, these were very emotional meetings, with a lot of shouting. At a meeting on January 23, 1961, Oscar Herron, a local Baptist pastor, delivered the sermon. A dozen women became so emotional that ushers removed them from the church. Fellow ministers and ushers then persuaded Herron to stop preaching, for fear that the meeting would break into pandemonium or result in a stampede. Three months later, when the April 17 meeting resulted in unusual emotional fervor and shouting, Shuttlesworth had to remind the audience "that this was not a church but a movement that had business to take care of."[5] The fervor of the mass meetings not only provided emotional release but also roused participants to find the courage to fight the forces of segregation in a hostile environment.

Spurred by their leader, the ACMHR relied on a new strategy that combined direct action and legal redress. Members of the group intentionally broke segregation laws and then challenged those ordinances in the courts. Shuttlesworth spearheaded this tactic, sometimes acting alone, going to jail, and then filing for court action. This represented a radical departure from prior civil rights activities in Birmingham in which groups would petition the city or go to court without having violated the law. The ACMHR championed numerous causes: the hiring of African American police officers; the integration of buses, waiting rooms, restaurants, public parks, schools, and other facilities; voting rights; and equity in hiring.

Despite the ACMHR's persistence and Shuttlesworth's courage, the struggle against segregation achieved limited results. Though the movement succeeded in integrating buses and transportation terminals, schools remained segregated; the city hired no black police officers; public accommodations were not integrated; and there was no increase in black employment. The city government, led by Police Commissioner "Bull" Connor, simply refused to make concessions. Realizing that he needed additional help if blacks were to bring segregation to an end, Shuttlesworth invited Martin Luther King Jr. and SCLC to come to Birmingham. "The only way this city was ever going to change," he told King, "was for their two organizations to join forces and do battle with sin and darkness here."[6]

At Shuttlesworth's urging, King decided to come to Birmingham to assist the ACMHR in achieving its goals. King convened his SCLC staff at Dorchester, Georgia, to plan the Birmingham campaign. The recent defeat at Albany, Georgia, inspired him to make more thorough preparations. King brought two important assets to the ACMHR-led movement in Birmingham: his national reputation and his ability to attract the national media. In addition, King's presence broadened the movement's base of support and enhanced the church culture that sustained the ACMHR movement.

Some segments of the black community, including prominent pastors and leading professionals, had not responded to Shuttlesworth's plea for activism. They viewed him as an interloper into their territory. King was more successful in attracting many of these community leaders. He formed an advisory committee composed of black professionals that gave them a voice in the decision-making process. This gained support from some and served to neutralize others. Similarly, King brought several key pastors with large congregations and facilities into the movement. John Porter, pastor of the Sixth Avenue Baptist Church, had served as King's assistant pastor while a student in Montgomery. When King came to Birmingham, Porter quickly joined the movement. John Cross, pastor of the Sixteenth Street Baptist Church, also joined the movement when King made an appeal at the Birmingham Baptist Minister's Conference. Porter and Cross brought Birmingham two largest black Baptist congregations into the movement, and their churches served as headquarters for future protests.

King's arrival also enhanced the religious dimension of the ACMHR and its church culture. With King's involvement, the ACMHR held meetings every night, instead of just on Mondays. Crowds grew larger at these highly spiritual and emotional meetings, and it became necessary to hold meetings in the larger churches. King, Shuttlesworth, and Abernathy shared center stage. Appeals inspired many people to volunteer to go to jail, just as converts might walk down the aisle to profess their newfound faith or to join African American churches. In addition, King's activities in Birmingham assumed a measure of religious symbolism. Arrested and jailed on Good Friday, the day for commemorating Christ's crucifixion, he wrote a letter similar to Paul's in which he explained the movement's purpose.

The climax of the movement in Birmingham began with the decision to use children in the demonstrations. Police Commissioner Bull Connor's response—deploying dogs and fire hoses against the young protestors—brought national media attention to the Birmingham civil rights movement and has been well documented by historians. On May 10, 1963, the white business community and black civil rights leaders reached a truce that the African American community interpreted as a victory. According to the agreement, lunch counters, restrooms, fitting rooms, and drinking fountains in the downtown stores would be desegregated within ninety days. Within sixty days, African Americans would be hired as salespeople and clerks in stores. Within two weeks a biracial committee would be established to improve communications between whites and blacks in the city. Many historians and scholars consider events in Birmingham as the turning point of the civil rights movement. The demonstrations made possible the Civil Rights Act of 1964 and firmly established the leadership role of Martin Luther King. The black church, led by black Baptist ministers, had achieved a great victory as well.

The Selma civil rights campaign developed somewhat differently from the movement in Montgomery and Birmingham. Although several black Baptist pastors provided local leadership, the major thrust came from national organizations. The Selma movement began in 1962 when Bernard Lafayette of SNCC, a Baptist minister and student at American Baptist College, arrived with his wife to support voter registration efforts. Out of a black population of 15,000, only 156 were registered. At that point, the Selma Voters League constituted the only organization to press for black voting rights and those efforts had achieved only limited success.

One of the first people to give support to Lafayette was Louis Lloyd Anderson, pastor of Tabernacle Baptist Church, who had succeeded David V. Jemison as pastor. Although Jemison had spoken out for equal rights for blacks as president of the Alabama Baptist Convention and the National Baptist Convention, Anderson was more militant. Jemison was more of a gradualist; Anderson wanted equality immediately. Anderson grew up in Pittsburgh, briefly pastored a church in Montgomery, and knew Martin Luther King. When the bus boycott began in Montgomery, he attended MIA meetings, spoke on a few occasions, and gave general support to the movement. In Selma, he had become a militant spokesman for human rights, often denouncing discrimination in the white South from his pulpit. Over the objections of his deacons, Anderson offered his church to Lafayette and SNCC to host a mass meeting.

The first mass meeting at Tabernacle helped spread Lafayette's message throughout Selma's black community. He went on to conduct mass meetings at several other churches, including the First Baptist Church and Brown Chapel African Methodist Episcopal Church. (Brown Chapel later became the headquarters of Selma's civil rights movement.) Lafayette attracted many young people and put pressure on the voting registrars by sending blacks to register to vote. When he left in midsummer to return to college, Selma had a few more registered voters and a hard core of predominately young civil rights activists. Lafayette had not, however, succeeded in enlisting the black middle class.

After Lafayette's departure, other members of SNCC came to Selma to continue the voting registration effort. Worth Long organized daily demonstrations at the courthouse with mass arrests occurring over a six-week period. Youngsters left school to participate. Many of the protestors who lined up at the courthouse were too young to vote. Age was irrelevant, however, because registrars were not going to register large numbers of blacks. Long's strategy sought to attract media attention by demonstrating, with long lines, that black people in Dallas County who wanted to register to vote were being denied that right. More than four hundred people went to jail that fall for unlawful assembly and parading without a permit.

As the movement gained momentum, several members of the Voter's League suggested they invite Martin Luther King and SCLC to Selma. Frederick Reese, pastor of the Ebenezer Baptist Church, supported the idea. Reese had attended Knox Academy and Alabama State University. After teaching in Wilcox County for a few years, he returned to Selma to teach at R. B. Hudson High School and to serve as a Baptist pastor. He quickly became president of the Selma Teachers Association and encouraged members of that group to qualify to vote. He also won increased benefits from the school board. A proud man, Reese despised the denials and degradations of segregation, especially when they were directed at intelligent black people with formal education. His concern for voting rights in Selma prompted him to join the Voter's League. He became head of its steering committee and later president of the organization. As a prominent leader in the Voter's League, Reese penned the letter inviting King to Selma.

The Selma invitation fit well into King's plans to concentrate on voting rights in the South. After obtaining the 1964 Civil Rights Act that outlawed discrimination in public accommodations, King had turned his attention to voting. One week after the 1964 presidential election, King convened a retreat at Birmingham's Gaston Motel to determine where SCLC should focus its efforts after the success of the Birmingham campaign. C. T. Vivian, director of affiliates, reminded King in that meeting that "the movement needed a rallying point around which to stir the entire nation about voting rights."[7]

Vivian, fellow staff member James Bevel, and other members of SCLC believed Selma would be the ideal place to launch a voting rights campaign. In addition to denying voting rights to black citizens, it was the home of Bull Connor, and the birthplace of Alabama's White Citizen's Council. Moreover, Sheriff James Clarke, who was known for his brutal treatment of civil rights workers, symbolized Southern white racism as much as Birmingham's Connor. In addition, counties adjacent to Selma, such as Wilcox and Lowndes, reported no black registered voters.

Martin Luther King sent C. T. Vivian to investigate Selma as the site for the SCLC's voting rights campaign. Vivian met with Frederick Reese, who believed SNCC's efforts had run their course and that the black community needed some rejuvenation. Other people also urged SCLC to come to Selma, including longtime activists Amelia Boynton and Mamie Foster. Vivian announced to the Voter's League in December 1964 that King was coming.

On January 2, 1965, King arrived in Selma and announced an SCLC voter registration drive to a crowd of seven hundred people gathered at Brown Chapel African Methodist Episcopal Church. In addition to his interest in registering local blacks to vote, King also wanted to challenge racial exclusion in the South and to force President Lyndon Johnson to enact a federal voting statute. King and his staff began a series of marches to the courthouse that would be covered by the national media.

Reverends L. L. Anderson and F. D. Reese were two Baptist pastors who were quite active during the 1965 protest. Anderson led several marches to the courthouse and engaged in verbal confrontations with police officials. On Friday, January 22, Reese led a group of one hundred teachers to protest the unfair voter registration system that had denied blacks the ballot. School officials tried unsuccessfully to persuade them to leave; the group returned to Brown Chapel only after Sheriff Clark and his deputies began prodding them with billy clubs. Reese and Anderson were also part of the negotiation team that met with white leaders and explained to them the movement goals and the need for black voting rights.

As the Selma demonstrations gained momentum, King decided to expand the voting campaign to other cities in the Black Belt, such as Marion in Perry County and Camden in Wilcox County. In Marion on Thursday night, February 18, Vivian led a column of marchers down the sidewalk toward the courthouse. Suddenly the street lights went out, and Alabama troopers began to beat the demonstrators. Jimmie Lee Jackson, a local youth, was shot by a state trooper who had pursued him, his mother, and several others into a café. After some delay, Jackson was taken to a Selma hospital where he died eight days later.

SCLC workers proposed a march from Selma to Montgomery and a meeting with Governor George Wallace to protest Jackson's killing. When marchers crossed the Edmund Pettus Bridge on Sunday, March 5, Alabama state troopers assaulted them. National reaction to the attack on Bloody Sunday worked to the benefit of those advocating a voting rights bill. Shortly after 9:00 p.m. one national television network interrupted the evening movie for a long film report showing Alabama troopers wielding clubs and stampeding horses against the quiet column of protestors. Outraged members of Congress and religious leaders throughout the country publicly protested the police brutality. Sympathy marches took place in key cities such as New York, Boston, and Chicago.

Responding to the growing national outrage, President Johnson announced at a press conference on March 15 that he was sending a voting rights bill to Congress. In a nationally televised speech to that body, he called for speedy passage of the bill. On March 25 nearly twenty-five thousand people gathered outside Montgomery to welcome the three hundred marchers who had made the trek from Selma to Montgomery. The march concluded with a giant rally on the steps of the Alabama capitol. After weeks of debate, Congress passed the Voting Rights Act.

The Selma campaign marked the culmination of the civil rights movement in the South. Blacks won the right to vote in Selma, and the number of black voters rose in the South from 1 million in 1964 to 3.1 million in 1968. The Voting Rights Act contributed to the transformation of the South, altered the balance of political power, and affected the politics of the entire nation. The black church in general, and black Baptists in particular, had provided leadership, theology, church culture, volunteers, and charisma for the events that unfolded in Montgomery, Birmingham, and Selma.

Black Baptists and a Culture of Change

The civil rights movement of the 1950s and 1960s had a profound effect on the black church in Alabama and beyond. First and foremost, black Baptist churches reaffirmed their protest tradition. In a real sense, protest had been a part of the black religious tradition from the beginning. During slavery, Nat Turner, a self-styled black minister, led a slave revolt in North Hampton, Virginia. Other ministers such as Denmark Vesey and Gabriel Prosser were implicated in other revolts. Black pastors were leaders in the northern abolitionist societies. After slavery, blacks left white churches and formed their own. Black pastors also served as political leaders during Reconstruction. During the difficult years following the Reconstruction era black leaders such as Henry McNeal Turner spoke out vigorously against racial discrimination and suggested that blacks return to Africa. While protest continued in one form or another with black pastors speaking out for justice, the need to conserve black institutions often took precedence over militant activism following Reconstruction. With the coming of the civil rights movement greater emphasis was placed on the church's role as an agent of political and social change. Pastors began to see themselves not only as preservers of institutions but as leaders who had a responsibility to challenge segregation and other forms of racial discrimination.

This emphasis on protest and social change reached the association and convention levels in Alabama. The Alabama convention, which had often taken a gradualist approach, became more supportive of the civil rights movement. It began to give funds to organizations that fostered first-class citizenship. For example, at the 1955 meeting of the state convention, funds from the convention budget were given to W. C. Patton, state president of the NAACP, in response to his appeal. The convention also adopted several resolutions of support, reaffirming the need for an immediate end to segregation. The 1957 convention endorsed the struggle for first-class citizenship and condemned mob action by those seeking to intimidate and physically harm people engaged in that struggle. That same year, a goodwill committee from the convention met with whites who believed in the principles of Christianity to promote better relations and greater understanding among all citizens. The next year, the goodwill committee sought aid from the federal Civil Rights Commission for a thorough investigation of violations of voting rights.

Leadership in denominational organizations generally devolved on men who were not only successful pastors but also advocates of social and political change. M. W. Whitt, one of Birmingham's most outspoken advocates of change, became moderator of the Mt. Pilgrim Association in the 1950s. On the convention level, people like A. W. Wilson, a leader in the Montgomery boycott; James L. Ware, outspoken advocate in Birmingham; and Uriah J. Robinson of Mobile, who sued Clarke County over a racial incident, assumed leadership positions. People who were not supportive of an immediate end to racial discrimination had no chance of assuming leadership in black Baptist work.

The emergence of militant activists in the black Baptist churches produced a new theological emphasis: what became known as black liberation theology. Led by James Cone of Union Theological Seminary in New York, the emphasis was on liberation as the major theme in the Bible. In the Old Testament, the exodus experience was highlighted; in the New Testament Jesus was viewed as a great religious liberator. Since blacks made up the most oppressed people in the country, Cone asserted "that any message that was not related to the liberation of the poor especially poor blacks is not Christ's message. In a society where men are oppressed because they are black, Christian theology must become Black Theology."[8] Although the rank and file of black pastors in Alabama did not read Cone, younger seminary graduates brought his theological bent into the state. Liberation theology began to appear more and more in sermons. On the national level, the emergence of organizations such as the National Committee of Black Churchmen signaled this new theological focus.

The civil rights movement also heralded a new relationship between white and black Baptists in the South. Historically, whites had given token funds to black schools, and the white Alabama convention had established a department of special missions. However, during the 1950s and 1960s, with few exceptions, the white Alabama convention opposed the civil rights movement. Led by the editor of the *Alabama Baptist*, Leon Macon, many southern Baptist leaders viewed integration as unchristian and communist inspired. The civil rights movement led to a different kind of relationship. With their new sense of black self-determination, blacks insisted that any relationship with white southern Baptists must be conducted on a basis of mutual respect. This new emphasis would be one factor in the creation of the Inter-Baptist Fellowship Committee and the Human Relations Conference. The Fellowship Committee was designed to plan such projects as the 1976 joint conventions, foster cooperation between white and black churches in transitional neighborhoods, and distribute disaster relief. It also developed biracial teams for the statewide, biracial revival "Good News, Alabama." All these activities were planned with equal input from black and white Baptists.

Black Baptist laymen sought a greater voice on the church, association, and convention levels. Although the civil rights movement was led by black pastors, laymen were significant participants. Laymen who had been deacons and trustees in local churches now insisted on having greater influence in association and convention levels. The Alabama convention formed a statewide organization of laymen in the 1930s that became more visible in the 1950s. This organization met concurrently with the state convention and district associations. Laymen were also placed on the trustee boards of Selma University and Birmingham Baptist College. Increasingly, laymen began to demand a voice in convention affairs.

As an increasing number of blacks graduated from college, some churches had gravitated toward more formal services. In some of these "class churches," traditional black worship patterns were frowned upon. With the emergence of the black power phase of the civil rights movement, there was greater emphasis on blacks maintaining their culture. Celebratory worship was a part of this new orientation. Middle-class churches began to sing more gospel songs. Preachers in these churches took on a less structural style of worship. Celebratory worship became almost universally accepted in black churches as the religion of black people.

Civil Rights and a New Convention

During the civil rights era a new convention emerged among black Baptists. In 1953 Joseph H. Jackson was elected president of the National Baptist Convention, USA, with the understanding that he would implement a policy of tenure. This meant the president would serve for four years and then leave office. In 1956 a tenure question came before the convention, but Jackson was able to avoid a floor vote. The 1956 convention adjourned with no resolution of the matter and for the next several years rumblings of discontent continued. Meanwhile, Jackson consolidated his power as his opponents considered strategies for removing him from office.

A civil rights issue was also a point of contention between Jackson's supporters and opponents. The issue centered on methods advocated by Martin Luther King. Jackson supported King and the Montgomery boycott in 1956, sending money from his church in Chicago while urging other Baptist churches across the nation to do the same. When nine pastors were arrested in February 1956, Jackson sent a telegram to Governor James Folsom asking him to use his influence to achieve a just resolution to the conflict.

As the civil rights movement gained momentum, Jackson's support of King waned. King's meteoric rise to prominence within the National Baptist Convention and throughout the black community appears to have created some envy on Jackson's part. And on a philosophical level, they had differences about the nature of civil disobedience. King accepted, indeed promoted, willful defiance of unjust laws; Jackson preferred a limited protest methodology. For

Jackson the right to petition for redress of grievances was laid out in the Bill of Rights and the Constitution, but citizens should not go beyond that. To do so threatened to bring about confusion and risked the destruction of an ordered society. Jackson urged blacks to move from protest to production as the key to black progress. Although he never referred to King by name in his writings and speeches, Jackson made it clear that he favored a more gradual approach than that espoused by the undisputed leader of the civil rights movement.

These issues coalesced around the presidency of the convention and moved to an unfortunate climax. Those opposing Jackson's presidency and civil rights philosophy continued to organize in the late 1950s. To gain support for his tactics, King wanted a more activist president. He and other opponents of Jackson supported Gardner C. Taylor, pastor of the Concord Baptist Church in Brooklyn, New York. The clash of opposing forces culminated at the Philadelphia convention of 1960 and ended with each group electing its own candidate. At the 1961 convention in Kansas City, Reverend A. G. Wright of Detroit died after he was accidentally pushed off the stage. Wright's death dampened the reformers' zeal, and when a court-ordered election was held that year, Jackson won with a vote of 2,721 to 1,519. Jackson immediately stripped King of his position as vice president of the Sunday School and BTU Congresses and ousted other leading pastors who supported King. He also accused King of being responsible for Wright's death, a charge that greatly upset King and that he vehemently denied.

Because of the bitter struggle and the revengeful actions of Jackson, no reconciliation was possible. Later that year L. V. Booth, pastor of the Zion Baptist Church of Cincinnati, called a meeting at his church in order to form a new convention. Twenty-three pastors, representing twenty-two churches in twelve states, attended the special meeting and founded the Progressive National Baptist Convention. Charter members spelled out several guiding principles including tenure limitations and civil rights advocacy.

Shortly after the formation of the Progressive Convention, a group met to form an Alabama branch. The state convention was never very large, consisting of only about fifteen churches. Among its presidents in Alabama were V. Hawkins, R. C. Mullins, and Nelson Smith. Smith, pastor of the New Pilgrim Baptist Church, Birmingham, served as national president for two years but was unable to rally Alabama churches into a strong convention. By the year 2000, the Progressive Convention no longer existed in Alabama.

Several reasons explain the lack of participation by Alabama Baptists in the new organization. The National Baptist Convention, USA, began in Alabama; several Alabamians had served as president; and convention officers always included some Alabama Baptists. These officers remained loyal to Jackson and urged pastors to do the same. Many Alabama pastors considered Jackson a great preacher and believed he was uniquely qualified to continue in office. Furthermore, Alabama Baptists had no tenure limitations in their own convention, and many leaders and members deemed the issue unimportant. Some Alabama Baptists refrained from endorsing one view of civil rights over another. Many felt that both civil disobedience and an emphasis on production were important strategies. Jackson, to them, was as concerned about black rights as King though his approach was different, which is why pastors such as A. W. Wilson of Montgomery and M. W. Whitt of Birmingham, who were strong civil rights activists, could also support Jackson.

Civil Rights and Reorganization of the Alabama Convention

While the Alabama convention viewed the civil rights struggle as important and the work of God, other issues received equal attention. Two key concerns were the election of new leadership and the reorganization of the convention. In 1953 David V. Jemison died, having served as president of the Baptist convention in Alabama for thirty-seven years. The next annual convention meeting was significant because black Baptists would choose a new leader. The three major candidates were E. W. Williams, Dennis C. Washington, and Uriah J. Robinson. Williams, pastor of the First Baptist Church, Fairfield, had served as vice president and assumed the presidency after Jemison's death. Washington was secretary of the Selma University board of trustees and pastor of the Seventeenth Street Baptist Church in Anniston. Robinson was secretary of the Alabama convention and pastor of the Franklin Street Baptist Church in Mobile. Robinson won the election and became the fourteenth president of the Alabama Colored Baptist State Convention.

Born on September 15, 1883, in Whatley, Clarke County, Alabama, Robinson was one of ten children, and his father, Reverend Charlie L. Robinson, was a Baptist pastor and one of the founders of the Colored Bethel District Association of Clarke County. Robinson was converted in 1893 and was baptized into the membership of the First Baptist Church, Whatley. After receiving his grammar school education from the Thomasville Baptist Academy, he entered Selma University in 1900 and finished his normal school course three years later. While attending Selma, he was called and ordained to the gospel ministry. Robinson served as a teacher in the public schools and as pastor of churches at Coals Bluff in Wilcox County, Bethel Baptist Church of Pleasant Hill, and the Union Baptist Church at Marion. Wanting to further his theological training, he returned to Selma University and graduated with the bachelor of divinity degree in 1912.

Soon after earning his degree, Robinson was called to the Mt. Olive Baptist Church in Anniston. There he guided construction of a new building and increased the membership from one hundred to five hundred. During World War I, the Mt. Olive congregation granted him a leave of absence to serve as a chaplain in the U.S. Army. He served with the 365th Infantry Regiment from the time of its organization until it was demobilized nearly two years later. Robinson, who saw more than ten months service in France and Belgium, was with the 92nd Division in the Argonne Forest, Metz, and other famous WWI battles. Robinson's service record was impressive. He was wounded at Metz but refused to leave the field. After his discharge from active duty, he continued as a chaplain of the reserve officer's corps.

Following World War I, Robinson returned to the pastorate of the Mt. Olive Baptist Church. Several churches sought his services, but he remained at Mt. Olive until called to the Franklin Street Baptist Church in Mobile. While at Franklin Street, Robinson remained active in denominational work. He served the state convention as both secretary and vice president. He became first assistant secretary of the National Baptist Convention in 1932, and was unanimously elected recording secretary in 1947. Robinson was elected president of the Alabama Colored Baptist State Convention in 1954.

At that convention Arthur W. Wilson, pastor of the Holt Street Baptist Church and director of Christian education, was elected vice president. James L. Ware, president of the Birmingham Baptist Minister's Conference, was elected secretary. Reverend M. C. Cleveland, pastor of the Day Street Baptist Church and moderator of the Montgomery Antioch District Association, continued as chair of the Selma University board of trustees. Because supporting Selma University was the chief goal of the convention, the chair of the trustee board wielded much power and influence in the convention.

As the newly elected convention president, Robinson provided the primary vision for reorganizing the state convention. Through their cooperative program, white Southern Baptists in Alabama were raising millions of dollars for missions and education, as well as supporting two accredited colleges. After conferring with the executive secretary, Dr. A. H. Reid, and other officials of the white convention, Robinson believed that black Baptists could benefit from a similar unified approach. Through the cooperative program all local church contributions would be sent to a central headquarters and then dispersed to various agencies. This replaced the old system in which local contributions went to different boards that allocated funds according to their needs. Charles A. Lett, pastor of the Macedonia Baptist Church of Daphne, was elected executive secretary for the cooperative program, and a convention office was established on the campus of Selma University.

In order to promote the cooperative program, President Robinson appointed a new budget committee with Luke Beard, pastor of the Sixteenth Street Baptist Church, Birmingham, as chairman. The first united budget called for the convention to raise $242,284 in 1955. Of that amount, $102,000 would be given to Selma University for operations and $100,000 for capital improvements. Projected budgets for the 1950s and 1960s would remain around $200,000 but the convention raised less than $100,000 per year. For example, in 1957 the convention raised $82,000 through its headquarters, and Selma University received $54,000 of that amount. By the mid-1960s the convention had increased its emphasis on stewardship, and a steadily expanding national economy resulted in better financial support. In 1965 $143,000 was given through the headquarters, and Selma University received $65,000 of that amount. The convention borrowed money for buildings and other improvements, and stewardship remained a major concern for advancing the convention's programs.

The convention made other changes as well. The date for the annual meeting was moved from the week of Thanksgiving to the week preceding the third Sunday in November. And the convention's fiscal year was changed to run from November 1 to October 31. In most other respects, the convention program remained the same. The convention continued to operate through four boards: executive, publishing, education, and missions. Convention auxiliaries included the women's convention, laymen's department, and the Sunday School and BTU Congresses. The major difference in the reorganization was that each group deposited their funds with headquarters and received a budget for its operation.

Education and Selma University

In spite of the emphasis on integrating public schools during the civil rights era, Alabama's black Baptists continued to support their own schools, which they thought served special needs. Baptists of Mobile and Birmingham operated their institutions with support from local Baptist associations and churches. These schools also maintained their original mission and leadership. Mobile's Cedar Grove Academy continued to offer night classes for ministers. Its day school awarded a high school diploma, but increasingly served students who had been dismissed from regular high school programs for academic or disciplinary reasons. At Cedar Grove, black students were given a second chance for a high school education. Charles A. Tunstall, pastor of the Stone Street Baptist Church, remained principal, and retired teachers and local pastors served as instructors.

Birmingham operated two schools devoted to the training of pastors. Easonian Baptist Seminary maintained a small student body during the 1950s and 1960s, usually fewer than seventy-five students. The seminary continued to train pastors for churches of the New Era Progressive Convention in Alabama, which was the major source of its funding. Similarly, Birmingham Baptist College, which traced its beginnings to 1904, continued to train ministers and Christian workers. Talmadge D. Bussey remained president during the 1950s and 1960s, and the institution operated several programs: high school, Bible certificate and diploma, Christian education certificate and diploma, and bachelor of theology degree. In the 1960s Birmingham Baptist instituted a night program that resulted in increased enrollment. By 1970 the institution's enrollment exceeded one hundred students and provided churches in Birmingham and North Alabama with many of its pastors and lay leaders.

Selma University consumed the attention of the Alabama Colored Baptist State Convention. Many of its leaders had graduated from the institution and they wanted to see it become a first-rate college. In fact, the convention's reorganization was designed to provide better support for Selma University. In the last years of the administration of David V. Jemison, the school had become a junior college with a separate School of Religion. That arrangement continued through the 1960s. President Robinson and his administration pressed for the accreditation of Selma University. Believing that the school could achieve accreditation more readily as a junior college than as a four-year college, the trustees invited an accreditation team from the Southern Association of Colleges and Schools (SACS) to evaluate the institution. SACS cited the need for improved teacher salaries, for buildings to house a library and science laboratory, and for restructuring the academic program. President Robinson and the trustees' board sought to accomplish these goals.

The building program constituted the most ambitious and successful part of the new accreditation thrust. From 1954 to 1970 four new buildings were added to the campus: Stone-Robinson Library, Jemison-Owens Auditorium Gymnasium, and two dormitories, Hood-Ware for men and Jackson-Wilson for women. Stone Hall was torn down in 1960 to make room for the new library, and the convention borrowed money to build the auditorium-gymnasium. Two dormitories were erected in 1970 with funds borrowed from the U.S. Department of Education.

By 1962 the trustees and administration had divided the institution into three departments: social science, business, and religion. Harvard and Wayne State Universities provided books that assisted in meeting accreditation requirements. Major areas of noncompliance were increased teacher qualifications and salaries, and proper science facilities. Financial support from the convention and other sources simply could not provide the funding necessary for attracting qualified faculty. The ambitious building program increased the institution's debt and construction of a science building was not completed until 1978. Thus, in spite of strenuous efforts, Selma University remained an unaccredited institution.

Even without accreditation, Selma University increased its enrollment and expanded its programs after a brief period of decline. In his 1955 report, acting president Richard Ellis reported that the school had an enrollment of 151 with 34 living on campus. By 1968 the institution was participating in several federal programs that assisted veterans and economically disadvantaged students. Among these were the national student loan, veterans education, and college work study programs. Federal assistance helped increase enrollment to 310 by 1968, and the addition of dormitories in 1970 contributed to further increases.

Three people served as president of Selma University during the civil rights era: William Ryan, James H. Owens, and M. W. Akins. Ryan, academic dean of the institution, served one year as acting president when C. L. McAllister resigned in 1955. James H. Owens became president in 1956, and served during the days of the Selma civil rights demonstrations. Convention leaders and trustees believed that Owens, a veteran educator and former president of Leland College in Louisiana, was qualified to lead the institution toward accreditation. Although supportive of equal rights for blacks, Owens did not approve of Selma University students taking part in the demonstrations or of civil rights leaders coming on campus. He argued that "you can't go around walking in the face of white people one day and then beg them the next day to donate money to your school. You are not going anywhere in this world without the help of white people and you might as well face it." He threatened to expel students if they participated in meetings and demonstrations. He told them, "Don't get involved, it will hurt the school." Several students, including Benny Tucker and Willie C. Robertson, did not heed Owens's admonition and became major recruiters of other students. This produced conflict between Owens and the students. Owens also had conflicts with the board of trustees. An impasse developed and Owens left the school in 1967. His departure took some momentum away from the accreditation emphasis. He was succeeded by William Akins, academic dean. An older man, Akins developed health problems and was forced to resign after serving three years as president. Because of internecine conflict the institution lacked executive leadership at a crucial time in its history.[9]

Despite inadequate funding and a lack of accreditation, Selma University continued to make a valuable contribution to the black Baptists in the state. The School of Religion educated pastors for Alabama churches, and many poor students in the Black Belt received their junior college training there and moved on to four-year colleges. In 1965 President Owens reported that seven students graduated at the end of the summer term. Of that number six were from Black Belt counties. Six of the seven graduates students had been accepted at either Alabama State or Alabama A&M. The remaining student stayed at Selma to work toward a bachelor of theology degree in the university's School of Religion.

By the early 1960s Selma university presidents and trustees, convention leadership, and a broad denominational constituency had arrived at a consensus concerning the school's future. Of utmost concern was the need for accreditation. Convention president Uriah J. Robinson stressed this need in every address he made before the convention. Selma University presidents Ryan and Owens also emphasized the need for accreditation. In his 1955 report to the convention, Ryan thanked the Women's Missionary Union for library books, stating that "the books were used in all accredited colleges which Selma University was on its way to becoming."[10] President Owens speaking to the Alabama Convention in 1964 informed the group that a visiting team from SACS had just left the university. He insisted that accreditation was paramount if the school were to remain competitive with other colleges in the state. He also urged the convention to make larger donations for improving the faculty and increasing salaries.

Maintaining Selma University as a Christian college was also a priority. Ministerial training was a primary goal from inception, and teachers prepared as both academicians and Christians. The 1955 trustee report was similar to all reports during this era in its emphasis on Christian values and origins: "Selma University plans to keep in a straight path, close to the concept of the founding fathers, and to the New Testament." Two years later the trustees reiterated that "Selma University would remain Christian not only in name but also in fact."[11] During the civil rights era, dancing and card playing, activities that had become common on many black college campuses, were not allowed at Selma University.

A third commitment called for Selma University to remain under black control, specifically the control of the Alabama Colored Baptist State Convention. Accepting the recommendation of President Robinson, the convention agreed to place A. H. Reid, executive secretary of the white Alabama Baptist State Convention, on the board of trustees. Other white Baptist convention officials were invited to attend trustee meetings and to give advice when needed. Robinson appreciated Reid's advice and believed that blacks could learn from the successes of white Baptist educational institutions. Robinson's actions were criticized by some militant black pastors in the convention. He made it clear in his 1965 annual address to the convention that "whites gave only advice, and the decision making remained in the hands of blacks and would continue to do so."[12]

Another major consensus within the convention advocated preserving Selma University as a Baptist institution. This emphasis stemmed from Landmarkism, the belief that the Baptist church and its denominational structure constituted the only true church. Landmarkism continued to prevail among many black Baptists in the state. Trustee reports stressed the need to train Baptist youth and ministers in the Baptist faith. The 1965 report confirmed the need for Selma University because Baptists must to be trained in a Baptist school. "We cannot," the report said, "train good Baptists by sending them to good Catholic, Presbyterian, or Methodist schools."[13]

While education remained an important focus for the state convention, particularly the enhancement of Selma University, black Baptists also made vital contributions to the civil rights movement by providing local leadership, funding, and the spiritual culture necessary to sustain important local movements. The success of the civil rights movement brought significant changes to blacks throughout the state. The desire to perpetuate and expand the convention and its causes would continue as a guiding principle among Alabama's black Baptists.

11
Continuity, Preservation, and Challenge

On April 4, 1968, in Memphis, Tennessee, Martin Luther King Jr. was assassinated while leading a campaign for employee benefits and better salaries for garbage workers. Although historians disagree on exactly when the modern civil rights movement ended, the period from King's death to the present has come to be known as the post–civil rights era. Black Alabama Baptists were primarily concerned with expanding the political and civil rights of African Americans in the state and preserving the institutions of the denomination. Except for tenure in office, the convention made few changes in its constitution or basic structure. Education continued to be the most important emphasis. Baptist schools in Birmingham and Mobile, Alabama's two largest cities, made progress and continued to serve vital needs in those communities. The state convention struggled to keep the doors of Selma University opened, a task that dominated much of the convention's time and energy.

Meanwhile, relations between black and white Baptists improved. Dialogue increased, and many churches cooperated on various programs. However, black and white Baptists continued to be divided on social and political issues. In many white Southern Baptist churches an unfortunate dark undercurrent of racism persisted. Blacks were forbidden membership and black ministers were barred from pulpits. Alabama's black Baptists also faced many challenges to maintain their position as the largest denomination among African Americans.

Preserving Political and Civil Rights Gains

The civil rights movement brought significant changes in African American life in Alabama. Legal segregation was destroyed and blacks could vote without intimidation or threat. These changes came about because of the 1964 Civil Rights Act and the 1965 Voting Rights Act. Black Baptist pastors urged their congregants to take advantage of the new rulings. In addition, pastors championed school integration, ran for political office, supported black political leaders, and remained active in civil rights organizations.

One of the most significant sections of the Civil Rights Act mandated desegregation in all public facilities. This act reversed legal segregation that had relegated blacks to separate sections in most public facilities and denied them access to hotels, restaurants, and other places. In spite of the law, many blacks were afraid to take advantage of the new opportunities. Consequently, black pastors led by example and encouraged blacks to use public facilities. During the civil rights movement in Selma, Martin Luther King was among the first blacks to stay at the Albert Hotel. Selma pastors F. D. Reese and L. L. Anderson led small groups of blacks to restaurants and hotels that had not been integrated. In Birmingham, pastors Abraham Woods and Fred Shuttlesworth led the way. In Gadsden, E. W. Jarrett, pastor of the Galilee Baptist Church, emerged as a leading force in testing the new laws. In Anniston, Baptist pastors N. Q. Reynolds and John Nettles were among the most aggressive in leading blacks to take advantage of the laws. In Bessemer, Leon Glover, pastor of the Starlight Baptist Church, was extremely forceful in urging African Americans in that city to frequent restaurants and hotels that had previously been off limits to blacks.

The 1965 Voting Rights Act eliminated all impediments to black voting that had been a part of the 1901 Alabama Constitution. "One man, one vote" became a reality in the state. However, many blacks were reluctant to vote, and the black Baptist pulpit became a platform from which pastors urged their members to vote. Some pastors endorsed candidates from their pulpits—and reminded them of the price paid for their right to vote. Convention presidents endorsed the use of the pulpit for political purposes, with Julius Scruggs as one of the most active in this regard. A graduate of Vanderbilt University with a doctoral degree in theology, he was a strong advocate of the Social Gospel. In his doctoral dissertation Scruggs stated unequivocally that religion should be socially relevant. On June 11, 2002, Scruggs wrote a letter to black Baptist pastors in the state endorsing Julian McPhillips for the U.S. Senate because his record on civil rights was better than his opponent.

Two black pastors—Charles Nevett and John Porter—were successful in their runs for the state legislature. Nevett, pastor of the First Baptist Church of Fairfield, served one term. Porter, pastor of the Sixth Avenue Baptist Church, served one term and then several terms on the Board of Pardons and Parole. The relatively short tenures of these pastors reflected their desire to serve their churches. Nevett and Porter found that serving in the legislature took too much time away from their pastoral duties.

Even though the overwhelming majority of pastors refrained from running for elective office, many were active in urging other African Americans to run and in supporting worthy candidates. In Birmingham, as in most southern cities, blacks had historically been denied the right to vote because of disfranchisement and the white primary. The 1965 Voting Rights Act allowed blacks to vote, but it remained difficult for blacks to be elected to county and state offices. Election proved problematic because candidates were required to run from the entire city or county rather than from districts where they lived. For example, in the 1970 election for state offices, four candidates ran for the state legislature from Birmingham and Jefferson County: Lucius Pitts, J. Mason Davis, Chris McNair, and Wilson Fallin Jr. These candidates forced a runoff but each was defeated in the general election because whites comprised the majority of the county voters.

With Birmingham's increasing black population, blacks could be elected to the city council from an at-large city vote. In 1971 Richard Arrington, a professor at Miles College, won a seat on the Birmingham City Council. Advocating affirmative action and defense for blacks against police brutality, Arrington became increasingly popular in the black community. A shooting involving Bonita Carter, an unarmed black girl, by a police officer known for brutality against blacks prompted Arrington to consider running for mayor when Mayor David Vann refused to fire the police office. E. W. Jarrett, pastor of the Trinity Baptist Church, and other black ministers urged Arrington to campaign for the city's top office. Arrington announced his candidacy for mayor at Jarrett's church, and with strong support from black pastors, Arrington was elected the first black mayor of Birmingham in 1979.

Arrington's campaign and election heralded an even closer relationship with the black church. Arrington was a frequent speaker at church programs and banquets, and he often attended events at Birmingham Baptist Bible College. Several black pastors were among his closest advisers: E. W. Jarrett, Abraham Woods, Nelson Smith Jr., and V. C. Provitt, president of the Birmingham Baptist Minister's Conference. In the 1980s, with the support of Mayor Arrington, Jarrett formed an organization called Clergy That Care. This organization received grants from the city of Birmingham in order to provide counseling and summer jobs for youth. The Clergy That Care organization provided strong support for Mayor Arrington and his initiatives during his twenty years as mayor.

School integration also became a high priority of several black Baptist ministers after the Supreme Court decision outlawing the segregation of public schools. However, because of the implementation clause in the 1954 decision that mandated "with all deliberate speed" and President Dwight Eisenhower's negative reaction to the decision, opposition leaders generated massive resistance in the South, which slowed school integration. In the 1960s the quest for integrated schools accelerated in the black community, and ministerial groups supported this effort. The Bessemer Baptist Minister's Conference worked closely with the NAACP and attorney David Hood to achieve school integration. The group raised funds for legal fees, and pastors urged parents to enroll their children in Bessemer's former all-white institutions. During the 1970s the all-black Dunbar High School was closed, and all high school students, black and white, attended the recently constructed Jesse Lanier High School.

Two black Baptist pastors who were also school administrators succeeded in becoming principals of recently integrated schools rather than being passed over for whites with less experience. After several years of struggle, Selma's public schools were finally integrated. Frederick Reese, pastor of the Ebenezer Baptist Church and principal of a black school, became principal of Selma High School because of his longer tenure. In Dothan, James Smith, black Baptist pastor of two local churches and principal of a local black high school, went to court in order to become principal of the integrated Northview High School.

A group of black Baptist pastors remained active in the Southern Christian Leadership Conference as well. Founded by Martin Luther King Jr., the organization of pastors was dedicated to achieving racial justice through nonviolent means. SCLC continued to operate after the death of King, and pastor John Nettles demonstrated intense devotion to King's vision. A graduate of Morehouse School of Religion, Nettles was a vigorous advocate of the Social Gospel. As pastor of the Mt. Olive Baptist Church in Anniston, he began a career in civil rights activism. For many years he served as president of the Alabama Southern Leadership Conference and as a member of the Alabama Board of Pardons and Parole. Other active SCLC leaders in Alabama included Abraham

Woods of Birmingham and King Solomon Baker of Hueytown. Woods became president of the Birmingham chapter, and Baker led the West Jefferson chapter. Both men and others, like Nettles, shared King's dream for an integrated and just society and wanted to see that dream fulfilled. Like others in SCLC they testified that "the vision of Martin Luther King was only partially realized and they needed to continue to work to redeem the soul of America," which was the general theme of SCLC.[1]

Alabama Missionary Baptist State Convention

Continuity characterized the convention work of Alabama black Baptists during the post–civil rights period. In 1970 there were four conventions in the state: the New Era Baptist State Convention, the New Era Progressive Baptist State Convention, the Progressive Baptist State Convention, and the Alabama Missionary Baptist State Convention.

The New Era Convention, formed in 1898, was concerned with black control of Selma University, rural versus urban pastors, and educated versus uneducated pastors. Today this convention includes approximately forty churches and four associations in the Birmingham area and supports Birmingham-Easonian Baptist Bible College, formerly known as Birmingham Baptist College.

The New Era Progressive Convention of Alabama resulted from a 1915 split in the National Baptist Convention over ownership of the publishing board. Those favoring control of the publishing house by Richard Boyd left to form the National Baptist Convention of America. In 1920 a group of Alabama churches favoring the position of the National Baptist Convention of America including several in the New Era Convention of Alabama formed the New Era Progressive Convention. In the 1930s this convention made Easonian Baptist Seminary its primary educational objective. In 1997 the school merged with Birmingham Baptist Bible College to become Birmingham-Easonian Baptist Bible College.

The Progressive Baptist Convention did not survive the 1990s in Alabama. With the death of Joseph H. Jackson and the emergence of tenure limits in the National Baptist Convention, USA, reasons for its existence were no longer as relevant. As a result, many former members in Alabama lost interest and the convention ceased to operate in the state.

The Alabama Missionary Baptist State Convention, formerly known as the Alabama Colored Baptist State Convention, continued as the largest convention and exerted the most influence. By the year 2000 it had one hundred associations and claimed 450,000 members throughout the state. The convention kept its basic operational structure and continued its quest to preserve Selma University.

Five men served as president of the Alabama Baptist Missionary State Convention between 1970 and 2002, and each administration endeavored to liquidate debts on the convention incurred because of its attempt to keep Selma University afloat. Arthur W. Wilson served the longest, from 1971 to 1984. A native of Thomasville and a graduate of Selma University, Wilson rose to vice president in 1953, the same year that U. J. Robinson became president. Upon Robinson's death, Wilson became president. Several developments transpired during the Wilson tenure that plunged the convention into increasingly heavy debt: a $500,000 loan to refurbish Dinkins Hall; a $2 million judgment against Selma University for misuse of federal funds; and the burning of Foster Hall, a women's dormitory. Wilson struggled with this debt as would convention presidents who followed him. During Wilson's tenure, the name of the convention was changed from Alabama Colored Baptist State Convention to Alabama Missionary Baptist State Convention, and the convention's program expanded to include a pastor's conference and a moderator's division.

Willie F. Alford succeeded Wilson when he resigned in 1984. Like Wilson, a pastor in Montgomery, Alford had been a faithful member of the convention, serving as president of the Southeast District State Convention for many years. Alford's solution to the convention's money problems centered on a consolidation loan of $2 million. However, his plan proved unsuccessful because of the poor financial status of the convention. When he died of a heart attack in 1989, Vice President Charles Nevett was elected president. Nevett resigned after serving only two years, and Felix N. Nixon, a York resident and Birmingham pastor, became president in 1991. Nixon's presidency was characterized by growing debt.

By 1995 a group of pastors believed that a change in the presidency was necessary if the convention were to overcome its debt. They convinced Julius Scruggs, pastor of the First Baptist Church, Huntsville, to run for president, a position he won. Scruggs asserted that "the convention could not borrow its way out of debt. The solution was to pay and pray."[2] Under Scrugg's leadership, the convention and Selma University filed bankruptcy under chapter eleven. With increased funding and improved management, the convention under Scruggs's leadership made progress toward liquidating its debts.

In addition to dealing effectively with the debts of the convention and Selma University, President Scruggs led a movement to revise the constitution to allow for tenure limits. With the exception of a few other minor modifications, the work of the convention has remained virtually unchanged. As in the past, three boards make up the heart of the convention work: education, publishing, and missions. The state convention maintained its four districts: southeast, southwest, northeast, and northwest. These wings provided income for the state convention program, and each included a women's and laymen's department. In addition to the three main boards and four wings of the convention, there were three convention auxiliaries: laymen, Sunday school and BTU, and women. The laymen's division coordinated the work of Baptist laymen in the state. The Sunday School and BTU Congresses were responsible for boosting the work of Sunday schools and Baptist training unions in the state. The largest auxiliary of the convention was the Women's Convention. Its membership increased and it continued to be one of the biggest supporters of Selma University.

Two women served as president during this period: Mrs. Annie M. Wilson and Mrs. Ethel Fallin. Mrs. Annie M. Wilson grew up in Bessemer and married A. W. Wilson who became president of the Alabama State Missionary Baptist Convention. Mrs. Wilson served in many capacities: secretary, vice president, and, at the death of Mrs. E. M. Morton in 1964, president. Under Mrs. Wilson's direction, the Women's Convention moved its meetings to Selma University. The convention had grown so large that no local church could host it. The university gymnasium, which could seat approximately two thousand people, seemed to be a logical venue. President Wilson also instituted a pantry shower, in which women brought food for students at the midwinter board meeting, started a summer camp for youth, and promoted a special fund-raising effort for Selma University during the annual convention meeting.

When Mrs. Wilson resigned in 1985, Vice President Ethel Fallin became president and served to 2002. Over the years, Mrs. Fallin had held several positions within the convention: counselor of the matrons, lecturer in the general women's department, and then vice president. On the national level, she served as southern director of the Young People's Department and later as a vice president. Mrs. Fallin's most outstanding achievement was in significantly enhancing the growth of the convention, raising more money for Selma University, and providing new equipment for the university. Under her leadership, the women's convention began contributing more than $100,000 to the state convention program, the most in its history. When Mrs. Fallin resigned in 2002, Mrs. Gertie Lowe became the new convention president.

Preservation of Selma University

The preservation of Selma University remained the heart and soul of the convention's work. In the post–civil rights era the school struggled to survive. It experienced growth, received full accreditation from the Southern Association of Colleges and Schools, and then lost that accreditation.

Six people served as president during the post–civil rights era. The ups and downs the school experienced were reflected in their tenures. Marshall C. Cleveland Jr., the son of M. C. Cleveland, who served as chair of the trustee board for more than thirty years, served for many years as dean of theology. He became president in 1970 and remained in that position until 1982. The early years of his administration witnessed increased enrollment because of the GI bill and other federal programs. In the late 1970s, mishandling of federal funds, a debt of $2 million to the Department of Education, and a fire that destroyed Foster Hall put the university in jeopardy. These events occurred when the convention had borrowed $500,000 to repair Dinkins Hall and was struggling to pay that debt. The university's very survival was in question.

In 1982 I assumed the presidency of the university. My father, Wilson Fallin Sr., who graduated from the institution in 1934, instilled in me a great love of the school. I had often heard him speak of the greatness of R. T. Pollard, a former president, and of his own love of the school. Because of my success with Birmingham Baptist Bible College, the trustees believed I could do the same at Selma University. I articulated three primary goals: "to produce greater operating funds; to increase enrollment; and to move the school toward accreditation with the Southern Association of Colleges and Schools."[3]

Funds increased with the reorganization of the alumni, the establishment of Selma University Days throughout the state, and greater foundation and individual giving. The school's financial report for 1984 showed that more than $500,000 had been received from donations, the greatest amount in the school's history. Enrollment increased to 450 students, including those in extension courses and a Bible study for the community on Monday nights, which I established and taught. Under my leadership, the institution embarked on a vigorous program toward accreditation with the Southern Association of Colleges and Schools, achieving both correspondence and candidacy status. However, my aggressive program generated conflict with some of the convention officials who were convinced that university fund-raising efforts were taking funds away from the convention headquarters. In 1986, I returned to the presidency of Birmingham Baptist Bible College, which had declined since my departure.

B. W. Dawson succeeded me as president of Selma University. Dawson had served as academic dean and vice president under me, and remained dedicated to accreditation efforts. In 1968, Selma University achieved full accreditation with the Southern Association of Colleges and Schools. Unfortunately, because of internal conflicts among faculty, trustees, and convention officials Dawson resigned. The major issue centered around the hiring of Michael Ellis, a financial consultant from Knoxville, Tennessee, to oversee recruitment and certain financial dealings. Ellis had been employed by the trustees and convention president F. N. Nixon. Dawson believed that hiring Ellis without his approval undermined his authority as president. J. Herbert Spencer, chair of the board of trustees, also resigned in protest.

Willie Muse, professor of religion, succeeded Dawson in 1994. His most important achievement was the beginning of an endowment fund. However, school debts increased, largely due to the policies and activities of Michael Ellis. The school lost its accreditation and its fortunes plummeted. The loss of accreditation meant the loss of a number of students and all federal programs. Muse resigned in 1998 and James C. Carter became interim president. He succeeded in holding the school together during turbulent times. Alvin Cleveland, who once served as chair of the religion department, became president in 1999. Because of the herculean efforts of Julius Scruggs, president of the Alabama Baptist State Convention, Selma University's debts have been eliminated and the institution is working toward accreditation by the American Association of Bible Colleges.

Black Baptist Education in Birmingham and Mobile

In Mobile, Cedar Grove Academy continued to focus on providing high school education for those students who had been dismissed from public schools. The school also continued to offer classes for ministers at night. Two events were of particular importance in the advancement of the institution: a multipurpose building was constructed on campus, and the institution was successful in obtaining funds from the state of Alabama. In 1995 Mrs. Gloria York became principal of the school and Reverend Howard Johnson became dean of the night theological school. Both continue to serve in those positions as of the publication of this book. Financial support continued from the Mobile Sunlight Association.

Birmingham Baptist College also made great strides during this period despite a fire that destroyed the school's administration building in 1970. The trustees and President T. D. Bussey undertook a building program, and two structures were planned: a chapel and a new administration building. With the new buildings nearly completed, President Bussey resigned because of ill health. Bussey believed that a younger man was needed. The institution had raised around $10,000 the previous year and the yearly mortgage payment would be almost double that amount, which did not include the operating budget. I was chosen by the trustees to become president. Only twenty-four years old at the time, I had recently graduated from Colgate Rochester Divinity School and returned to the community to pastor the New Zion Baptist Church in Bessemer. I was also an adjunct professor of religion at Miles College.

My first tenure as president, 1971 to 1983, was highlighted by three achievements. Funding for the college increased to $150,000, allowing the mortgage to be reduced and the institution to become financially stable. The name was changed to Birmingham Baptist Bible College to more clearly denote the school's mission. And the curriculum was brought into line with other Bible colleges throughout the nation. The institution offered Bible certificates, diplomas, a B.A. degree, and a B.Th. degree in Bible. The name change provided the school a stronger sense of identity, as well as greater recognition in the Birmingham community and across Alabama. The student body doubled, to around two hundred students, before I left to assume the presidency of Selma University. George Cook served for one year and Cecil McNear served three years as interim president.

Financial problems mounted during this time, and I returned to Birmingham Baptist Bible College in 1986. I reversed the financial picture of the institution, and by 2000 the institution was raising $300,000 from churches and friends. The student body increased to between 250 and 300 students with extension programs in Gadsden, Anniston, Mobile, Ohatchee, and Greenville. The school received both veterans and foreign immigration approval. When the Department of Justice approved the enrollment of students from other countries, the institution opened relations with Baptist conventions in Kenya and Tanzania. By 2000 approximately twenty-five ministerial students from those and other African and Caribbean countries were enrolled in the college.

The most outstanding achievement during my second tenure was the merger of Birmingham Baptist Bible College and Easonian Baptist Seminary. These schools were essentially providing the same service in the Birmingham community. Joint committees were formed in 1997 to begin merger talks. The merger was completed that year and the name of the school was changed to Birmingham-Easonian Baptist Bible College. Today it is one of the largest black Bible colleges in the nation and is the largest trainer of black ministers in the state of Alabama.

Race: Black and White Baptists

Race continued to be a major issue in Alabama during the post–civil rights era. Blacks and whites differed on many political, social, economic, and religious issues and lived in separate worlds. White attitudes were probably best expressed in the idea that too much had been done for blacks. Blacks tended to think that whites wanted to overturn the advances that had been made. These divergent attitudes were exacerbated because most whites knew almost nothing about the history of black oppression in the state.

Racism in Alabama, as in the rest of the nation, was expressed in institutional forms. Blacks earned less income, received poorer medical care, were more likely to be incarcerated, and received less funds for black educational institutions. Blacks and whites continued to vote differently. Blacks perceived the resurgence of the Republican Party in Alabama as an attempt to stop their progress, and most continued to vote the Democratic ticket.

Racial dynamics in Alabama during this era can be traced through the history of relations between two Baptist institutions: Southern Baptists (white) and National Baptists (black). When the Southern Baptist Convention was formed in 1845 approximately 100,000 of the 350,000 Southern Baptists were black. After the Civil War, blacks who had worshipped in biracial churches controlled by whites left to form their own churches. Blacks wanted to be treated as equals (which whites were not prepared to do), to worship in their own way, and to chart their own course. Southern Baptist relations with blacks between 1865 and 1900 were hampered by financial problems and by the inability of Southern Baptists to rise above traditional racial attitudes. Even so, the Home Mission Board expressed some interest in helping educate black ministers. For example, in 1894 the board appointed Robert T. Pollard, a black minister in Alabama and president of Selma University, to serve as a theological professor at Selma University. Beyond this appointment and assisting black students with scholarships and institutes, little else was done.

Between 1900 and 1950 relations between white and black Baptists in Alabama and throughout the South reached a low ebb. On the whole, Southern

Baptists supported black disfranchisement, advocated legal segregation, and tolerated lynchings of blacks. White Baptists upheld racist presuppositions and social traditions. But, even in the midst of a gloomy situation, there were positive contacts. One of the most positive was the founding of American Baptist Seminary to train black ministers, which was jointly supported by the National Baptist and the Southern Baptist Conventions.

The 1950s heralded a new day for relations between the Southern Baptist Convention and blacks. Two black churches, one in California and the other in Alaska, joined Southern Baptist associations. Although black Baptists were extremely disappointed with the actions of Southern Baptist leaders and churches during the civil rights movement of the sixties, black churches continued to join the Southern Baptist Convention. In 1968 the number of black churches in the Southern Baptist Convention reached fifty-seven, and the Home Mission Board hired Emmanuel McCall to work with National Baptists. A man of integrity, McCall maintained good relations with National Baptists while cultivating the respect of Southern Baptists. He kept the issue of race relations alive among Southern Baptists and helped them mature in their views. In 1974 McCall was elected director of the Black Church Relations Department of the Home Mission Board. Throughout the 1970s the board continued to work with National Baptists. Rather than Southern Baptists setting the agenda, the two groups began to work together.

Between 1970 and 2002, cooperative work between black and white Baptists increased in Alabama. Inter-Baptist committees were formed, and blacks were hired to serve as ministry directors in Mobile and Birmingham. In Birmingham, the committee sponsored an interracial citywide revival and supported other joint projects as well. The white Alabama Baptist Convention began to hire African American staff members, and in 1968 the state board of missions employed a black campus minister at Alabama A&M University in Huntsville. Another African American was hired by the state board of missions in 1993 to work with the twenty-two predominantly black Alabama Baptist State convention churches. By 1996 the professional staff of the state board of missions included three African Americans.

Black Baptist churches in Alabama began to join Southern Baptist associations. Some black pastors felt they needed the resources and services these associations provided. Most of these churches remained dually aligned, maintaining their membership in black associations and conventions. In addition, a few churches such as Westside in Montgomery, Baptist Church of the Covenant in Birmingham, and New Song Community Church in Mobile, integrated and chose to stay in the inner city rather than moving to the suburbs as blacks moved into their communities.

While positive things have occurred at the denominational level, a dark undercurrent of racism still prevails in many local Southern Baptist congregations. Many churches refuse to accept blacks as members or allow them to preach. In 1994 and again in 2001, African American and African students from Samford University and Beeson Divinity School were prevented from preaching in local Southern Baptist churches.

On the other hand, some black pastors were reluctant to become involved with white Baptists. One group believed that white Southern Baptists wanted only token relationships and were unwilling to tackle the problems of institutional racism and other critical issues. Some felt that Southern Baptists needed to get their own churches integrated before trying to build relations with blacks. Still others believed that Southern Baptists needed to cleanse their communities of prejudice and racism before they could effectively relate to blacks. Many civil rights leaders objected when Southern Baptists were unwilling to join them in causes of economic and political justice.

Most fundamental in the persistent separation of white and black Baptists was their differing understanding of the Bible. While the two have much in common—belief in strong family values, the need for a conversion experience, opposition to abortion, and even the Bible as the inerrant word of God—these beliefs have not translated into the same political orientation. Most black Baptists churches interpret the Bible as a book of liberation, equality, and social compassion. Thus, black Baptists are more likely than their white Southern Baptist counterparts to oppose all forms of discrimination and to favor social programs to help the poor. Southern Baptists often foster an individualistic ethic without social content. Morality is reflected in personal terms rather than challenging political and economic structures that oppress groups of people and create social problems.

Challenges

Black Baptists today remain the largest denomination among people of color in the state. It is estimated that half of black church members in Alabama belong to the Baptist church. Some churches continue to experience growth. These churches are primarily urban, have full-time pastors with vision, emphasize evangelistic programs, and practice celebration worship. Despite these impressive numbers, the Baptist church in the state is being challenged both from within and without.

The Jehovah's Witnesses have developed a program of extensive evangelism and won people away from the Baptist church. The Pentecostal church experienced the greatest growth in the black community in the twentieth century and made inroads into black Baptist memberships with their strong emphasis on celebration worship and a more liberal view toward women clergy. Recently, new churches have emerged that stress "health" and "wealth." These churches promise that if a person follows certain principles they can achieve financial security and achieve freedom from sickness and disease. Through television and unique interpretations of select Bible passages, they have been able to attract large numbers of blacks, especially young black women. Few black Baptist churches have not experienced some loss in membership from one of these groups and most of these churches are filled with ex-Baptists.

The greatest challenge to black Baptists in Alabama, however, is from within. Numerous problems continue to beset a successful witness by the denomination against those groups that have gained some of its membership. Stewardship remains a major problem for both denominational progress and the enhancement of the local church. Black Baptist churches have never provided adequate resources to finance and enhance their denominational institutions. For this reason denominational objectives such as Selma University and the *Baptist Leader* have struggled throughout their history. Stewardship has also been at the center of other denominational problems. The lack of stewardship has made it impossible to develop a comprehensive convention program to provide for many of the needs of churches. The convention and its auxiliaries continue to operate with part-time workers. There is no adequate retirement or insurance program.

The lack of stewardship has caused understaffing in local black Baptist churches. The result has been insufficient or nonexistent staffs to meet the needs of churches. Ministries such as counseling, family ministries, and outreach initiatives have gone unrealized because of the lack of staff to assist pastors. Pastors are often overwhelmed with responsibilities. Stewardship has also caused poor pastoral support, a primary reason for the overwhelming number of bivocational pastors.

Black Baptist churches have historically focused on celebration worship at the expense of Christian education programs. Today in Alabama there is a decline in Sunday school and Baptist Training Union attendance. Among the reasons are breakdown in the black family structure, an anti-intellectual atmosphere, and lack of pastoral concern. Some pastors simply do not see Christian education programs as important. Getting people converted, rather than Christian nurture and growth, is often viewed as the most important goal. A lack of Christian education programs is one of the major factors in the flight of black Baptists to cults who prey on ill-informed black Baptists.

Family ministries are another challenge for black Baptist churches. As C. Eric Lincoln and Lawrence H. Mamiya have said, "the historic black church was a gathering of families and extended families worshipping in a sanctuary they erected, and buried in a churchyard hallowed by memories of past generations."[4] Today the church no longer maintains the strong family focus. Black teenage females have the highest pregnancy rates in the world, and black males have the highest homicide and incarceration rates in the United States. The church needs to become more active in revitalizing poor communities and families that breed such maladies. A great need exists for male youth enhancement programs, prison ministries, and black female support groups for pregnant teenagers.

No issue is more troubling for black Baptists in Alabama than gender. Traditionally, Baptists have been among the most conservative groups on this issue. In the 1980s the Alabama convention authorized the writing of a small booklet on why women should not be allowed to preach, stating that "female clergy could not be supported in the Bible."[5] Several associations passed resolutions against female clergy, and some association groups expelled churches that had licensed or ordained women. Beginning in the 1990s liberal pastors began to license and ordain women. Some of these churches also ordained female deacons. In a few cases, churches voted over the pastor's objection to license women. In 2004 a black Baptist congregation in Birmingham called a black female as its pastor. The issue remains a volatile one among black Baptists. It is also one that will not likely go away. Seminaries in Alabama and adjacent states have a growing enrollment of black females. Often female aspirants for the pastorate are more highly trained than black males. Unfortunately, the issue has the potential to create splits and schisms in local churches and associations. Several associations and ministers' conferences have come to the conclusion that it is a church issue and not one that should be a criteria for membership in their organizations, a position that has brought some normalcy among these bodies. It is important that black Baptists come to some common policy on this issue that will accommodate most of its constituency. The ability of black Baptist churches to grow in the future will be determined by how they meet the challenge of gender—as well as other issues.

Conclusion
Serving the Needs of the People

From slavery to the present, black Baptists in Alabama have made invaluable contributions to the state in general and to African Americans in particular. As the state's largest black denomination, Baptists remain at the heart of the community that blacks developed after slavery by providing an Afro-Baptist theology, religious and civic leadership, educational and benevolent institutions, protesters, and civil rights movement leadership that brought the state into the mainstream of American life.

During slavery the Afro-Baptist faith provided a theology of spiritual power and liberation. Combining their West African sacred cosmos with the theology of Baptist evangelicals, black Baptists stressed the importance of a conversion experience that resulted in spiritual rebirth. This theology assured blacks of their salvation and of God's deliverance from slavery. Black sermons and spirituals emphasized the deliverance of the Israelites. Moses, Joshua, and Jesus were pictured as deliverers. Just as God delivered the Israelite nation from slavery, he would deliver them. This theology gave slaves hope and an understanding of their slavery. Blacks turned to this liberation theology to sustain them in times of crisis.

During Reconstruction, black Baptists left white churches and formed their own congregations with black ministers as pastors and leaders. The desire to worship as they pleased and the reluctance of whites to give equality in the churches were the major reasons for this split. Black Alabama Baptists formed a state convention and local associations. Churches—Baptist, Methodist, and other denominations—became the central institutions for blacks in Alabama. Black Baptists demanded a conversion experience and a holy life as the basis for church membership. Because the church represented the only institution controlled by blacks, it became the center of social, economic, and political life. Having developed spiritual leadership skills in biracial and semi-independent churches, black Baptist ministers emerged as political leaders as well.

Armed with their Afro-Baptist theology, which taught patience and the ultimate victory of God's justice, black Baptists continued to develop and expand their denomination in the post-Reconstruction period from 1875 to 1900. Baptists formed most of their major convention auxiliaries, and religious and educational institutions. Selma University, the convention's most ambitious project opened in 1878.

The nadir of race relations, from 1900 to 1917, saw blacks subjected to violence and intimidation, segregation and disfranchisement, and further estrangement from white Baptists. Education for blacks deteriorated as the state decreased the already meager funds it had provided for black education. Black Baptist associations responded by forming numerous academies that augmented the work of the state. Strenuous efforts were made to enhance and build a greater Selma University, the major focus of the state convention. Meanwhile, black Baptists protested segregation and disfranchisement, and urban churches ministered to black migrants who moved to the cities. Several pastors, inspired by Booker T. Washington, established businesses and other institutions.

Despite disfranchisement and legal segregation, Baptist pastors and secular leaders supported both World War I and World War II. After the Second World War pastors became more militant as they insisted on full rights for blacks. Ministers expressed this newfound militancy by leading protests from ministers' conferences and by providing leadership for many NAACP chapters.

Beginning in the 1950s, a group of black Baptist pastors led the civil rights movement in Alabama, which resulted in the passage of the 1964 Civil Rights Act and the 1965 Voting Rights Act and an end to disfranchisement and legal segregation. The state convention supported the civil rights movement but also focused on reorganizing, with the main purpose being to achieve accreditation for Selma University.

In the post–civil rights era, a group of black Baptist pastors sought to maintain and expand the gains of the civil rights era. However, financial problems continued to plague both the convention and Selma University. Leaders also attempted to bridge the gap between black and white Baptists in the state, but progress was slow because of the fundamentally different ways the two groups interpreted the Bible. They continued to differ over social, political, economic, and religious issues.

Today, black Baptists face many challenges. In spite of these challenges, black Baptists continue to be a mighty force in Alabama. Black Baptist pastors remain in the forefront in speaking out for social justice and the rights of the poor. Their churches sponsor day care centers, head start programs, and other agencies to assist the community. Although poorly funded, black Baptist institutions serve valuable educational needs. Baptist churches, because of their size and location, are often the places for political meetings and community social gatherings.

As black Baptists proceed into the twenty-first century, their continued effectiveness in the state will depend largely upon how they respond to various challenges. Challenges from inside and outside the church remind black Baptists of the need to build strong programs of stewardship and evangelism, to keep alive vibrant celebration worship, and to develop effective public relations. A reexamination of traditional views on gender and new music forms in worship may also prove beneficial. Black Alabama Baptists must continue to be a voice for the poor and oppressed—and to serve the physical, emotional, and spiritual needs of their people.

Notes

Chapter 1

1. Mechal Sobel, *Trabelin' On: The Slave Journey to an Afro-Baptist Faith* (Princeton: Princeton University Press, 1988), 10.

2. George P. Rawick, ed., *The American Slave: A Composite Autobiography,* series 1, vol. 1, *Alabama Narratives* (Westport, Conn.: Greenwood, 1973–77), 20.

3. Ibid., vol. 6, *Alabama and Indiana Narratives,* 7, 10.

4. Ibid., 6:22.

5. Ibid., 6:300.

6. Ibid., vol. 5, *Texas Narrative,* 5:132–33.

7. Ibid., vol. 7, *Oklahoma and Mississippi Narratives,* 7:171–72.

8. Howard F. McCord, *Baptists in Bibb County* (Tuscaloosa, Ala.: Privately printed, 1979), 24.

9. Nancy Claiborne Roberson, "The Negro and Baptists of Antebellum Alabama" (master's thesis, University of Alabama, 1954), 74.

10. *South-Western Baptist,* March 2, 1854.

11. Rawick, *American Slave,* 6:5.

12. Ibid., 6:300.

13. Bayliss E. Grace, *My Autobiography,* Manuscript Division, Southern History Department, Birmingham Public Library.

14. Charles O. Boothe, *Cyclopedia of the Colored Baptists of Alabama: Their Leaders and Their Work* (Birmingham: Alabama Publishing, 1895), 209–10.

15. Ibid., 174–75.

16. *Birmingham Free Speech,* December 28, 1901.

Chapter 2

1. *Minutes of the Alabama Baptist State Convention, 1865,* 10.

2. Karen Stone, *Prattville's First Baptist Church: Sharing Our Past with a Vision of the Future, 1838–1988* (Montgomery: Brown Printing, 1988), 30–31.

3. George E. Brewer, *A History of the Central Association of Alabama: From Its Organization in 1845 to 1895* (Opelika, Ala.: Post Publishing, 1895), 24.

4. *History of the Coosa Valley Association,* 104, Manuscript Division, Samford University Library, Birmingham.

5. B. B. Williamson Jr., *Big Bigbee's First 125 Years, 1852–1976* (privately printed, 1976), 48.

6. Quoted in Lee N. Allen, *First 150 Years, 1829–1979, First Baptist Church, Montgomery* (Montgomery: First Baptist Church, 1979), 88–89.

7. Boothe, *Cyclopedia,* 142–43.

8. *Minutes of the Alabama Colored Baptist State Convention, 1869,* 16–17

9. Ibid., *1868,* 2.

10. *Minutes of the Forty-Sixth Annual Session of the Alabama Baptist State Convention,* 11.

11. *Minutes of the Alabama Colored Baptist State Convention, 1870,* 10–11.

12. Boothe, *Cyclopedia,* 39.

13. *Minutes of the Alabama Colored Baptist State Convention, 1868,* 10; *1869; 1872.*

14. Quoted in Bailey, *Neither Carpetbaggers Nor Scalawags: Black Officeholders during the Reconstruction of Alabama, 1867–1878* (Montgomery: R. Bailey Publishers, 1991), 44.

Chapter 3

1. Glen Sisk, "Negro Churches in the Alabama Black Belt, 1875–1900," *Journal of Presbyterian Historical Society* 33 (June 1955): 87–88.

2. *History of the Antioch Baptist Church, Greensboro, Alabama,* in the author's private collection.

3. Theodore Rosengarten, *All God's Dangers: The Life of Nate Shaw* (New York: Random House, 1974), 332–34, 410–11.

4. Ibid., 410–11.

5. Portia Smiley, "'The Foot Wash' in Alabama," *Southern Workman* (April 1896): 101 2.

6. Notes on funerals in *Southern Workman* (January 1897): 18–19.

7. *Minutes of the 1886 Session of the Eufaula District Association,* 18.

8. Charles J. Davis, "History of the State Mission Board of the Alabama Colored Baptist State Convention" in the *Jubilee Volume of the Fiftieth Annual Session of the Alabama Colored Baptist State Convention,* 112.

9. E. W. Pollard, "History of the Women's Baptist State Convention of Alabama in *Jubilee Volume of the Fiftieth Annual Session of the Alabama Colored Baptist State Convention,* 98–99.

10. *Minutes of the Fifteenth Annual Session of the Women's State Convention,* 23–24.

11. *Minutes of the Fourth Annual Session of the Women's State Convention,* 16; *Minutes of the Seventh Annual Session of the Women's State Convention,* 10.

12. Hardie Martin, "How the Church Can Best Help the Condition of the Masses," *National Baptist Magazine* (October 1896–January 1897): 279–81.

13. *Minutes of the Colored Bethlehem Baptist Association, 1891,* 12.

14. Robert E. Praytor, "From Concern to Neglect: Alabama Baptists' Relations to the Negro, 1823–1870" (master's thesis, Samford University, 1971).

15. Lewis G. Jordan, *Negro Baptist History, U.S.A.* (Nashville: Sunday School Publishing Board, NBC, 1930), 260–63.

Chapter 4

1. *Minutes of the Canaan-Pickensville Association, 1893,* 10.

2. *Minutes of the Snow Creek Baptist Association, 1890,* 18.

3. *Minutes of the Alabama Colored Baptist State Convention, 1878,* 22.

4. *Minutes of the Early Rose Baptist Association, 1889,* 4.

5. Quoted in Boothe, *Cyclopedia,* 39.

6. Harrison Woodsmall, "The Theological and Bible Teaching Work of the Alabama Baptist Normal and Theological School," in *Minutes of the Eleventh Annual Session of the Spring Hill Baptist Association, 1885,* 19–23.

7. Quoted in James McPherson, *The Abolitionist Legacy: From Reconstruction to the NAACP* (Princeton: Princeton University Press, 1975), 289.

8. *Minutes of the Colored Baptist State Convention of Alabama, 1898,* 45–47.

9. Cited in Wayne Flynt, *Alabama Baptists: Southern Baptists in the Heart of Dixie* (Tuscaloosa: University of Alabama Press, 1998), 237.

10. *Minutes of the Alabama Colored Baptist State Convention, 1897,* 21.

11. *Minutes of the Alabama Association, 1893,* 10.

12. *Minutes of the Mt. Pilgrim Baptist Association, 1897,* 34–35.

Chapter 5

1. Charles O. Boothe, *Plain Theology for Plain People* (Philadelphia: American Baptist Publication Society, 1890), 11–12.

2. *Minutes of the Alabama Colored Baptist State Convention, 1878,* 22; *1895,* 14.

3. Rufus Perry, *The Cushite; or, the Descendants of Ham as Found in the Sacred Scriptures* (Springfield, Mass.: Wiley, 1893), ix.

4. *Minutes of the Alabama Colored Baptist State Convention, 1887,* 10; *Baptist Leader,* July 16, 1937, 2.

5. Boyd quoted in Nathaniel H. Pius, *An Outline of Baptist History* (Nashville: National Baptist Publishing Board, 1911), 55; Elias Camp Morris, *Sermons, Addresses, and Reminiscences, and Important Correspondence* (New York: Arno, 1980), 27; Edward M. Brawley, ed., *The Negro Baptist Pulpit* (Philadelphia: American Baptist Publication Society, 1890), 11–16.

6. *Minutes of the Mt. Pilgrim Baptist Association, 1887,* 12; *Minutes of the Eufaula Baptist Association, 1891,* 21.

7. *Jubilee Volume of the Fiftieth Annual Session of the Alabama Colored Baptist State Convention, 1917,* 107.

8. Boothe, *Cyclopedia,* 10.

9. Boothe, *Plain Theology for Plain People,* 14, 22.

10. Ibid., 125, 187.

11. Edward Crowther, "Charles O. Boothe: Apostle of Uplift," *Journal of Negro History* 78 (Spring 1993): 113–14.

12. *Jubilee Session of the Alabama Colored Baptist State Convention, 1917,* 108.

Chapter 6

1. August Meier and Elliott Rudwick, "The Boycott Movement against Jim Crow Streetcars in the South, 1900–1906," in Meier and Elliott, *Along the Color Line: Explorations in the Black Experience* (Urbana: University of Illinois Press, 1976), 268.

2. John Sparks, "Alabama Negro Reaction to Disfranchisement, 1901–1904" (master's thesis, Samford University, 1973), 22–23.

3. Horace Mann Bond, *Negro Education in Alabama: A Study in Cotton and Steel* (New York: Octagon Books, 1969), 168–70.

4. *Union Leader* (Anniston, Ala.), 1901.

5. Ibid.

6. *Minutes of the Alabama Colored Baptist State Convention, 1902,* 4.

7. *Minutes of the Morning Star Baptist Association, 1906,* 10.

8. *Alabama Baptist,* April 26 and May 17, 1900, and October 24, 1901; Flynt, *Alabama Baptists,* 302–5.

9. *Minutes of the Alabama Colored Baptist State Convention, 1901,* 10.

10. Ibid., *1907,* 22, 24.

11. Ibid., 4–5.

12. Ibid., *1909*, 14.

13. Bond, *Negro Education*, 229–39.

14. George Wade Prewett, "The Struggle for School Reform in Alabama, 1893–1939" (Ph.D. diss., University of Alabama, 1993), 89, 98.

15. *Minutes of the Alabama Colored Baptist State Convention, 1904*, 16.

16. Ibid., *1910*, 37.

17. Prewett, "Struggle for School Reform," 98, 100.

18. *Minutes of the Alabama Colored Baptist State Convention, 1906*, 18–19; *1910*, 10.

19. Ibid., *1904*, 18–20.

20. Ibid., *1907*, 72; *1912*, 72.

21. Ibid., *1907*, 17.

Chapter 7

1. Isabel Dangaix Allen, "Negro Enterprise: An Institutional Church," *Outlook* (September 1904): 183.

2. Walter Pitts, *Old Ship of Zion: The Afro-Baptist Ritual in the African Diaspora* (New York: Oxford University Press, 1993), 23.

3. Boothe, *Cyclopedia*, 77–78.

4. U.S. Congress, Senate, *Report of the Committee on Relations between Capital and Labor* (Washington, D.C.: Government Printing Office, 1885), 10.

5. Charles L. Fisher, *Social Evils: A Series of Sermons* (Jackson, Miss.: Truth Publishing, 1899), 23–35.

6. Ibid., 49–61.

7. Ibid., 62–72.

8. Ibid., 73–88.

9. *Minutes of the Alabama Colored Baptist State Convention, 1912*, 12.

10. *Minutes of the Sunday School Convention of Alabama, 1901*, 28–29.

11. *Minutes of the Alabama Colored Baptist State Convention, 1901*, 31.

12. Ibid., *1905*, 18.

13. Ibid., *1909*, 11–12.

14. *Minutes of the Wills Creek Baptist Association, 1903,* 4–5; *Minutes of the Mt. Pilgrim Baptist Association, 1909.*

15. *Birmingham News,* December 31, 1902.

16. William R. Pettiford, *Guide to the Representative Council* (Birmingham: Willis Printing, n.d.), 2–6; Charles A. Brown, "Alabama Blacks in Jones Valley," *Birmingham Mirror,* February 9, 1975, p. 10.

17. Clement Eaton, "The Nestor of Negro Bankers," *Southern Workman* 43 (November 1914): 608–9.

18. William Pettiford, "How to Help the Negro Help Himself," in *Twentieth Century Negro Literature; or, A Cyclopedia of Thought on the Vital Topics Relating to the American Negro,* ed. D. W. Culp (Atlanta: J. L. Nichols, 1902), 468–72.

19. Arnett G. Lindsay, "The Negro in Banking," *Journal of Negro History* 14 (April 1929): 170–71.

Chapter 8

1. The notion of the deradicalization of the black church comes primarily from books by two prominent theologians of black religion: James Cone, *Black Theology and Black Power* (New York: Seabury Press, 1969), and Gayraud Wilmore, *Black Religion and Black Radicalism,* 2nd ed.(Maryknoll, N.Y.: Orbis Books, 1983). In my view, neither Cone nor Wilmore has presented a convincing argument. Future studies of denominational and local religious histories will determine the accuracy or inaccuracy of my view. As for black Baptists in Alabama, there was more continuity with the past than discontinuity. Leaders were conscious that they were following in the footsteps of those who had come before them.

2. *Minutes of the Alabama Colored Baptist State Convention, 1917,* 33–34.

3. William Warren Rogers, Robert David Ward, Leah Rawls Atkins, and Wayne Flynt, *Alabama: The History of a Deep South State* (Tuscaloosa: University of Alabama Press, 1994), 425–29; Robert G. Sherer, *Subordination or Liberation? The Development and Conflicting Theories of Black Education in Nineteenth-Century Alabama* (University: University of Alabama Press, 1977); James D. Anderson, *The Education of Blacks in the South, 1860–1935* (Chapel Hill: University of North Carolina Press, 1988). The quote is in Sherer.

4. *Minutes of the Alabama Colored Baptist State Convention, 1919,* 122.

5. Ibid., *1921,* 40–41.

6. Ibid., *1927,* 31; *1930,* 30.

7. Ibid., *1935,* 41.

8. "Third Annual Message of President David V. Jemison," in Joseph H. Jackson, *A Story of Christian Activism: A History of the National Baptist Convention, U.S.A., Inc.* (Nashville: Townsend Press, 1980), 183–84.

9. *Minutes of the Alabama Colored Baptist State Convention, 1925,* 110–11.

10. Ibid., *1921,* 48–49.

11. *A Collection of Sermons and Speeches by John W. Goodgame, Pastor of the Sixth Avenue Baptist Church, Birmingham, Alabama* (Birmingham: Privately printed, n. d.), 22, in the author's private collection.

12. *History of the Twenty-third Street Baptist Church,* in the author's private collection.

13. *Minutes of the Alabama Colored Baptist State Convention, 1927,* 19–20.

14. Ibid., *1921,* 35; *1929,* 22–25.

15. Ibid., *1921,* 77.

16. Baccalaureate sermon, "Man's Preeminence," delivered in 1927 by Robert T. Pollard, president of Selma University, in the author's private collection.

17. *Minutes of the Alabama District Association, 1892,* 11–13.

18. Ibid., *1927,* 69.

19. *Baptist Leader,* January 1938.

20. *Minutes of the Alabama Colored Baptist State Convention, 1927,* 115–16, 119.

21. Ibid., 156–62.

22. Robert J. Norrell, *The Other Side: The Story of Birmingham's Black Community* (Birmingham: Birmingfind, n.d.)

Chapter 9

1. *Proceedings of the National Baptist Convention, USA, Inc., 1941,* 52–53.

2. *Birmingham World,* November 6, 1952.

3. Quoted in Roberson, "Fighting the Good Fight," 194.

4. *Birmingham World,* July 11, 1941.

5. *Alabama Citizen,* April 14 and May 5, 1951.

6. Ibid., December 22, 1951.

7. *Birmingham World,* October 31, 1947; November 11, 1949; August 15, 1950; April 3, 1953. Ware quoted in April 3, 1953 issue.

8. *Minutes of the Colored Baptist State Convention of Alabama, 1949*, 37.

9. *Baptist Leader*, July 17, 1950; *Alabama Citizen*, July 17, 1950.

10. Amos Jones Jr., *In the Hands of God: An Autobiography of the Life of Dr. J. Robert Bradley as Told by Amos Jones, Jr.* (Nashville: Townsend Press, 1993).

11. Interview with Thelma McLin, July 7, 2003.

12. Interview with Susie Rembert, March 5, 2003.

13. *Baptist Leader*, June 26, 1940.

14. Ibid., January 13, 1939.

Chapter 10

1. Morgan quoted in *New York Times*, January 7, 1972; Abernathy quoted in Pat Watters, *Down to Now: Reflections on the Southern Civil Rights Movement* (New York: Pantheon, 1971), 175.

2. Jo Ann Robinson, *The Montgomery Bus Boycott and the Women Who Started It: The Memoir of Jo Ann Gibson Robinson* (Knoxville: University of Tennessee Press, 1978), 54.

3. Stephen B. Oates, *Let the Trumpet Sound: The Life of Martin Luther King, Jr.* (New York: Penguin Books, 1985), 202.

4. Glen Eskew, *But for Birmingham: The Local and National Movements in the Civil Rights Struggle* (Chapel Hill: University of North Carolina Press, 1997), 196–97.

5. *Birmingham Police Report of the ACMHR*, April 17, 1961, Southern History Archives, Birmingham Public Library.

6. Oates, *Let the Trumpet Sound*, 202.

7. David J. Garrow, *Bearing the Cross: Martin Luther King, Jr., and the Southern Christian Leadership Conference* (New York: William Morrow, 1986), 358.

8. James H. Cone, *A Black Theology of Liberation* (New York: J. B. Lippincott, 1970), 11.

9. J. L. Chestnut and Julia Cass, *Black in Selma: The Uncommon Life of J. L. Chestnut, Jr.* (New York: Bantam Doubleday Dell, 1990), 153–54.

10. *Minutes of the Alabama Colored Baptist State Convention, 1955*, 201.

11. Ibid., 200–201; *1957*, 53–54.

12. "Annual Address of U. J. Robinson, President of the Alabama Colored Baptist State Convention, 1965," in the author's private collection.

13. *Minutes of the Alabama Colored Baptist State Convention, 1965*, 72.

Chapter 11

1. Adam Fairclough, *To Redeem the Soul of America: The Southern Christian Leadership Conference and Martin Luther King, Jr.* (Athens: University of Georgia Press, 1987), 32.

2. *Minutes of the Alabama Baptist Missionary Convention, 1995,* 52.

3. Trustee Minutes of Selma University, June 2, 1982, in the author's private collection.

4. C. Eric Lincoln and Lawrence H. Mamiya, *The Black Church in the African American Experience* (Durham: Duke University Press, 1990), 402.

5. J. Herbert Spencer, "Why Women Should Not Be Allowed to Preach," in the author's private collection.

Bibliographical Essay

In 1975 the Reverend A. W. Wilson, then president of the Alabama Missionary Baptist State Convention, appointed me to chair a committee to write a history of the convention. I began to collect histories of churches and associations in anticipation of completing this book. Because of many competing obligations, it has taken me more than thirty years to complete this task. However, in a real sense, I have been writing this book all my life. Born in an Alabama Baptist parsonage, pastoring two churches in the state, serving as president of its two colleges, becoming a professor of history at one of the major universities in the state has given me a compelling albeit belated desire to place in print the story of black Baptists in Alabama.

This narrative has relied on a number of primary and secondary sources. This bibliographical essay contains a general discussion of the major types of sources used in writing this history and a chapter by chapter discussion of the major sources used. It does not purport to give all of the sources, merely a summary of the most important works.

Several archives proved indispensable. The American Baptist Historical Collection in Rochester, N.Y., located on the campus of the Colgate Rochester Divinity School contains the most complete collection of nineteenth-century literature dealing with black Baptist history. It has copies of the *Baptist Leader,* the official paper of the Alabama Baptist State Convention. There are also copies of publications like the *Mission Herald* that has information about Selma University. A limited number of biographies of outstanding Alabama black Baptists are included, along with microfilmed copies of Alabama association and convention minutes. The papers of the Southern Baptist Convention in Nashville, Tennessee, contain minutes of the National Baptist Convention. The speeches of D. V. Jemison, a longtime president of the Alabama Convention who also served as president of National Baptist Convention, are housed there. In addition, it holds biographies of several outstanding black Alabama Baptists.

The Samford University archives in the library of Samford University in Birmingham contain minutes of the (white) Alabama Baptist State Convention and its associations. There are also a large number of histories of white churches in Alabama, many of which were biracial churches during slavery. It also has microfilmed copies of Alabama association and convention minutes. The Alabama historical archives in Montgomery contain a WPA study that collected histories of white and black churches in Alabama during the Depression years, especially for Birmingham and Jefferson County. The library of the Martin Luther King Center in Atlanta contains the most important collection of material on the role of black Baptists in the civil rights movement. Sermons and speeches by people such as Martin Luther King Jr., Ralph Abernathy, and Fred Shuttlesworth, all Alabama civil rights leaders, were very useful for the chapter on civil rights and black Baptists in Alabama. The library of Selma University holds some information on the history of Selma University. Among this material are old catalogs and presidents' reports. It also has minutes of the Alabama Baptist State Convention, including journals of the Alabama Baptist Women's Convention and the Alabama Baptist Sunday School and Baptist Training Union Congress.

Some periodicals provided useful material. The *Baptist Leader,* official organ of the Alabama Colored Baptist State Convention, contains sermons and addresses of leaders, in addition to news of the convention and its associations. The *National Baptist Voice,* a publication of the National Baptist Convention, has sermons and addresses of Alabama Baptists because many of them were national leaders. The *Southern Workman* contains meaningful information on the religious practices of Alabama Baptists in their early years of slavery and Reconstruction. The *Birmingham World* has sermons and activities of pastors not only in Birmingham but throughout Alabama. The *Emancipator* includes sermons and addresses by Montgomery pastors and generally shows the actions of black churches in 1917–19.

Because I have been collecting information on Alabama Baptists for thirty years, I have a rather extensive private collection that contains church histories, association histories, souvenir programs of Baptist meetings, and speeches of Baptist leaders.

Knowing firsthand many of the leaders of the convention, I collected countless interviews of people who were leaders and were present at important events of the convention and associations. Other interviews were collected from people who knew key participants in the history of black Baptists in the state.

Another valuable source was general histories that provided a broad context for this book. Among the most helpful were William E. Montgomery, *Under Their Own Vine and Fig Tree;* Carter G. Woodson, *The History of the Negro Church;* E. Franklin Frazier, *The Negro Church in America;* Benjamin E. Mays and John W. Nicholson, *The Negro's Church;* and C. Eric Lincoln and Lawrence H. Mamiya, *The Black Church in the African American Experience.*

Chapter 1

No recent history of slavery in Alabama exists. The best narrative on this subject is the book by James Benson Sellers, *Slavery in Alabama.* Although published in 1950 and written in the traditionalist mode that pictured slavery as a paternalistic institution, it contains the most comprehensive study of the subject. A recent history of Alabama, *Alabama: The History of a Deep South State* by William Warren Rogers, Robert David Ward, Leah Rawls Atkins, and Wayne Flynt, provides a more up-to-date discussion of the institution of slavery as it developed in the state.

A summary of the religion of West Africa is found in John Mbiti, *African Religions and Philosophy;* Albert Raboteau, *Slave Religion;* Mechal Sobel, *Trabelin' On;* and Geoffrey Parrinder, *West African Religion.*

Descriptions of life and religion in the slave community in the South that show how African slaves maintained much of their African culture are based on John Blassingame, *The Slave Community;* George Rawick, *The American Slave;* and Charles Joyner, *Down by the Riverside.*

An account of religion in the Alabama slave community came from slave narratives found in Rawick, *The American Slave.* These narratives came the closest to giving primary accounts of Alabama slaves' versions of their religious practices. Sobel's book *Trabelin' On* provided the best source for a discussion of the Afro-Baptist faith that slaves developed. Most of his discussions on conversion, the Holy Spirit, and baptism are confirmed by the narratives of Rawick. *God Struck Me Dead,* edited by Clifton Johnson, discusses the primacy of conversion in black slave religion and contains testimonies of slave conversion.

The best source for a discussion of slaves in white churches is the book edited by John Boles, *Masters and Slaves in the House of the Lord.* A number of histories of white churches in Alabama are found in the library of Samford University. These histories outlined the place of blacks in these churches. Especially helpful was Wayne Flynt's compiled minutes of Mt. Hebron Baptist Church in Leeds, *A Special Feeling of Closeness.*

The story of the development of semi-independent churches in Alabama is taken from Edward R. Crowther's article "Independent Black Baptist Congregations in Antebellum Alabama." Charles Boothe's classic work *Cyclopedia of the*

Colored Baptist of Alabama gives brief discussions of a few of these churches. In my private collection, I have a history of the Stone Street Baptist Church written by church members.

Information about slave preachers licensed or ordained by white churches is found in several publications. One of the best is Charles O. Boothe's history, which has biographies of the pioneers of black Baptists in Alabama, many of whom were slaves. A good discussion of the slave preacher Job is found in James H. Walker Jr.'s book *Roupes Valley*. The story of William Ware, another pioneer slave preacher, is found in the now defunct black Birmingham newspaper *Birmingham Free Speech*.

Chapter 2

The best book giving a general picture of Reconstruction in Alabama is Peter Kolchin, *First Freedom*. Walter L. Fleming's book *Civil War and Reconstruction in Alabama* contains much helpful information, but it is written from the perspective of the traditionalist view and its conclusions are often biased.

Two types of material proved helpful in the discussion of blacks leaving white churches. The first was histories of black churches, some in my private collection and others at the Alabama state archives. These histories help establish when churches began and the circumstances that caused the separation. The second major source was histories compiled by white congregations. Some of these are book-length histories and are found in the archives at Samford University in Birmingham. Wayne Flynt's book *Alabama Baptists* includes a discussion of black separation from white churches. Katherine Dvorak's book *After Apocalypse, Moses* is useful in giving a general picture of black separation from white churches in the South, but little of the information deals directly with Alabama.

Factors leading to the formation of the Alabama Colored Baptist State Convention and its leaders in the early years of the movement are found in Boothe's *Cyclopedia*. Minutes of the first ten years of the convention are helpful in showing that order, missions, education, and morality were primary motives. Information on the leaders of Montgomery's First Colored Baptist Church, who would in turn serve as initiators and leaders of the convention, is found in three sources: Lee N. Allen, *First 150 Years*; C. A. Stakely, *History of First Baptist Church*; and Alfred Lewis Bratcher, *Eighty-Three Years*. James Melvin Washington's classic book *Frustrated Fellowship* provides valuable insight into the Consolidated American Baptist Missionary Convention and its leaders who helped Alabama black Baptists form their convention.

The account of black Baptist ministers and laymen affiliated with the Alabama Colored Baptist State Convention who were key political leaders is found in several sources. Much of the information on Holland Thompson came from the book edited by Howard Rabinowitz, *Southern Black Leaders*. Richard Hume's "Negro Delegates to the State Constitutional Conventions" in that book contains a brief discussion of black leaders in Alabama. *Neither Carpetbaggers Nor Scalawags* by Richard Bailey has biographical information and discusses the political philosophy and activities of black legislators in Alabama during Reconstruction, including those who were black Baptists. Charles A. Brown's articles on Lloyd Leftwich and other black Baptist legislators are found in the *Negro History Bulletin*. Boothe's *Cyclopedia* offers brief biographies of Baptist political leaders.

The account of the growth of black Baptists during Reconstruction owes much to Joe M. Richardson, *Christian Reconstruction*, which compares the slow growth of the Congregational Church in Alabama to the rapid growth of black Baptists. My book *The African American Church in Birmingham, 1815–1963* discusses the fast pace of growth of black Baptists in Birmingham over other denominations during Reconstruction. William E. Montgomery's study of the African American Church, *Under Their Own Vine and Fig Tree*, gives a general picture of the reasons for black Baptist growth in the South.

Two books showing the different ways that black and white Baptists interpreted the Civil War and emancipation are Daniel Sowell, *Rebuilding Zion*, and Paul Harvey, *Redeeming the South*.

Chapter 3

The discussion on black Baptists in the Black Belt is based on Glen Sisk's dissertation, "Alabama Black Belt." Sisk also wrote an article on the subject titled "The Negro Church in the Black Belt." Charles S. Johnson's book *Shadow of the Plantation* contains much relevant material on the church in the Black Belt. Theodore Rosengarten's biography of Nat Shaw, an Alabama sharecropper, recounts Shaw's conversion experience and baptism, which was similar to those of other black Baptists during this period. Several articles in the *Southern Workman* discuss foot washings, revivals, and funerals in Alabama.

The story of the growth of churches and associations came from church histories I collected through the years and those found in the Alabama state archives. Boothe's early history was also valuable as well as association histories found in the microfilmed material compiled by the American Baptist Historical Society.

Histories of organizations established by the Alabama Colored Baptist State Convention are found primarily in the *Jubilee Volume* of the convention that met in Birmingham in 1917 and in several issues of the *Baptist Leader,* along with information from Boothe and Reid. Evelyn Brooks Higgenbotham's classic study of women in the National Baptist Convention, *Righteous Discontent* contains valuable information on Alabama Baptist women. Minutes in the library of Selma University and in the American Baptist Collection were of assistance in telling the story of the founding of the Alabama Women's Convention.

The discussion on denominational concerns came from association and convention minutes. Sowell's *Rebuilding Zion* helped clarify why Southern Baptists in Alabama refused to continue a meaningful relationship with black churches. Other works include Robert E. Praytor's master's thesis, "From Concern to Neglect," and Edward R. Crowther, "Interracial Cooperative Missions among Alabama's Baptist, 1868–1882."

Several books provided information on Alabama Baptists in the formation of the National Baptist Convention: Lewis G. Jordan, *Negro Baptist History;* Leroy Fitts, *A History of Black Baptists;* and Joseph H. Jackson, *A Story of Christian Activism.*

Chapter 4

The story of black Baptist educational efforts was taken from convention and association minutes. Several histories of academies are in my private collection. The history of Selma University and its presidents came from A. W. Pegues, *Our Baptist Ministers and Schools;* L. Fitts, *A History of Black Baptists;* and William Simmons, *Men of Mark.* A. F. Owens's speech at the jubilee session of the convention, "A Brief History of Selma University" is found in the *Jubilee Volume* and gives some personal insights by graduates of the school. A few catalogs of Selma University during this period were of assistance in following the development of the college to 1900.

An understanding of the emergence of black nationalism in the black religious community came from several books: Montgomery, *Under Their Own Vine and Fig Tree;* Edwin S. Redkey, *Black Exodus;* and Stephen Angell, *Bishop*

Henry McNeal Turner. An account of the Alabama convention split, as well as a discussion of black Baptist sociopolitical concerns during this period, is found in association and convention minutes.

Chapter 5

The liberation theology of black Baptists is found in the Alabama narratives of Rawick's *American Slave,* where slaves often spoke of their love for spirituals and their desire to be free. The strong biblicism is echoed in statements by black Baptist leaders in convention and association minutes.

Discussion of Ethiopianism among the leaders of the black religious community is located in several works: Rufus Perry, *The Cushite or the Descendants of Ham;* Albert J. Raboteau, "Ethiopia Shall Soon Stretch Forth Her Hands"; and Timothy Fulop and Albert J Raboteau, "The Future Golden Day of the Race."

On the importance of Landmarkism in black religion, I am indebted to Lawrence H. Williams, *Black Higher Education in Kentucky,* and James Brawley, ed., *Negro Baptist Pulpit.* Brawley's book contains sermons by himself and other Baptist leaders who advocated Landmarkism. In Alabama, sermons by Baptist leaders and catalogs of Selma University show the strong Landmarkist support.

Information on the life and accomplishments of Charles O. Boothe came from his published works and from Edward Crowther's article "Charles Octavius Boothe: An Alabama Apostle of Uplift."

Most of the information on William McAlpine came from convention minutes. Information is also found in the history of *Dexter Avenue Baptist Church* and William Simmons, *Men of Mark.* Boothe's history of black Baptists of Alabama also contains much useful material.

Chapter 6

Alabama's move toward disfranchisement and legal segregation is found in several works: Horace Mann Bond, *Negro Education in Alabama;* Malcolm McMillan, *Constitutional Development in Alabama;* and George Wade Prewett, "The Struggle for School Reform in Alabama."

Several sources examine the reaction of blacks to disfranchisement and legal segregation: John Sparks, "Alabama Negro Reaction to Disfranchisement"; August Meier and Elliott Rudwick, "The Boycott Movement against Jim Crow Streetcars"; and McMillan, *Constitutional Development in Alabama.* The Alabama state archives contain the *Journal of the Proceedings of the Constitutional Convention of the State of Alabama,* which recorded the debate and the four black protest resolutions.

Several publications discuss the effect the 1901 Constitution had on black education in the state. Among these is an excellent discussion in Rogers, Ward, Atkins, and Flynt, *Alabama.* Information about the formation of additional black Baptist academies, as well as black Baptist reaction to many of the social and political issues of the Progressive Era, is found in convention and association minutes.

The progress and struggle of Selma University during this era is discussed in presidential reports to the Alabama convention. Descriptions of the presidents of Selma University are located in several places: Clement Richardson, ed., *The National Cyclopedia of the Colored Race;* Simmons, *Men of Mark;* and Boothe, *Cyclopedia.*

Chapter 7

An account of the growth of churches in Birmingham comes from the *Birmingham City Directory* and also from my private collection of church histories that show the splits that occurred in black congregations. Richardson's *National Cyclopedia of the Colored Race* includes a good discussion on William Madison and the Day Street Baptist Church of Montgomery. Likewise, Isabel Allen, "Negro Enterprise," describes the ministry of T. W. Walker and the Shiloh Baptist Church of Birmingham. Both authors describe these as institutional churches fulfilling the needs of urban blacks. Several papers in Birmingham, including *Wide Awake, Hot Shots,* and the *Truth,* contain advertisements from Birmingham churches and other valuable information from the Progressive Era. These papers also describe the activities of several ministers and the businesses they operated. An unpublished biography of T. W. Walker is in the archives of the American Baptist Historical Society. My book on the African American Church in Birmingham also discusses several Baptist ministers who were active in business endeavors.

Three books by well-known Baptist pastors show how the church sought to fulfill the moral and spiritual needs of urban blacks: Charles L. Fisher, *Social Evils,* and W. R. Pettiford, *Divinity in Wedlock* and *God's Revenue System.*

Books and articles on the life and ministry of W. R. Pettiford include my *African American Church in Birmingham;* Simmons, *Men of Mark;* Boothe, *Cyclopedia;* Pegues, *Our Baptist Ministers and Schools;* Charles A. Brown, "Alabama

Blacks in Jones Valley"; Clement Richardson, "The Nestor of Negro Bankers"; Lynne Feldman, "Black Business in Birmingham"; and John N. Ingham and Lynne B. Feldman, *African American Business Leaders*. Speeches by Pettiford were gathered from several sources: addresses delivered by Pettiford before the first, sixth, and thirteenth annual conventions of the Negro Business League; "How to Help the Negro Help Himself"; *Hampton Negro Conference* no. 7 (July 1903). Speeches and statements of Pettiford are also found in convention minutes and those of the Mt. Pilgrim District associations.

Chapter 8

The discussion on black Baptist support for World War I came primarily from convention minutes. The story of Dexter Avenue Baptist Church is based on a doctoral dissertation by Houston B. Roberson, "Fighting the Good Fight." Christopher Hamlin's book *Behind the Stained Glass* was helpful in showing the struggles of Sixteenth Street Baptist Church and its pastors during the Depression and the interwar years.

General information on hard times for blacks and the Ku Klux Klan in Alabama during the Depression came from Rogers, Ward, Atkins, and Flynt, *Alabama;* David Chalmers, *Hooded Americanism;* William Robert Snell, "The Ku Klux Klan in Jefferson County"; and Robin D. G. Kelley, *Hammer and Hoe.*

A discussion of the convention leadership of D. V. Jemison is found in convention minutes and speeches. Especially helpful were speeches found in the minutes of the National Baptist Convention. Books detailing the life of Jemison include J. H. Moorman and E. L. Barrett, eds., *Leaders of the Colored Race in Alabama* and a brief biographical sketch of Jemison found in Reid, *History of the Colored Baptists in Alabama.*

Several publications provided invaluable information on the life and work of Robert T. Pollard: Pegues, *Our Baptist Ministers and Schools;* Chan C. Garrett and William T. Moore, *Speaking to the Mountain;* and *Dexter Avenue Baptist Church.* In addition, minutes of the convention and the Montgomery-Antioch Association were invaluable. Pollard's baccalaureate sermon "Man's Preeminence" is found in my private collection. My father, Wilson Fallin Sr., who was a student of Pollard's, gave helpful and personal insights into the personality and influence of Pollard during an interview in 1999. Interviews with Charles A. Lett and Chester Fredd, who were also students of Pollard, were also helpful. Pollard's reports to the Alabama convention described the growth, development, and struggle of Selma University.

Minutes of the Alabama Women's Convention provided most of the information on female work in the state. An interview with my mother, Ethel Fallin, who knew Henrietta Gibbs, helped give me additional understanding of her leadership style.

The account on the development of the emergence of varieties of religious expression among black Baptists came from several sources: Johnson, *Shadow of the Plantation;* Mays and Nicholson, *The Negro's Church;* Robert J. Norrell, *The Other Side;* and Christopher Hamlin, *History of the Sixteenth Street Baptist Church.*

The story of the growth of number two choirs in Alabama churches and their proclivity toward gospel music was found in church histories I collected and those in the Alabama state archives. General studies that deal with the growth of gospel music include Wyatt Tee Walker, *"Somebody's Calling My Name";* Eileen Southern, *The Music of Black Americans;* and Lawrence Levine, *Black Culture and Black Consciousness.*

Chapter 9

Discussion of growing militancy among Alabama pastors came from speeches found in the *Baptist Leader* and the *Birmingham World.* Vernon Johns is discussed in Charles Boddie, *God's Bad Boys;* Roberson, "Fighting the Good Fight"; Taylor Branch, *Parting the Waters;* and Martin Luther King Jr., *Stride toward Freedom.* J. L. Ware was discussed primarily in the *Birmingham World.* The militancy of W. B. Sheeley is in several sources: Reid, *History of the Colored Baptists of Alabama;* the *Alabama Citizen,* a local black newspaper published in Tuscaloosa; Anthony J. Blasi, *Segregationist Violence and Civil Rights Movements in Tuscaloosa.* Histories of the Trinity Baptist Church and the First African Baptist Church in my private collection provided important material on the militancy of Sheeley and Ware. Dorothy Autrey's dissertation, "National Association for the Advancement of Colored People in Alabama," provided insight into the growing participation of clergy, as did the *Birmingham World.*

The account of the Selma University controversy is found primarily in the minutes of the convention. Interviews with pastors such as W. M. Norwood and Charles A. Lett were also helpful. Information on Birmingham Baptist College and Cedar Grove Academy during this period came from catalogs and programs in my private collection. Accounts of the problems faced by urban churches in Alabama came from the *Baptist Leader.*

Chapter 10

The story of the different civil religions of black and white Baptists came primarily from two sources: Andrew Michael Manis, *Southern Civil Religions in Conflict*, and Flynt, *Alabama Baptists*.

The discussion of black Baptist participation and leadership in the three major civil rights campaigns in Alabama relied on a number of sources. The story of the Montgomery movement came from King, *Stride Toward Freedom;* David J. Garrow, *Bearing the Cross;* Jo Ann Robinson, *The Montgomery Bus Boycott and the Women Who Started It;* James A. Colaiaco, *Martin Luther King;* and Stephen B. Oates, *Let the Trumpet Sound.* In "Challenge and Response in the Montgomery Bus Boycott," J. Mills Thornton discusses what King learned from Montgomery.

The Birmingham movement is discussed in Fred Shuttlesworth, "An Account of the Alabama Christian Movement for Human Rights"; Glen Eskew, "The Alabama Christian Movement"; Lewis L. Jones, "Fred Shuttlesworth"; Glen Eskew, *But for Birmingham;* Adam Fairclough, *To Redeem the Soul of America.* Interviews with key leaders in the Birmingham movement were helpful, including Abraham Woods, Fred Shuttlesworth, Carlton Reese, Lola Hendrix, and Nelson H. Smith. The Birmingham police reports found in the Birmingham Public Library recorded actual proceedings of the Birmingham mass meetings. Shuttlesworth papers are in the Birmingham Public Library and the Martin Luther King Center for Social Change in Atlanta.

An account of the Selma movement came from David J. Garrow, *Protest At Selma;* J. L. Chestnut and Julia Cass, *Black in Selma;* Amelia Boynton Robinson, *Bridge across Jordan;* and Taylor Branch, *Pillar of Fire.* I also conducted interviews with L. L. Anderson and F. D. Reese.

The emergence of the Progressive National Baptist Convention was taken from Manis, *Civil Religions in Conflict;* William Booth, *A Call to Greatness;* Jackson, *A Story of Christian Activism;* Wallace C. Smith, "The Progressive National Baptist Convention," and from interviews with Nelson H. Smith and M. W. Williams, who were affiliated with the Alabama convention.

Accounts of the election in the Alabama Convention in 1954, the struggles of Selma University, and Robinson's goals as president were garnered from minutes of the convention. The life of Uriah J. Robinson was taken from Moorman and Barrett, eds., *Leaders of the Colored Race in Alabama.* Several of Robinson's speeches are in my private collection. Interviews were conducted with Wilson Fallin Sr. and Charles A. Lett, both of whom knew Robinson.

The discussion on the development of Birmingham Baptist College, Easonian Seminary, and Cedar Grove Academy during the civil rights era came from catalogs and other papers of the schools in my private collection.

Chapter 11

The discussion of pastors who were active in SCLC and other civil rights organizations dedicated to preserving and enhancing the civil rights movement came primarily from newspaper stories in the *Birmingham News, Birmingham World, Anniston Star,* and *Baptist Leader.* Interviews were conducted with Charles Nevett and John Porter, African American pastors who served in the Alabama State Legislature. Fairclough's book *To Redeem the Soul of America* provided a broader context in which to view pastors who sought to complete King's dream.

Most of the information on the work, goals, and leaders of the Alabama Baptist State Convention came from convention minutes and speeches. Speeches and minutes are in my private collection. Some minutes from this period are also available in the library at Selma University.

The story of Birmingham Baptist Bible College, Easonian Seminary, and Cedar Grove Academy during this period came from catalogs and other school papers in my private collection. The merger papers of Birmingham Baptist Bible College and Easonian Seminary are in the archives of the library at Birmingham-Easonian Baptist Bible College. My book, *The History of Birmingham-Easonian Baptist Bible College,* in the archives of Samford University, and the Birmingham-Easonian Baptist Bible College library contain extensive information on the merger.

The discussion of black and white Baptists in Alabama, especially since 1950, was based on Flynt, *Alabama Baptists,* and Edward L. Wheeler, "An Overview of Black Southern Baptist Involvements." Flynt's *Alabama Baptists* also contains information describing the relationship and activities between National and Southern Baptists in recent years.

Analysis of challenges faced by black Baptists in Alabama came basically from my own participation as a black Baptist pastor and educator, as well as interviews with various pastors and leaders. Two books were also helpful: Lincoln and Lawrence H. Mamiya, *The Black Church in the African American Experience,* and Anthony Pinn, *The Black Church in the Post–Civil Rights Era.*

Bibliography

Archival Sources

MANUSCRIPTS

Alabama Baptist Historical Society. Papers. Samford University, Birmingham, Alabama.

Birmingfind Collection. Department of Archives and History, Birmingham Public Library, Birmingham, Ala.

Birmingham Police Surveillance Papers. Birmingham Public Library, Birmingham, Ala.

Connor, T. Eugene "Bull." Papers. Birmingham Public Library, Birmingham, Ala.

King, Martin Luther, Jr. Papers. Martin Luther King Jr. Center for Nonviolent Social Change, Atlanta, Ga.

Shuttlesworth, Fred. Papers. Birmingham Public Library, Birmingham, Ala.

———. Papers. Martin Luther King Jr. Center for Nonviolent Social Change, Atlanta, Ga.

Works Progress Association. Papers. Alabama Department of Archives and History, Montgomery, Ala.

CHURCH AND ASSOCIATION MINUTES

Coosa Valley Baptist Association, Sylacauga, Ala.

Eufaula Baptist Church, Eufaula, Ala.

First Baptist Church, Tuscaloosa, Ala.

Society Hill Baptist Church, Tuskegee, Ala.

A Special Feeling of Closeness: The Minutes of the Mt. Hebron Baptist Church, Leeds, Alabama during Slavery. Compiled by Wayne Flynt. Special Collections. Birmingham Public Library, Birmingham, Ala.

Secondary Sources

Abernathy, Ralph David. *And the Walls Came Tumbling Down: An Autobiography.* New York: Harper and Row, 1989.

Allen, Isabel Dangaix. "Negro Enterprise: An Institutional Church." *Outlook* (September 1904): 181–85.

Allen, Lee N. *First 150 Years, 1829–1979, First Baptist Church, Montgomery.* Montgomery: First Baptist Church, 1979.

Allen, Lee N., and Fanna K. Bee. *Sesquicentennial History of Ruhama Baptist Church, 1818–1869.* Birmingham: Oxmoor Press, 1969.

Anderson, James D. *The Education of Blacks in the South, 1860–1935.* Chapel Hill: University of North Carolina Press, 1988.

Angell, Stephen Ward. *Bishop Henry McNeal Turner and African American Religion in the South.* Knoxville: University of Tennessee Press, 1992.

Arnette, Casey W. *The Tie That Binds: History of the Alpine Baptist Church, 1832–1988.* Talladega: Alpine Baptist Church, 1988.

Atkins, Leah. *The Valley and the Hills: An Illustrated History of Birmingham and Jefferson County.* Woodland Hills, Calif.: Windsor, 1981.

Autrey, Dorothy. "National Association for the Advancement of Colored People in Alabama, 1913–1952." Ph.D. diss., University of Notre Dame, 1969.

Bacote, Samuel William. *Who's Who among the Colored Baptists of the United States.* Kansas City: Franklin Publishing, 1919.

Bailey, Richard. *Neither Carpetbaggers Nor Scalawags: Black Officeholders during the Reconstruction of Alabama, 1867–1878.* Montgomery: R. Bailey Publishers, 1991.

Bigelow, Mitchell. "Birmingham: Biography of a City of the New South." Ph.D. diss., University of Chicago, 1946.

Blasi, Anthony J. *Segregationist Violence and Civil Rights Movements in Tuscaloosa.* Washington, D.C.: University Press of America, 1980.

Blassingame, John W. *The Slave Community: Plantation Life in the Antebellum South.* New York: Oxford University Press, 1972.

Boddie, Charles. *God's Bad Boys.* Valley Forge: Judson Press, 1972.

Boles, John B. *Black Southerners, 1619–1869.* Lexington: University Press of Kentucky, 1963.

———, ed. *Masters and Slaves in the House of the Lord: Race and Religion in the American South.* Lexington: University Press of Kentucky, 1988.

Bond, Horace Mann. *Negro Education in Alabama: A Study in Cotton and Steel.* New York: Octagon Books, 1969.

Booth, William D., ed. *A Call to Greatness: The Story of the Founding of the Progressive National Baptist Convention.* Lawrenceville, Va.: Brunswick Publishing, 2001.

Boothe, Charles O. *Cyclopedia of the Colored Baptists of Alabama: Their Leaders and Their Work.* Birmingham: Alabama Publishing, 1895.

———. *The Life Above: Address to Ministers Conference.* Birmingham: Willis Publishing, 1913.

———. *Plain Theology for Plain People.* Philadelphia: American Baptist Publication Society, 1890.

———. *Systematic Theology.* Philadelphia: American Baptist Publication Society, 1925.

Braden, Anne. "The History That We Made: Birmingham, Alabama, 1956–1979." *Southern Exposure* 7 (Summer 1979): 48–54.

Branch, Taylor. *Parting the Waters: America in the King Years, 1954–63.* New York: Simon and Schuster, 1988.

———. *Pillar of Fire: America in the King Years, 1963–65.* New York: Simon and Schuster, 1998.

Bratcher, Alfred Lewis. *Eighty-three Years: The Moving Story of Church Growth.* Montgomery: Paragon Press, 1950.

Brawley, Edward M. "Report on Selma University." *Home Mission Monthly* 21 (November 1890): 22–25.

———, ed. *The Negro Baptist Pulpit.* Philadelphia: American Baptist Publication Society, 1890.

Brewer, George E. *A History of the Central Association of Alabama: From Its Organization in 1845 to 1895.* Opelika, Ala.: Post Publishing, 1895.

Brittain, Joseph M. "Negro Suffrage and Politics in Alabama since 1870." Ph.D. diss., Indiana University, 1958.

Brown, Charles A. "A. H. Curtis: An Alabama Legislator, 1870–1876, with Glimpses into Reconstruction." *Negro History Bulletin* 25 (February 1962): 99–101.

———."Alabama Blacks in Jones Valley." *Birmingham Mirror*, February 9, 1975.

———. *Biographical Sketches of Presidents of the Alabama Baptist State Sunday School and Baptist Training Union Congress.* Birmingham: Gray Printing, 1974.

———. "John Dozier: Member of the General Assembly of Alabama, 1872–1873 and 1873–1874." *Negro History Bulletin* 26 (December 1962).

———. "Lloyd Leftwich: Alabama State Senator." *Negro History Bulletin* 26 (December 1962): 211–12.

———. "Mansfield Tyler: A Member of the Alabama House of Representatives." *Negro History Bulletin* 36 (March 1963): 199–200.

———. "Reconstruction Legislators." *Negro History Bulletin* 36 (May 1963): 198–99.

Brown, Virginia Pounds, and Helen Morgan Akins. *Alabama Heritage.* Huntsville: Strode Publishers, 1967.

Carter, Dan. *Scottsboro: A Tragedy of the American South.* Baton Rouge: Louisiana State University Press, 1969.

Carter, Harold. *The Prayer Tradition of Black People.* Baltimore: Gateway Press, 1982.

Cathcart, William, ed. *The Baptist Encyclopedia: A Dictionary of Baptists in All Lands.* Philadelphia: Louis H. Everts, 1881.

Chalmers, David M. *Hooded Americanism: The History of the Ku Klux Klan.* Durham: Duke University Press, 1978.

Chestnut, J. L., and Julia Cass. *Black in Selma: The Uncommon Life of J. L. Chestnut, Jr.* New York: Bantam Doubleday Dell, 1990.

Cochran, Lynda Dempsey. "Arthur Shores: Advocate for Freedom." Master's thesis, Georgia State University, 1977.

Colaiaco, James A. *Martin Luther King, Jr.: Apostle of Militant Nonviolence.* New York: St. Martin's Press, 1993.

Cones, James H. *Black Theology and Black Power.* New York: Seabury Press, 1969.

———. *A Black Theology of Liberation.* New York: Lippincott, 1970.

Cooper, William J., and Thomas E Terrill. *The American South: A History.* New York: McGraw-Hill, 1991.

Corley, Robert Gaines. "Quest for Racial Harmony: Race Relations in Birmingham, Alabama." Ph.D. diss., University of Virginia, 1979.

Crowther, Edward R. "Charles Octavius Boothe: An Alabama Apostle of Uplift." *Journal of Negro History* 78 (Spring 1993): 110–16.

———. "Independent Black Baptist Congregations in Antebellum Alabama." *Journal of Negro History* 72 (Summer–Fall 1987): 66–75.

———. "Interracial Cooperative Missions among Alabama's Baptists, 1868–1882." *Journal of Negro History* 90 (Summer 1995): 131–39.

Dalfiume, Richard M. "The Forgotten Years of the Negro Revolution." *Journal of American History* 55 (June 1968): 90–97.

Dexter Avenue Baptist Church, 1877–1977. Ed. Zelia S. Evans with J. T. Alexander. Montgomery: Dexter Avenue Baptist Church, 1978.

Drago, Edmund L. *Black Politicians and Reconstruction in Georgia: A Splendid Failure.* Baton Rouge: Louisiana State University Press, 1982.

Dvorak, Katherine. "After Apocalypse, Moses." In *Masters and Slaves in the*

House of the Lord: Race and Religion in the American South, 1740–1870, ed. John Boles. Lexington: University Press of Kentucky, 1988.

Eason, James H. *Sanctification vs. Fanaticism: Pulpit and Platform Efforts.* Nashville: National Baptist Publishing Board, 1899.

Eaton, Clement. "The Nestor of Negro Bankers." *Southern Workman* 43 (November 1914).

Eskew, Glenn. "The Alabama Christian Movement for Human Rights and the Birmingham Struggle, 1956–1963." Master's thesis, University of Georgia, 1987.

———. *But for Birmingham: The Local and National Movements in the Civil Rights Struggle.* Chapel Hill: University of North Carolina Press, 1997.

Fallin, Wilson, Jr. *The African American Church in Birmingham, 1815–1963: A Shelter in the Storm.* New York: Garland, 1997.

———. *The History of Birmingham-Easonian Baptist Bible College: One Hundred Years of Christian Education in Birmingham's Black Community.* Birmingham: Ebsco Media, 2004.

Fairclough, Adam. *To Redeem the Soul of America: The Southern Christian Leadership Conference and Martin Luther King, Jr.* Athens: University of Georgia Press, 1987.

Feldman, Lynne B. *A Sense of Place: Birmingham's Black Middle-Class Community, 1890–1930.* Tuscaloosa: University of Alabama Press, 1999.

———. "Black Business in Birmingham." Master's thesis, Florida State University, 1993.

Fisher, Charles L. *Social Evils: A Series of Sermons.* Jackson, Miss.: Truth Publishing, 1899.

Fitts, Alston. *Selma: Queen City of the Black Belt.* Selma: Clairmont Press, 1989.

Fitts, Leroy. *A History of Black Baptists.* Nashville: Broadman Press, 1985.

Fleming, Walter L. *Civil War and Reconstruction in Alabama.* New York: Columbia University Press, 1949.

Florence, Mary, and Arthur Wood. *Big Springs: A History of a Church and a Community in Randolph County, Alabama.* LaGrange, Ga.: Family Tree Press, 1980.

Flynt, Wayne. *Alabama Baptists: Southern Baptists in the Heart of Dixie.* Tuscaloosa: University of Alabama Press, 1998.

———. "'A Special Feeling of Closeness': Mt. Hebron Baptist Church, Leeds, Alabama." In *American Congregations,* ed. James P. Wind and James W.

Lewis. Vol. 1, *Portraits of Twelve Religious Communities*. Chicago: University of Chicago Press, 1994.

Franklin, Jinnie Lewis. *Back to Birmingham: Richard Arrington, Jr., and His Times*. Tuscaloosa: University of Alabama Press, 1989.

Frazier, E. Franklin. *The Negro Church in America*. New York: Schocken Books, 1963.

Fulop, Timothy, and Albert J Raboteau. "The Future Golden Day of the Race: Millennialism and Black Americans in the Nadir, 1877–1901." In *African American Religion: Interpretive Essays in History and Culture*, ed. Fulop and Raboteau. New York: Routledge, 1997.

Garrett, Chan C., and William T. Moore. *Speaking to the Mountain*. Atlanta: Austin Printing, 1982.

Garrow, David J. *Bearing the Cross: Martin Luther King, Jr., and the Southern Christian Leadership Conference*. New York: William Morrow, 1986.

———. *Protest at Selma: Martin Luther King, Jr., and the Voting Rights Act of 1965*. New Haven: Yale University Press, 1978.

Genovese, Eugene D. *Roll, Jordan, Roll: The World the Slaves Made*. New York: Random House, 1974.

God Struck Me Dead: Religious Conversion Experiences and Autobiographies of Negro Ex-Slaves. Ed. Clifton Johnson. Philadelphia: Pilgrim Press, 1969.

Going, Allan Johnston. *Bourbon Democracy in Alabama, 1874–1890*. University: University of Alabama Press, 1951.

Griffin, Lucille. *Alabama: A Documentary History to 1900*. University: University of Alabama Press, 1966.

Hamlin, Christopher M. *Behind the Stained Glass: A History of Sixteenth Street Baptist Church*. Birmingham: Crane Hill Publishers, 1998.

Hanlin, Katherine Hale. *The Steeple Beckons: A Narrative History of the First Baptist Church, Trussville, Alabama, 1821–1971*. Trussville: First Baptist Church, 1971.

Harvey, Paul. *Redeeming the South: Religious Cultures and Racial Identities among Southern Baptists, 1865–1925*. Chapel Hill: University of North Carolina Press, 1997.

Harvey, William J. *Bridges of Faith across the Seas*. Philadelphia: Foreign Mission Board of the National Baptist Convention, USA, 2000.

Hatcher, Andrew. *Two Nations: Black and White, Separate, Hostile, Unequal*. New York: Ballantine Books, 1992.

Heilbut, Arthur E. *The Gospel Sound: Good News and Bad Times.* New York: Limelight Editions, 1958.

Higgenbotham, Evelyn Brooks. *Righteous Discontent: The Women's Movement in the Black National Baptist Church, 1880–1920.* Cambridge: Harvard University Press, 1993.

History of the First African Baptist Church, 1868–1986. Tuscaloosa: Weatherford Printing, 1968.

Holcombe, Hosea. *A History of the Rise and Progress of the Baptists of Alabama.* Philadelphia: King and Baird, 1840.

Holifield, E. Brook. *Gentlemen Theologians: American Theology in Southern Culture, 1795–1860.* Durham: Duke University Press, 1978.

Hollis, Daniel Webster. *A History of the First Baptist Church, Jacksonville, Alabama, 1836–1986.* Jacksonville: Printed by First Baptist, Jacksonville, 1986.

Holt, Thomas. *Black over White: Negro Political Leadership in South Carolina during Reconstruction.* Urbana: University of Illinois Press, 1977.

Hume, Richard L. "Negro Delegates to the State Constitutional Conventions of 1867–1869." In *Southern Black Leaders of the Reconstruction Era,* ed. Howard N. Rabinowitz. Urbana: University of Illinois Press, 1982.

Ingham, John N., and Lynne B. Feldman. *African American Business Leaders: A Biographical Dictionary.* Westport, Conn.: Greenwood, 1993.

Jackson, Joseph H. *A Story of Christian Activism: A History of the National Baptist Convention, U.S.A., Inc.* Nashville: Townsend Press, 1980.

Johnson, Charles. *Shadow of the Plantation.* Chicago: University of Chicago Press, 1969.

Jones, Allan Woodrow. "Alabama." In *The Black Press in the South, 1865–1979,* ed. Henry Lewis Suggs. Westport, Conn.: Greenwood, 1983.

Jones, Amos, Jr. *In the Hands of God: An Autobiography of the Life of Dr. J. Robert Bradley as told by Amos Jones, Jr.* Nashville: Townsend Press, 1993.

Jones, Lewis L. "Fred Shuttlesworth: Indigenous Leader." In *Birmingham, Alabama, 1956–1963: The Black Struggle for Civil Rights,* ed. David J. Garrow. Brooklyn: Carlson Publishing, 1989.

Jones, Terry L. "Attitude of Alabama Baptists toward Negroes." Master's thesis, Samford University, 1968.

Jordan, Lewis G. *Negro Baptist History.* Nashville: Sunday School Publishing Board, NBC, 1930.

Journal of the Proceedings of the Constitutional Convention of the State of Alabama. Montgomery: Brown Printing, 1901.

Joyner, Charles. *Down by the Riverside: A South Carolina Slave Community.* Urbana: University of Illinois Press, 1984.

Kelly, Robin D. G. *Hammer and Hoe: Alabama Communists during the Great Depression.* Chapel Hill: University of North Carolina Press, 1990.

King, Martin Luther, Jr. *Stride toward Freedom: The Montgomery Story.* New York: Harper and Row, 1958.

Kolchin, Peter. *First Freedom: The Response of Alabama's Blacks to Emancipation and Reconstruction.* Westport, Conn.: Greenwood, 1972.

Levine, Lawrence. *Black Culture and Black Consciousness: Afro-American Folk Thought from Slavery to Freedom.* New York: Oxford University Press, 1977.

Lincoln, C. Eric, and Lawrence H. Mamiya. *The Black Church in the African American Experience.* Durham: Duke University Press, 1990.

Lindsay, Arnett G. "The Negro in Banking." *Journal of Negro History* 14 (April 1929).

Logan, Rayford W. *The Negro in American Life and Thought: The Nadir, 1877–1901.* New York: Dial, 1954.

Longenecker, Stephen L. *Selma's Peacemaker: Ralph Smeltzer and Civil Rights Mediation.* Philadelphia: Temple University Press, 1987.

Manis, Andrew Michael. *Southern Civil Religions in Conflict: Black and White Baptists and Civil Rights, 1947–1957.* Athens: University of Georgia Press, 1987.

Martin, Hardie. "How the Church Can Best Help the Condition of the Masses." *National Baptist Magazine* (October 1896–January 1897).

Martin, Patricia Thomas, Warren T. Martin III, and Angie Sigler. *Cubahatchee Baptist Church of Christ.* Privately printed, 1992.

Matthews, Donald. *Religion in the South.* Chicago: University of Chicago Press, 1977.

Mays, Benjamin Elijah, and John William Nicholson. *The Negro's Church.* New York: Arno, 1969.

Mbiti, John. *African Religions and Philosophy.* London: Heineman, 1969.

McCord, Howard F. *Baptists of Bibb County.* Tuscaloosa, Ala.: Privately printed, 1979.

McMillan, Malcolm. *Constitutional Development in Alabama, 1798–1901: A Study in Politics, the Negro, and Sectionalism.* Chapel Hill: University of North Carolina Press, 1955.

———. *Yesterday's Birmingham.* Miami: E. A. Seeman, 1975.

McPherson, James M. *The Abolitionist Legacy: From Reconstruction to the NAACP.* Princeton: Princeton University Press, 1975.

Meier, August, and Elliott Rudwick. *Along the Color Line: Explorations in the Black Experience.* Urbana: University of Illinois Press, 1976.

———. "The Boycott Movement against Jim Crow Streetcars in the South, 1900–1906." In Meier and Rudwick, *Along the Color Line: Explorations in the Black Experience.* Urbana: University of Illinois Press, 1976.

Mims, Glover. *William Jemison Mims: Soldier and Squire.* Birmingham: Birmingham Publishing, 1972.

Mixon, W. H. *History of the African Methodist Episcopal Church in Alabama with Biographical Sketches.* Nashville: A.M.E. Church Sunday School Union, 1902.

Montgomery, William E. *Under Their Own Vine and Fig Tree: The African-American Church in the South, 1865–1900.* Baton Rouge: Louisiana State University Press, 1993.

Moorman, J. H., and E. L. Barrett, eds. *Leaders of the Colored Race in Alabama.* Mobile: News Publishing, 1928.

Morris, Aldon D. *The Origins of the Civil Rights Movement: Black Communities Organizing for Change.* New York: Free Press, 1984.

Morris, Elias Camp. *Sermons, Addresses, and Reminiscences, and Important Correspondence.* New York: Arno, 1980.

Myrdal, Gunner. *An American Dilemma: The Negro Problem and Modern Democracy.* New York: Harper and Row, 1942.

National Cyclopedia of the Colored Race. Montgomery: National Publishing, 1919.

Noll, Mark A. "The Bible and Slavery." In *Religion and the American Civil War,* ed. Randall Miller, Harry S. Stout, and Charles Reagan Wilson. New York: Oxford University Press, 1998.

Norrell, Robert J. *The Alabama Journey: State History and Geography.* Tuscaloosa: Yellowhammer Press, 1998.

———. "One Thing We Did Right: Reflections on the Movement." In *New Directions in Civil Rights Studies,* ed. Armstead L. Robinson and Patricia Sullivan. Charlottesville: University Press of Virginia, 1991.

———. *The Other Side: The Story of Birmingham's Black Community.* Birmingham: Birmingfind, n.d.

Oates, Stephen B. *Let the Trumpet Sound: The Life of Martin Luther King, Jr.,* New York: Penguin Books, 1985.

Painter, Nell Irvin. *Narrative of Hosea Hudson: His Life as a Negro Communist in the South.* Cambridge: Harvard University Press, 1979.

Parker, Arthur H. *A Dream That Came True: The Autobiography of Arthur Harold Parker.* Birmingham: Industrial High School Printing Dept., 1932.

Parrinder, Geoffrey. *West African Religion.* London: Epworth Press, 1961.

Pendleton, James M. *Reminiscences of a Long Life.* Louisville: Press Book Concern, 1891.

Pegues, A. W. *Our Baptist Ministers and Schools.* Springfield, Mass.: Springfield Printing and Binding, 1892.

Perry, Rufus. *The Cushite; or, the Descendants of Ham as Found in the Sacred Scriptures.* Springfield, Mass.: Wiley, 1893.

Pettiford, William R. *Divinity in Wedlock.* Birmingham: Alabama Publishing, 1895.

———. *God's Revenue System.* Birmingham: Alabama Publishing, 1896.

———. *Guide to the Representative Council.* Birmingham: Willis Printing, n.d.

———. "How to Help the Negro Help Himself." In *Twentieth Century Negro Literature; or, A Cyclopedia of Thought on the Vital Topics Relating to the American Negro,* ed. D. W. Culp. Atlanta: J. L. Nichols, 1902.

Pinn, Anthony B. *The Black Church in the Post–Civil Rights Era.* Maryknoll, N.Y.: Orbis Books, 2002.

Pipes, William H. *Say Amen, Brother! Old-Time Negro Preaching: A Study in American Frustration.* Detroit: Wayne State University Press, 1992.

Pitts, Walter F. *Old Ship of Zion: The Afro-Baptist Ritual in the African Diaspora.* New York: Oxford University Press, 1993.

Pius, Nathaniel H. *An Outline of Baptist History.* Nashville: National Baptist Publishing Board, 1911.

Porch, Luther Q. *History of First Baptist, Tuscaloosa, 1818–1968.* Tuscaloosa: Drake Printers, 1968.

Posey, Walter Brownlow. *The Baptist Church in the Lower Mississippi Valley, 1776–1845.* Lexington: University Press of Kentucky, 1957.

Praytor, Robert Earl. "From Concern to Neglect: Alabama Baptists' Relations to the Negroes, 1819–1870." Master's thesis, Samford University, 1971.

Prewett, George Wade. "The Struggle for School Reform in Alabama, 1893–1939." Ph.D. diss., University of Alabama, 1993.

Rabinowitz, Howard N. "Holland Thompson and Black Political Participation in Montgomery, Alabama." In *Southern Black Leaders of the Reconstruction Era,* ed. Rabinowitz. Urbana: University of Illinois Press, 1982.

———, ed. *Southern Black Leaders of the Reconstruction Era.* Urbana: University of Illinois Press, 1982.

Raboteau, Albert. "Ethiopia Shall Soon Stretch Forth Her Hands." In *A Fire in the Bones: Reflections on African-American Religious History.* Boston: Beacon Press, 1995.

———. *Slave Religion: The "Invisible Institution" in the Antebellum South.* New York: Oxford University Press, 1978.

Rawick, George P. *From Sundown to Sunup: The Making of the Black Community.* Westport, Conn.: Greenwood, 1972.

———, ed. *The American Slave: A Composite Autobiography.* Series 1. Westport, Conn.: Greenwood, 1973–77.

Redkey, Edwin. *Black Exodus: Black Nationalist and Back-to-Africa Movements, 1890–1910.* New Haven: Yale University Press, 1969.

Reid, S. N. *History of the Colored Baptists in Alabama: Including Facts about Many Men, Women and Events of the Denomination Based upon the Careful Study of the Highest Recognized Authority within Reach.* Gadsden, Ala.: S. N. Reid, 1949.

Richardson, Clement, ed. *The National Cyclopedia of the Colored Race.* Montgomery: National Publishing, 1919.

Richardson, Joe M. *Christian Reconstruction: The American Missionary Association and Southern Blacks, 1861–1890.* Athens: University of Georgia Press, 1980.

———. *A History of Fisk University.* University: University of Alabama Press, 1980.

Riley, B. F. *A Memorial History of the Baptists of Alabama.* Philadelphia: Judson Press, 1932.

Roberson, Houston. "Fighting the Good Fight: A History of Dexter Avenue Baptist Church." Ph.D. diss., University of North Carolina, 1997.

Roberson, Nancy Claiborne. "The Negro and Baptists of Antebellum Alabama." Master's thesis, University of Alabama, 1954.

Robinson, Amelia Boynton. *Bridge across Jordan.* Washington, D.C.: Schiller Institute, 1991.

Robinson, Jo Ann. *The Montgomery Bus Boycott and the Women Who Started It: The Memoir of Jo Ann Gibson Robinson.* Knoxville: University of Tennessee Press, 1978.

Rogers, William Warren, Robert David Ward, Leah Rawls Atkins, and Wayne

Flynt. *Alabama: The History of a Deep South State*. Tuscaloosa: University of Alabama Press, 1994.

Rosengarten, Theodore. *All God's Dangers: The Life of Nate Shaw*. New York: Random House, 1974.

Scruggs, Julius R. "Comparison of the Theology of Harry Emerson Fosdick and Martin Luther King, Jr." D.Min. diss., Vanderbilt University, 1971.

Sellers, James Benson. *Slavery in Alabama*. University: University of Alabama Press, 1950.

Sernett, Milton C. *Black Religion and American Evangelicalism: White Protestants, Plantation Missions, and the Flowering of Negro Christianity, 1787–1865*. Metuchen, N.J.: Scarecrow Press, 1975.

Shepperson, George. "Notes on Negro American Influences on the Emergence of African Nationalism." *Journal of African History* 2 (1960): 302–10.

Sherer, Robert G. *Subordination or Liberation? The Development and Conflicting Theories of Black Education in Nineteenth-Century Alabama*. University: University of Alabama Press, 1977.

Shuttlesworth, Fred. "An Account of the Alabama Christian Movement for Human Rights." In *These Rights They Seek: A Comparison of Goals and Techniques of Local Civil Rights Organizations*, ed. Jacqueline Johnson Clarke. Washington, D.C.: Public Affairs Press, 1962.

Simmons, William. *Men of Mark: Eminent, Progressive, and Rising*. New York: Arno, 1968.

Sisk, Glen. "Alabama Black Belt: A Social History, 1875–1917." Ph.D. diss., Duke University, 1950.

———. "Negro Churches in the Black Belt, 1875–1900." *Journal of Presbyterian Historical Society* 33 (June 1955): 87–98.

Smiley, Portia. "'The Foot-Wash' in Alabama." *Southern Workman* (April 1896).

Smith, Simon J., and Fanna K. Bee. *Canaan, Garden Spot by the Cuttachoee*. Bessemer, Ala.: Canaan Baptist Church, 1972.

Smith, Wallace C. "The Progressive National Baptist Convention: The Roots of the Black Church." *American Baptist Quarterly* 19 (September 2000): 248.

Snell, William Robert. "The Ku Klux Klan in Jefferson County, 1916–1930." Master's thesis, Samford University, 1976.

Snow, Malinda. "Martin Luther King's Letter from the Birmingham Jail as Pauline Epistle." In *Martin Luther King, Jr.: Civil Rights Leader, Theologian, Orator*, ed. David J. Garrow. New York: Carlson, 1989.

Sobel, Mechal. *Trabelin' On: The Slave Journey to an Afro-Baptist Faith.* Princeton: Princeton University Press, 1988.

Southern, Eileen. *The Music of Black Americans: A History.* 2nd ed. New York: W. W. Norton, 1983.

Sowell, Daniel. *Rebuilding Zion: The Religious Reconstruction of the South.* New York: Oxford University Press, 1998.

Spain, Rufus. *At Ease in Zion: A Social History of Southern Baptists, 1865–1900.* Nashville: Vanderbilt University Press, 1961.

Sparks, John. "Alabama Negro Reaction to Disfranchisement, 1901–1904." Master's thesis, Samford University, 1973.

Stakely, C. A. *History of First Baptist Church, Montgomery.* Montgomery: Paragon Press, 1930.

Stone, Karen. *History of First Baptist, Wetumpka.* Montgomery: Brown Printing, 1996.

———. *Prattville's First Baptist Church: Sharing Our Past with a Vision of the Future, 1838–1988.* Montgomery: Brown Printing, 1988.

Thomas, E. L. *A History of the National Baptist Convention: The Program, Personalities, and Power Base.* Nashville: Townsend Press, 1999.

Thornton, J. Mills, III. "Challenge and Response in the Montgomery Bus Boycott of 1955–1956." *Alabama Review* 33 (July 1980): 163–235.

Torbet, Robert G. *A History of Baptists.* Valley Forge: Judson Press, 1936.

Townsend, William, ed. *Gospel Pearls.* Nashville: Sunday School Publishing Board, National Baptist Convention, USA, 1921.

Tucker, David M. *Black Pastors and Leaders: Memphis, Tennessee, 1918–1972.* Memphis: Memphis State University Press, 1975.

U.S. Congress, Senate. *Report of the Committee on Relations between Capital and Labor.* Washington, D.C.: Government Printing Office, 1885.

U.S. Office of Education. *Negro Education: A Study of the Private and Higher Schools for Colored People in the United States. Prepared in Cooperation with the Phelps-Stokes Fund under the direction of Thomas Jesse Jones, Specialist in the Education of Racial Groups.* Vol. 2. Washington, D.C.: Government Printing Office, 1917.

Vincent, Charles. *Black Legislators in Louisiana during Reconstruction.* Baton Rouge: Louisiana State University Press, 1976.

Walker, Charles. *Miss Lucy.* Nashville: Townsend Press, 1993.

Walker, James H., Jr. *Roupes Valley: A History of a Pioneer Settlement of Roupes*

Valley Which Is Located in Tuscaloosa and Jefferson Counties, Alabama. Bessemer, Ala.: Montezuma Press, 1971.

Walker, Wyatt Tee. *"Somebody's Calling My Name": Black Sacred Music and Social Change.* Valley Forge: Judson Press, 1979.

Washington, Booker T. *The Booker T. Washington Papers.* Ed. Louis Harlan. 14 vols. Urbana: University of Illinois Press, 1984.

Washington, James Melvin. *Frustrated Fellowship: The Black Baptist Quest for Social Power.* Macon, Ga.: Mercer University Press, 1986.

Watters, Pat. *Down to Now: Reflections on the Southern Civil Rights Movement.* New York: Pantheon, 1971.

Wheeler, Edward L. "An Overview of Black Southern Baptist Involvements." *Baptist History and Heritage* 16 (July 1981): 3–11.

———. *Uplifting the Race: The Black Minister in the New South, 1865–1902.* Landham, Md.: University Press of America, 1983.

White, Walter Belt. *History of the Talladega Baptist Church: Its Pastors, People, and Programs throughout One Hundred Fifty Years, 1835–1985.* Macon, Ga.: Omni Press, 1985.

Williams, Lawrence H. *Black Higher Education in Kentucky, 1879–1930: The History of Simmons University.* Lewiston, N.Y.: Edwin Mellen Press, 1987.

Williams, Walter L. *Black Americans and the Evangelization of Africa, 1877–1900.* Madison: University of Wisconsin Press, 1982.

Williamson, B. B., Jr. *Big Bigbee's First 125 Years, 1852–1976.* Privately printed, 1976.

Wilmore, Gayraud. *Black Religion and Black Radicalism.* 2nd ed. Maryknoll, N.Y.: Orbis Books, 1963.

Wilson, Harold. "Basil Manley, Apologist for Slavocracy." *Alabama Review* 15 (January 1962): 38–53.

Wilson, Mabel Ponder, Dorothy Youngblood Woodyerd, and Rosa Lee Busby, comps. *Some Early Alabama Churches.* Birmingham: Parchment Press, 1973.

Wolters, Raymond. *The New Negro on Campus: Black College Rebellions of the 1920s.* Princeton: Princeton University Press, 1975.

Woodson, Carter G. *The History of the Negro Church.* 3rd ed. Washington, D.C.: Associated Publishers, 1972.

Woodward, C. Vann. *The Origins of the New South.* Baton Rouge: Louisiana State University Press, 1971.

Index

cal campaigns with national implications, 222; and a new black Baptist convention, 237–39; and new relationship between black and white Baptist in Alabama, 236; religious dimensions of, 221; and reorganization of Alabama Convention, 239–41; three major campaigns in Alabama, 223. *See also* black Baptist ministers, civil rights era and beyond; black Baptists in Alabama, civil rights era and beyond

civil rights organizations, 165

Civil War, end of, 29

Clarke, C. A. W., 211

Clarke, James, 233

"class" churches, 166, 237

Clay, Dr. Collier P., 201

Clergy That Care, 248–49

Cleveland, Alvin, 254

Cleveland, M. C., 203, 240, 253

Cleveland, Marshall C. Jr., 253

Cobb, Ned, 60; baptism of, 61

Collins, Ella, 204

Collins, Etta, 204

Collinsville High School, 129

Colonization Society, 11

Colored American Magazine, 91

Colored Baptist Missionary Convention of Alabama, 38–42; hired missionary to carry out evangelical initiative, 40; leaders stressed the need for doctrine and education, 41–42; morality as major concern, 42; period of rapid growth post-Reconstruction, 58; purpose and structure, 41; Sunday School Congress, 42; twenty-six delegates present at the initial 1868 convention, 39. *See also* Alabama Colored Baptist State Convention

Colored Baptist Union Association, 74

Colored Bethel Union Association, 72, 80, 239

Colored Bethlehem Baptist Association, 43, 73, 81

Colored Comfort Committee, 166

Columbus Street Baptist Church, Montgomery, 37, 40

Commission on Interracial Cooperation, 170

Communist Party, 170

Compere, Lee, 10

Cone, James, 236; *Black Theology and Black Power,* 270n1

congregational splits, 139, 174; often result of tensions between pastors and deacons, 216–17; over pastoral issues, 175

conjuring, 7

Connor, "Bull," 229, 233

Consolidated American Baptist Missionary Convention, 37–38, 38

conversion: central concept in Afro-Baptist Christianity, 21; importance of to black Baptists in Alabama, 262; as a rite of passage in rural black communities, 60; of slaves, 21; testimonies, 60

convict lease system, 108

Cook, George, 255

Cooley, William W., 78, 112

cooperationists: black Baptist leaders as, xii, 91; called for continuing relationship with white northern mission boards, 90; debate with separatists caused schisms, 90–91; increase in number between 1970 and 2002, 257

Coosa River Baptist Association, 31

Cottage Grove Academy, 129

cotton production, depended on slave labor, 10

Courtland Academy, 81, 83

Cravath, Erastus Milo, 110

Cross, John, 230

Crozer Theological Seminary, 101, 224